"A Tree Does Not Make A Forest"
Anonymous

Relationships: Caveat Emptor
What You Should Know and Do Before You Enter Into One...and After.

Dr Joel Akande MBBS, MBA, LLB

Reproductive Biologist and Psychiatrist

Strategic Insight Publishing
Part of Strategic Insight Solutions Ltd and Myeexpert
6 Woodgates Close
Horsham RH13 5RU. West Sussex
Website: www.myeexpert.com

© Dr Joel Akande 2009. All rights reserved

No part of this book may be reproduced, stored in a retrieval system, or transmitted by any means without the written permission of the author.

First published by Strategic Insight Publishing
On 27 July 2009

ISBN 13:   978-0-9532332-2-9.   *ISBN 10:* 0-9532332-2-7

British Library Cataloguing-in-Publication Data
A catalogue record for this book is available from British Library

Printed in the United Kingdom

This book is printed on acid-free paper

ACKNOWLEDGEMENT

I am indebted to many of you who have visited my website, http://www.myeexpert.com, to read my earlier articles on many of the subjects of this book. Some of you have sent me questions for answers and some have sought counselling for your pressing personal problems. I have been greatly inspired by your determination in pursuit of solutions to your challenges, most of which stemmed from one form of relationship or the other. It is in the course of providing you with answers that I have been moved to write this book. On account of that, I am grateful to you and I hope this book will further help cement credible solutions --- which you may have found --- to your difficulties.

I am once again grateful to some friends and family members who, despite the odds that were so brazenly stacked against me in many ways, understood the mission I am pursuing.

Many thanks go to Matt Murphy of SOAS, University of London.
He was meticulous in the course of editing this book. In this respect, if there is any lingering error in the book, I take responsibility for the same.

I must not forget the many academic sources, writings and authorities which I have refered to in this book. Without them, assumptions and some of my views will be unsupported. In some cases, where some works have appeared in this book and perhaps the same have not been referenced or credited, due to inadvertent oversight on my part, I apologise. I do not mean to cause harm to anyone.

I also wish to thank you the reader for reading this book. The aim and joy of an author is to have his book read, worldwide.

TABLE OF CONTENTS

Acknowledgement	6
Dedication	11
Introduction: Every Human Dilemma	12

SECTION I
Intimate Relationships

Chapter One:
Names Do Matter — 24

Chapter Two:
The Root of Relationships and the Crucible of Controversy — 29

Chapter Three:
The Purpose of Marriage — 36

Chapter Four:
The Choice of Spouse and Partner:
Free Will and the Choices that We Make — 45

Chapter Five:
Why Marriages and Relationships Fail or Succeed — 52

Chapter Six:
Adolescent Relationship: The Turbulent Years — 64

Chapter Seven:
Is this Love or Deceit? Why Does *"Love"* Hurt so Badly? — 75

Chapter Eight:
Advantages and Disadvantages of Marriage And Partnership/Co-habitation Relationships, With Legal, Medical, Social, Implications — 84

Chapter Nine:
Consequences of Broken Marriages and
Broken Relationships   113

Chapter Ten:
Broken Marriages: Effects on Children   132

Chapter Eleven:
Broken Marriages/Partnerships: Effects on
Relatives, Friends and In-laws   141

Chapter Twelve:
Broken Marriages: Effects on Society   146

Chapter Thirteen:
Anger and Frustration: Causes,
And Management in Relationships   153

Chapter Fourteen:
There is Power in Knowing: Talking Frankly with You   167

Chapter Fifteen:
Relationship Questionnaire/Assessment   181

Chapter Sixteen:
Conflict Resolutions in Relationships   196

Chapter Seventeen:
Sex in Relationships: Snare or Serenity?
Is Sex Necessary?   220

Chapter Eighteen:
Gender Differences: What You Should Know   237

Chapter Nineteen:
Sample of Marriage/Partnership Agreement   253

SECTION II
Platonic Relationships
(Non-Sexual Relationships)

Chapter Twenty:
Friendships   265

Chapter Twenty One:
Children, Siblings and Extended Family Relationships   273

Chapter Twenty Two:
Business Relationships   290

SECTION III
Value

Chapter Twenty Three:
Maintenance of Relationships   301

Chapter Twenty Four:
Instances of One-Sided Relationships:
Abuse of Relationships   306

Chapter Twenty Five:
Stories of Successful and Dreadfully Failed Relationships 320

Twenty Six:
Conclusion   334

***

References   338

Index   353

DEDICATION

To all those who have so painfully let me down
And
Those who have helped me and not betrayed the trust;
You have both strengthened my resolve to succeed.

INTRODUCTION
Every Human Dilemma
"There is power in knowing..." Joel Akande

Thank you for choosing to read this book. You are holding in your very hands, a book like no other. You are about to unravel, as never before published, stunning insights into the influences that shape human relationships---personal and business---influences that may lead a relationship ---personal or business---into either failure or success, a happy finale or an acrimoniously sad ending. These are influences that you can not escape from; they will in one way or another affect your association with other individuals. I will rather prefer that you know about them, make use of them and avoid the traps that lay ahead in difficult relationships. The same traps that have dogged many unwary people and confined their relationships into: "if I had known what I know now, I should have done things in a different way". This book is about what you need to "know now... so that you can do things in a different way".

I want to say right at the outset that this book is about you, holding and reading this book, advising you, in relationship terms, to look before you leap as well as helping you to assess with a view to improving your existing relationships at home with your spouse, with your children and at work with your boss and your friends at large. The book is not a defence for nor attack on one relationship or the other. This is an open book written to help you live better and to help you improve your decision-making process.

Let me say right now that you need relationships if you are ever to make progress in this life. You need the right ones too. For example, if you happen to live next to the wrong neighbour, you may be in trouble for a long time. Yet, no one is an island or a beacon of "all in all". You can not go through this life on your own, as a single person, without being in one form of relationship or the other. It may not necessarily be an intimate relationship.

***

In spite of the foregoing argument, you are at liberty to choose to live in isolation. There are benefits in doing so. I, however, bet that living in seclusion from others is, in the image of Greek terms, a Herculean task. Of course that is the dilemma and the object of this book: to shed light into how you can either best live in isolation or in association. The choice is yours. If you choose to live a life of loneliness, you will find comfort in this book. Also if you decide to live in association, you will find great help in this book. You decide.

If you have existing relationships, this book will also help you to decide if you are on the right track or not. Should you not be on the right track, from this book, you can draw your conclusions as to what you can do to improve things. These are simple and straightforward, logical and well-proven truths and facts.

***

The aim of the author is to put in the open, those things which you ought to know about before you ever take the first step to get involved with another person of the opposite gender, e.g. in the case of marriage, as well as those things which you the reader should consider doing before you enter into any form of relationship, be it platonic or sexual, business or ordinary friendship. Human beings, it may interest you, can hardly be depended upon to hold a particular position of principle for a long time. Faced with mild to severe danger or the need for pleasure and personal survival, a human being would, in a lot of cases, abandon the ship that contained the relationship and the other individuals that are in it. Yet, for you as a reader to survive well in this world, you need people, dependable people around you: That is called relationship, for short. You will need to trust and be dependent on others for your continued existence.

Most relationships would fail or do fail for the simple reason that the partners or individuals who are involved fail in their strategic foresight in knowing what the future holds or what is in store for them before they take the crucial and, as a friend of mine used to put it, "indelible" step of connecting with the other person. A human relationship also fails for the plain reason that each individual simply fails to "gel" with the other: either that the vision diverges or there is a division in the vision!

The basis for this, whilst, it's further explained in the book, can be found on the ground of failed intensions and desires of either or both parties to the relationship. How pleasant would it be, imagine, if a relationship could mirror a jigsaw or puzzle when it all fits snugly together in one piece---all in agreement in pursuit of a common purpose!

***

Now, regarding the authority of this book, I wish to state that, the book is borne out of the need to provide truthful and helpful information to the readers. On that basis, I have done extensive research in medical or clinical medicine, particularly psychological, as well as legal positions on relationships. In addition, I have considered the social effects and consequences of forming a relationship between individuals and why it so often ends up in conflicts.

I have taken a critical look at business relationships and what informs them too.

The outcome of this extensive work is borne out in this book.

Readers need not be anxious about technicalities regarding the various specialities which I have referred to above. I have not bothered to cite complex arguments in the book but just straightforward decisive information and examination to help you to make an informed decision about where you are heading: To know the very end before you begin is the aim of this book.

With this clarification, I can step forward to how the book is organised. Please trust and follow me in this pathway.

This book is divided into three sections. The first section deals with intimate relationships such as marriages and "partnerships" or as they are commonly called "co-habitation".

***

The second section of the books deals with platonic or non-intimate and non-sexual relationships, such as ordinary friendships, business relations and family connections including relations between parents and children. The second section also deals with relationship between siblings and extended families. Presumably, this is how the larger relationships between family (inter-families) relationships are formed and by extension, inter-communities and international relationships.

Crucially, similar principles underline them all. I discuss such principles in this book.

The third and final section is concerned with maintenance of our on-going relationships as well as abuses that may arise in our association with other people.

***

Now let me give a synopsis of some of the sections which I mentioned above.

Let me start with: Marriages and "partnerships" or "co-habitation".

The data on marriages in the last 100 years in Western Europe and America is not an encouraging read. At best, it's puzzling. Let us begin in the UK.

Here is an excerpt from the National Office of Statistics:

"In 2006, there were 275,140 weddings in the UK, a fall of 4 per cent since 2005. Marriages in England and Wales fell by 4 per cent in 2006 to 236,980, which is the lowest number of marriages since 1895. In Scotland, marriages dropped 3 per cent to 29,898, whilst in Northern Ireland marriages increased 1 per cent to 8,259. The long-term picture for UK weddings is one of decline from a peak of 480,285 marriages in 1972.

In England and Wales, the number of unmarried adults rose in 2006, but the number who chose to marry fell, producing the lowest marriage rates on record. In 2006, the marriage rate for men was 22.8 men marrying per 1,000 unmarried men aged 16 and over, down from 24.5 in 2005. The marriage rate for women in 2006 was 20.5 women marrying per 1,000 unmarried women aged 16 and over, down from 21.9 in 2005.

The number of marriages in England and Wales that were the first for both partners peaked in 1940 at 426,100 when 91 per cent of all marriages were the first for both partners. This number has since fallen to 144,120 in 2006, accounting for 61 per cent of all marriages.

Remarriages rose by about a third between 1971 and 1972 following the introduction of the Divorce Reform Act 1969 in England and Wales and then levelled off. In 2006, 92,870 marriages were remarriages for one or both parties accounting for 39 per cent of all marriages.

Since 1992, there have been more civil ceremonies in England and Wales than religious ceremonies. In 2006, civil ceremonies accounted for 66 per cent of all ceremonies, an increase from 59 per cent in 1996", according to the UK's official statistical records.

***

That's for marriages: What about divorce? The National Office of Statistics gave the following insight.

The average rate for the years between 1990 and 2000 is as follows: 1990 (36.8%) and Year 2000 (39.7). Though the report claimed the overall divorce rates had fallen in the UK compared to 2006, the latest estimates for 2007 are:

"For the fifth consecutive year both men and women in their late twenties had the highest divorce rates of all five-year age groups. In 2007 there were 26.6 divorces per 1,000 married men aged 25-29 and 26.9 divorces per 1,000 married women aged 25-29."

If you put these together, it means, that for every 22-23 people that get married, about 26 on average, divorce. That means, effectively, divorce is increasing whilst marriage is falling. The computation suggests that divorce is not only taking place amongst the relatively newly married but also in existing relationships. At the same time co-habitation is increasing.

The remaining data is staggering to read and I will not bother you with the rest. An interesting question is, could it be that couples choose the wrong person? The data, in my opinion, seems to suggest so and that is very important to discuss in this book and how to avoid falling into wrong decision.

The American data is even more mind-blowing: According to the National Centre for Health Statistics, the following are data for the 1990-2004 periods.
Number of marriages for the period stated above: 2,230,000. Marriage rate: 7.5 per 1,000 total population. Divorce rate: 3.6 per 1,000 populations (46 reporting States and D.C.). That means approximate 50% are divorcing!

Obviously, at the root of it all is that couples do not really know what they were getting into before jumping into marriage.
Therefore the objective of this book is to present how to encourage individuals to make credible informed decisions on this matter.
One significant observation is that relationships and marriages are failing at a very fast rate. Take for example, in the UK. One in every three marriages will end up in divorce. In the USA, the data is even worse: one in every two marriages will fail.

The economic impact on society of this fragmentation is staggering, not to mention the effects on physical and mental health which is, in simple terms, devastating.

***

This book will focus on these issues.
The paramount aim of this book is preventive. That is to say that, to avoid marriage and relationship failure, there is certain key steps that need to be taken and could indeed be taken. Marriage is fundamentally a pleasant thing as it was originally designed, if it's the choice of the reader to pursue the course of marriage. However it needs planning like a business, pre-marriage intelligence gathering, vision, strategies and tactics like any other business. The marital vision needs to be defended.

If you read simple answers to questions that were put to some married couples, in tabloid and glossy magazines, regarding if they were happy in their marriage and or relationships: Observations from their responses are like this: "I am not happy in my marriage" or "I am not a happy person…in my marriage". On the other hand, a stable and balanced couple would say: "I am happily married… thank you". Why these differences? We would look at these issues in this book.

**

Platonic Relationships
Let me begin this section with what could pass for why most individuals and relationships run into huge difficulties.

Before I continue, I should clarify a point for the sake of this section and for the rest of the book, in relation to drug and alcohol. I do not for any reason suppose that all illegal drug takers end up as criminals or end up in mental health problem. After all there are individuals who are now in or in the past were President or Secretaries of a nation. There are individuals in responsible positions in business in other public and private positions. Some of these individuals may have taken a bit of illegal drugs in the past. Many people also experiment with drugs. In spite of their success now, no reasonable individual will advocate such youthful exhuberance that carries such a risk to the health of others especially the health of vulnerable young brains. That said; let me illustrate the impact of relationships and substances.

Seeing patients in my clinics and wards has opened my literal and inner eyes to how human beings influence each other. Seeing a young boy who is now "mad" and who was on illegal drugs, I would ask the question: "How did you get into taking drugs?"

The almost always consistent answer is that someone somewhere they have had a relationship with introduced the damaging substance to them. In my experience, it could be either a "mate" while in school or at work or a street friend. It may, surprisingly, have been a parent or other member of the extended family. In short, as a rule, the introduction is usually by someone who they know, by association.

The lesson here is that for you to succeed or fail in life—in a good proportion of cases--- you will be influenced by someone near you and by someone who knows you or a person with whom you relate or live with. The name for this is relationship. You can not avoid them and you can not run away from them but you can make the best of them with strategic forethought.

This is true in business as it is true for men, women, school boys and girls. Evidence has shown that if a child is going to be harmed or abused, it is usually by someone with whom they have a trusting relationship. On the contrary, if a child is to be successful in life, you should take note of those with whom he or she associates with. These people could be parents, siblings or outside peers.

These associations and many more like them will be examined in the second section of the book. Suffice to say that your connection to other individuals may be for ill or for good, but choose your friends wisely. Now, I present a panoramic view for you to see ahead so that you may succeed in your relationships. Trust and follow me as I lay before you the dynamic nature of human conduct that influences relationships, but bear in mind as we go along that the words of Emily Kimbrough are ever so true even today: "we all stumble, every one of us. That's why it's a comfort to go hand in hand". But if you lay a solid foundation now, using this book, your stumbling may be at the barest minimum or none at all. It all depends on you.

***

A Note to Readers

Now, a note about morality: In this book, I have merely stated my candid views, supported as much as I could find, by credible evidence. Where I have little or no experience about an issue, I have minimised or omitted the issue especially if such an issue will not make any substantial difference to the overall theme of the book. Some individuals may feel excluded or not included in the discussion. My view is that I have provided a framework through which individuals can find their own positions. Also, where I have "rang the alarm bell to sound very loud", such as under drugs and substance misuse, it's a reflection of my concern judging from my clinical experience. I have no desire to seem sensational. I do not intend to lord over nor impose my own morality on anyone. I have merely stated dynamic, evidence-based human interactions. With these behind us, I wish you happy reading.

SECTION I

Intimate Relationships Involving Sex: Marriages and "Partnerships"/Co-habitation

Why You Should Not Enter into One Without Reading This Section

"Having someone wonder where you are when you don't come home at night is a very old human need".
Margaret Mead

CHAPTER ONE
Names Do Matter

*"What's in a name? That which we call a rose
by any other name would smell as sweet."*

Shakespeare: Romeo and Juliet (II, ii, 1-2)

There are many names that are used to refer to human associations with one another. Some of these names are very appropriate for the specific association. Some are diffuse and would need some unravelling. Therefore, as one of the tools that will help us to understand the discussion in this book, let us look at these names. Forgive me if you find this diversion unnecessary. But you will find this exercise useful since my assumption and your guess regarding these names may not necessarily converge at the same point, so we need a platform where we may both operate successfully and a point where we can begin to see eye-to-eye.

Before this is done, let us look at the differences between the word "relationship" and "marriage". While, relationship is the general terms that is applicable to all forms of connection between one person and another, marriage is not so, as we shall see later. Relationship implies a connection between one person and another or others.

A relationship can be son-father, daughter-father, daughter-mother, son-mother or between siblings or uncles, nephews etc. These are called blood relationships. A relationship can also be between friends who are either related by blood, or not. Some types of relationship may also end up in marriage (see below) or they may not. The type that ends up in marriage should strictly speaking be non-blood (it may well be, though rarely so). The reason why blood or biologically related individuals should not marry is that it constitutes what is called *incest*. This is outlawed in most countries in the World, though in reality, it does occur in some relatively advanced societies. There are some reports that to some extent, it does occur even in the US, where the beliefs of some religious organizations apparently allow it.

Besides, incest can spread ancestral and heritable or genetic diseases if marriage or child birth is allowed between blood relations. Reproduction, in other words, can spread dreadful genetic but otherwise preventable diseases. For example, if cystic fibrosis sufferers within the same family should marry each other, they may end up increasing the chances of their offspring inheriting the same disease. Also, imagine if two sickle cell disease sufferers in the same family should marry one another. Essentially, such a relationship may not necessarily put those in it at ease but rather, there are chances that both the children and the parents may endure a long periods of pain and distresses. It thus makes good social and biological sense that sexual intercourse and marriage should be between, presumably, two unrelated individuals. As a sign of what is to come, if you as a reader should understand the preceding point, you will avoid a lot of pitfalls as you enter into a relationship.

Also, relationships can be in the work place. They can similarly be in business partnerships. These types can occur between blood relationships or spouses and between friends, regardless of how close or distant they may be.

Relationships can also be emotional and intimate with sexual involvement. When such an intimate relationship is *formally and publicly* declared between two adults of opposite genders according to the rules establishing an agreement between two people to share each other's body (sex) as a union emotionally and physically, such a relationship is described as a *marriage*. Thus, marriage is an agreement that is, at first glance, apparently meant to be irreversible. Reversing a marriage is possible and it is a reality of marriage that dissolution may occur. While it happens to millions of couples every year around the world, such actions have caused and do cause considerable distress, as we shall see later in the book. The consequences of divorce can be far-reaching, touching not only the couples themselves but also their children, families, friends and society at large, as I shall discuss later.

***

Now when a relationship exists which includes sexual acts but without the "contract of marriage" --- a contract which may or may not necessarily be written down --- the social as well as the common terms for this are also called, somewhat ironically, a *relationship,* or the more acceptable form, *"co-habitation,"* if they live together. The individuals in this type of relationship are called *"partners"* or *"cohabitants"* while the individuals in marital relationships are called *"spouses"*. If potential marriage is underway, the individuals are called *fiancée* (female *engaged* to be married) and *fiancé* (male *engaged* to be married) respectively.

Any relationship without sexual involvement is in general called a *platonic* relationship. Platonic relationships could be between friends, siblings, parents and children, business partners and so forth. A platonic relationship could be spiritual as well such as a relationship between a priest or pastor and the worshippers

***

Legally, these differences matter a lot; for marriages have certain rights and social status that are not available to any other form of "relationships" (see later chapters). On the other hand, some of these relationships do enjoy certain privileges that are recognised by the society's culture, for example the relationship between son and father is a peculiar one and one between daughter and mother is a special bond too. They are peculiar because the decision to enter into this kind of relationship was decided by one side --- the parents --- and the children, strictly speaking, were helpless onlookers. If they were even present at all, it may be in such occasions as some adoptions in early years. At formation of the relationship, the children may not have been born. They did not take part in deciding if they like the idea of entering a relationship with a particular parent or not. They were thrusted into it. These types are mostly biological relationships that have social and legal consequences. Parent-child relationships may also arise from legal guardianship in which the child and guardian may or may not be related to one another.

An example of the latter may arise through adoption of another non-biological child, such as adopting from a different country.

Adoption is also possible in cases where the original parent of the child is dead, imprisoned, disabled or simply (often she but can be a he) does not want the child or can not care for the child. In such a case, the grandparent may "adopt" the grandchild. This latter scenario is common with adolescent parents, but can also occur with fully grown and experienced adults (see later chapters) who mistakenly enter parenthood without the means to support their children and maintain a child-parent relationship.

***

Lest we forget, there is another term that has *crept* (yes, crept) into the world of relationships. This word and behaviour is called an *"affair"*. Human beings are very smart indeed. The word "affair" is used to describe an ill-defined relationship. It acts as a cover for a form of relationship that is characterised by cheating, wrongs, extra-marital connections, treachery, back-stabbing, unfaithfulness, "getting back at him" or "getting back at her" and a clear evidence of dissatisfaction with an existing marriage or co-habitation relationship.

Affairs are undeniably a common occurrence before and during marriage and co-habitation. They even occur when there is no commitment between the two individuals, such as when two teenagers "cheat" on each other. Society has in fact, largely ignored the effects of "affairs" and more or less accepted them as a norm (part of the culture). Lest I should be crucified on this stand, "affairs" may also refer to situations when two perfectly innocent individuals are establishing what may also lead to perfect sexual relationship. Intercourse is almost always the target end and reason for any affair though some have cited as a reason, "someone who is there to listen and to care".

***

In this book, in the section that deals with sexual relationship (co-habitation or marriage) the focus will primarily be on marriage but with explanations or comparisons and emphasis on co-habitation and other specific relationships as may be required.

Welcome to the real world of unpredictable human character. That is the nature of human beings! Take your seat, hold the book with your two hands, focus and put away all distractions for you are about to enter a sphere where people stumble on a journey that they so much hoped, at the outset, would usher in a glorious end for them. Tread carefully for any journey of relationship is perilous. Avoid being taken by surprise for the booby traps are laid clear before you, except if you fail to notice them. In that case, you may be ensnared. Be an owl for the time being, with a 360 degree visual field. Help me: be an eagle also and therefore perch on the highest of trees. Have a panoramic view of the matter. If you are on your guard and you take hold of my words, you will come to notice that the net is spread in front of a vigilant bird in vain: That is, if you are alert, you can not fail nor be entrapped in a dangerous relationship. You hold in your hands the answers to many puzzling questions that people in relationships are seeking. You are also possessing between your fingers, palm and eyes, solutions to questions that individuals intending to enter into a potential relationship are asking. You only can decide what to make of it.

***

CHAPTER TWO
The Root of Relationships and the Crucible of Controversy
"Good beginnings always have a good ending".
English Proverb

Though not everyone will necessarily *agree* to the origin of marriage and relationship that I present here, nonetheless, it is a good starting point. We need a reference point. We can not float in the air without knowing where we are coming from or where we are going. The objective is to avoid any argument and to allow us to make an unobstructed search for the truth and thus to allow for extensions into all possible directions in view of this subject.

The first word that I need to explain so that it can be acceptable to you and me is the word "agree". I am conscious of the word *"agree"* which I have used here. There will be no book like this one that you are reading and there will be no divorce in marriages nor there a separation, if this simple word "agree" fully interpreted and complied with in all relationships. It's the word that will either hold a relationship together or on the contrary send it into different parts and pieces.

Dear reader, in case you have missed the point which I have just mentioned, that is the first important point which you should note at this stage as we go along. Therefore, please note it carefully as it is crucial to all successful or failed relationships regardless of shape or form. The bedrock of all failures in any relationship that involves a minimum of two people is the inability to follow the word *"agree"* to its logical conclusion. When a relationship fails, someone at least, has broken the rule. When a relationship succeeds, the parties have kept the rules of agreement, it may surprise you to note.

As a first step therefore, I want you my reader to at least avoid the stumbling block --- disagreement --- that has plagued all failed relationships and marriages during the time you will spend reading this book. Just *agree* with me for the time being.

Let us avoid unnecessary confrontation. We can avoid the crises and conflicts that so often typify business and personal relationships. To agree means to have united intentions and then a concerted set of actions in pursuit of a common objective.

***

With this behind us, let us start the difficult task of learning from history if we are to reach our intended destination, for a lesson in history will guide us against the traps and pitfalls that ensnared those great men and women who have gone before us. *"History,"* Norman Cousins once said*," is a vast early warning system."* I think we should heed that warning.

***

Where did marriage begin? Well, if you are looking for a material scientific answer to this question, you may not find one. There is no clear evidence, at least for now, from scientific studies to show where the first marriage and relationship was first formed. Charles Darwin, the icon of evolution, you may be disappointed, did not tell us either. No shred of evidence from evolution has shed light on where the first marriage was knotted. Should we be discouraged? Certainly not. Let us dig a bit further into history.

There are however claims with indirect evidence from anthropological studies (or studies of mankind) that, the first marriage and relationship, in all probability, took place in East Africa somewhere around the area of modern day Ethiopia/Kenya. If, as it is generally believed, the first human being came from East Africa, then it holds to logical reasoning that the first marriage could not have been from elsewhere. There is no indisputable evidence to support this even though it is said to have happened about 200,000 years ago. This is merely an assumption with some DNA backup. There is also the story of Lucy, found in East Africa in 1974, and the University of Arizona researchers have claimed her birth is dated to just less than 3.18 million years old. She was said to have died as an adult. This means Lucy was probably one of the first human beings and is a female. This runs contrary to all known and established knowledge. Well, this book is not about the origin of human beings. The interesting bit is how this claim has thrown everything we know to date, about the origin of relationships, into some apparent confusion. Also, the role of the male, how he came about and his subsequent relationships, as well as the issue of reproduction, if any, is missing from the Lucy story.

Much further north than Ethiopia though, some have said that the components of a modern family, including marriage, wedding ceremonies, and hence the formation of relationships, including the birth of children, goes back to Mesopotamia. The earliest date for this is put at about 4000BC.

***

Rewind if you like, and we know from available records that there is another history that predated or occurred before the Mesopotamia account. Everyone knows it and no one has offered contrary evidence.

A more generally satisfactory origin of marriage which is accepted across the world by both Christians, Muslims and even non-religious folks alike, is that marriage began somewhere in the Middle East in the Garden of Eden. The Bible put it clearly that after the formation of the first man, Adam, God decided to *give (Note: he, Adam did not ask for a wife)* him a wife as a "*help meet*"--- a *partner* to help him. Help him to do what? Obviously, Adam was probably being overtaxed in the job that he was given, it would appear. He needed a "helper", as the story goes.

Here is the declaration, we are told, and a ceremony that joined the two of them together that ultimately established the institution of marriage as we now know it:

"And the Lord God took the man, and put him into the garden of Eden to dress it and to keep it. And the Lord God commanded the man, saying, Of every tree of the garden thou mayest freely eat: But of the tree of the knowledge of good and evil, thou shalt not eat of it: for in the day that thou eatest thereof thou shalt surely die. And the Lord God said, *It is not good that the man should be alone; I will make him an help meet for him.* And out of the ground the Lord God formed every beast of the field, and every fowl of the air; and brought them unto Adam to see what he would call them: and whatsoever Adam called every living creature, that was the name thereof. And Adam gave names to all cattle, and to the fowl of the air, and to every beast of the field; but for Adam there was not found an help meet for him.

And the Lord God caused a deep sleep to fall upon Adam, and he slept: and he took one of his ribs, and closed up the flesh instead thereof; And the rib, which the Lord God had taken from man, made he a woman, and brought her unto the man. And Adam said, This is now bone of my bones, and flesh of my flesh: she shall be called Woman, because she was taken out of Man. Therefore shall a man leave his father and his mother, and shall *cleave* unto his *wife:* and they shall be *one flesh.* And they were both naked, the man and his wife, and were not ashamed".

(Note my italicised emphasis. They are very crucial to the institution of marriage which is a (1) Union of (2) male and female).

Incredulous as this may *seem to some*, human beings have not offered a credible alternative to this story. Therefore, it continues to be validly relied upon. Even looking at the Darwin's Theory of Evolution, it is clear to any logical thinker, that all said and done, life must have taken off, from somewhere with some ordering and sequencing of events. Besides, clearly, some events preceeded and predated evolution.

***

With this simple gesture, the very first sets of controversy on marriage arise.
    a) Some people including anthropologists tend not to *agree* to this order of things, questioning as it were:
i)   "How can *man* be created first?"
ii)   "How can a woman be a *help meet* to a man, with whom she is biologically equal?"

It becomes the question of the chicken and the egg and which of them came first. Science has not resolved these questions. Nevertheless, perhaps the story of Lucy which I cited above may give some comfort to those who doubt the story of Adam and Eve.

These two questions pre-suppose that women are *"the lesser of the two genders"* to men. Is this really so? There is no evidence in the Scripture and in science to suggest either that this is the case or if that was the intention.

What should also be noted in the Biblical account is that, Adam, really *never chose to have* Eve. He never took part in the decision-making process. The relationship was forced on him. He was helpless in this situation and he had no choice as he had to accept Eve at any rate. It was God's decision for Adam. And it was for Adam to manage and care for Eve as his, now, wife. This is the hidden question even up to this day that men and women have had battles with. In other words they ask: "Do I have to marry?" "When should I marry?" "Who do I marry?" "Will I get the right person (man or woman)?" "Will God give me my wife?" This book will answer these questions. You have the answers in your sight and in your hands, in this book. In modern times, the question which was until now at the fringes of human social fabric is "which gender.... I am confused... I am not sure where I belong". You will find comfort in this book to these questions.

Let us return a little while to the story of Eden. In this same Biblical account, there is another lingering scenario: The role of a *third* party after the supposed marriage. We are told that while Adam was away to work, and a person in the shape of a Snake (we now know this is an individual person, in our time and days) tricked Eve to also deceive Adam. An intruder and uninvited guest, whose advice was not sought but, who chose to give the advice anyway, had just had an opening into the *union*.

In case you missed that, welcome to the world of treachery and mutiny. "Snake", we can not on reflection conclude, was not content with the way things were going between Adam and Eve. Things were working out and events had been too peaceful, apparently. Then, it was time to strike a deadly blow at the very heart of the foundation of the relationship. Now it was time to cause offence and disruptions to the connection. It (or He) must have reasoned: "What if I entice Eve with something she is not used to? What if I use money? It could be advice. It could be food --- just anything". There began the sliding of relationships into deceit, conflict and crisis which has remained with us to this day.

The intention was clear: to deceive and to cause maximum damage. In the end, the three were found to be disobedient to the existing *rules* of relationship and marriage --- the rule to abstain from certain acts. Enough said of Adam and Eve. Let us return to our days, our time and our own reality.

To this day, these simple acts of betrayals, disobedience of the rules and interference by third parties persists in practically all relationships!

This account, I would assume, apparently, represents the global view and generally is the accepted account of the origin of marriage and relationships.

Interestingly, it also presents us with the birth of controversy in marriages and in human relationships. These delicate issues will be examined in this book. I will also introduce the reader to how these relationship storms can be best avoided. Suffice to say that as a general rule, all relationships which have failed from the origin to the present day have done so for one reason: Whenever something unpleasant and incompatible with the union came in-between the individuals and the union. Certain laws must have been breached by someone or both in the relationship. The rules must have been disregarded by someone somewhere.

This *thing* that causes so much disruption to the union is almost always external to the union but may also be something that helps sustain the relationship, ultimately, something that leads to frustration, anger and unhappiness: for example: money, sex, children, property, in-laws, career, illness, death etc. At the core of such frustration and third party intervention, is the shortsightedness of individuals to the marriage/relationship not to *agree* on the course of action to positively remedy the situation for the sake of the bigger reason for the relationship in the first instance ---*companionship* --- (company together) which I will examine later.

***

CHAPTER THREE
The Purpose of Marriage and Relationships

"We may have all come on different ships, but we're in the same boat now".
Martin Luther King Jr. (1929-1968)

I have been asked many questions in my clinical career, obviously, by my clients and patients. Amongst the most perplexing of the many questions are ones that concern the "purpose of things" and not least, the purpose of a marriage. A lot of the questions may actually be in the form of rhetorical questions.

Sometimes, I do feel, I should be the one asking the question as some of these patients could have been married even before I was born. Though they expect me to rely on my academic and clinical practice to provide the answers, I suppose, experience is the best teacher. Nonetheless, consider the fact that I have seen many couples in crisis. Often such crisis may either have been brought about by marital or relationship discord. It may also be an unrelated crisis that is complicated by disagreement in matrimony. It is therefore not surprising that my experience on having seen varied clients is called for to answer this essential question.

From a casual observation, any keen person should come to the conclusion that every material thing and every process that exists on earth and beyond has an intended purpose. I know this is so from the common reason that nothing can just exist for the sake of existing. We do not go to work or embark on a particular journey without a specific aim. If we do so, someone might say, we are aimless and a wanderer. I know some of the readers will certainly disagree with this view. Some may see chaos in all things or some may see order in the chaos of this world. Whatever your view, one thing is clear: There is a purpose in things and events. You simply need to look a bit closer with more attention to detail, as they say.

Working in Crisis Resolutions Teams in mental health in my encounters with patients, I have been asked by disappointed and bewildered spouses or "partners" in psychological pain:
"What is the purpose of marriage if I have to go through this, doctor?" By *"this"*, it means the troubles, the lack of support from the other spouse, the verbal and physical agony, the financial ruin, the illnesses, the embarrassment, the abandonment, the problem with children and the world that is falling apart around him or her. Now, I got used to hearing this kind of question from time to time, and sometimes, I simply nudge myself and say in silence, "Here we go again…How many times do I have to hear this in my career? I have heard this before".

I have also been sent many questions and I have answered many questions over the internet as to the meaning and purpose of marriage, or if you like, the "meaning of love". I shall provide detailed explanations in this book.

***

As we shall see, in subsequent chapters, marriage, like anything and everything else that exists on earth, is designed to achieve a specific purpose. A business is intended to achieve a desirable purpose. Marriage, it may surprise you, is a "business" with often unwritten vision statements and unstated mission declarations, as we often see in many established businesses. It may not be a business in the same sense as GE, Microsoft or Barclays bank with a lot of capital and financial input, with board meetings and the like. It nevertheless is a business for the couple and perhaps the family with the children are the board members, the earnings of the couple being their income, the project that they manage is actually the home, the children and the couple themselves. Indeed any marriage or relationship between people is not and could not be purposeless. Such a relationship, no matter how distant or even platonic, must have an aim of what the participants intend to achieve. No one can afford to labour for nothing. These businesses which I have mentioned as well as our private relationships, including cohabitation and marriage, are required to be managed by human beings.

Therefore, marriage (and *any* relationship for that matter) as an institution does not fail; it is human beings that fail, often for selfish reasons or what I will call self-preservation reasons. Such selfish reasons are the product of desires - lacking in consideration for the welfare of the other person. Sometimes, such desires would not take account of the harm that may be caused to the other person. Some of these desires run in direct conflict with the desire of the other spouse or partners. In the extreme, some of these desires may actually be illegal or the desires may be a morally bankrupt intention and action.

***

Let us once again return to the issue of the purpose of things. If we take a look around us, we would see that our home is meant to serve as a fortress (more or less) to secure us and as a shelter to serve as a place where we can have some rest. Our homes are meeting places for the family and also as stores in which to keep our belongings secure in the knowledge that it is our castle after all. Above all, a home is a place which we can call our own (either as the owner or tenant) where we feel secure and not threatened by outside forces - a place where we can run to when we need solace.

Similarly, if we take a closer look at the earth around us, we would see that things are ordered in certain manners. The seas are in their place, the mountains and other natural features in their natural locations. None of all these has overrun the other or breached the boundaries of the earth, except under natural order of changing the arrangement such as in tsunamis. In far away space, we can see, thanks to our space scientists, that the Sun is fixated in its place. The planets are going about their daily routines. The stars are doing their jobs. Some we are told are being "born" while others are "dying". In all these, one thing is certain: No matter which religious group we belong to, one thing is clear, human beings did not create this world and beyond. The same holds true even if you profess evolution --- human beings could not have made these things.

Now going by the observable human activities, we know that, these natural assets --- on earth, at least --- require maintenance and some work on them to transform them to other valuable things that human beings and animals can use for their own good. If you prefer, you may call these outcome of human activities as industrial products.

Remember, I did not make this "crucible of controversy" but it exists and one can not deny that fact. I am sure some readers may now want to take issue with my analysis here. The truth however, is palpable and undeniable.

The question thus arises: Who is going to administer these activities? Someone will have to do this job of management. From what is obvious to us as human beings, someone must take the lead. Human beings lead. Thus, *man* indeed takes the lead in some pursuits. In some other areas, *woman* must take the lead, biologically at least. Man, for all his envy of women and in spite of all the falsehoods about "men who became pregnant" in the media lately, can not be pregnant. True men --- bearing a set of XY genes --- are not endowed with the resources and organs to become pregnant and to sustain pregnancy. This is an absolute privilege reserved for women. It is a natural and specific advantage over men. I can therefore not see how the jealousy of women by men can go away in the foreseeable future. And on that account, the superiority of woman over man can not be challenged.

Now the questions are, can a man or a woman do the "job", alone? Can he or she do the job alone regardless of his or her strength? The job in question is management of the earth and its resources. This includes the management of waters, seas, sky, land, animals, plants, forests, other human beings, gold, diamond, platinum, oil reserves, light, darkness and so many other resources, including the space around the earth.

The modern trend in the UK provides the clearest answer. 75% of women, according to a publication from the UK's Home Office, of working age are now at work in one form or another, to supplement and complement the efforts of the men! This figure does not include those full time housewives who as the Law Court in the UK have now concluded in a lot of judgements brought before it, are also at work. Therefore, everyone is working if you look at it from a general perspective except of course, the unemployed.

This reality which I have presented here is regardless of the fact that culturally, men are still seen as the main breadwinner in many homes. The man (or woman) as we can now see, needs a supporter, a backer and a steadfast dependable ally. No one is an island, a paragon of the soul or heart of the party after all. We all need a partner, a friend, a spouse and a pillar to lean on. Someone to help us and to see us through the task we set before us: A trusted person to lighten the load. We need someone to provide a word of encouragement in times of discouragement or to act in sincerity to make the journey less difficult.

***

The next question is: Would you rather work with a stranger or with someone whom you know much better? The evidence from everyday working relationships tends to suggest that people are more content working with someone who would do the job in question but also as a matter of priority, people are more comfortable working with a person who is, for want of language of description, "a known quantity" --- in the common manner of speaking. That is, people like to work with someone that they know. At the minimum, someone whose CV supports his or her ability to do the job and who will not cause damage to the "project".

For me, I would choose the latter too---someone whom, not only do I know but someone who will do the job without harms to the "project". For increased productivity, the job at hand requires an intimate *meet* who can be *trusted* ("Trusted": another keyword to note) with confidential information on how things are supposed to work as well as an *encourager* and a person who will *defend the cause* at any rate. Would you want to be partners with someone who will discourage you on a regular basis? If you do, you will either remain stationary or go backwards. Then your journey through this world may end up not as planned. You need someone who will share the same vision of where you are both heading. If this joint effort works as planned and the two partners share the same vision and challenges of the mission, it is called *compatibility*. If it happens to you and you get to successfully grasp this point, you are a lucky person and the chance of you failing in your intimate relationship is very thin indeed, if not completely nought.

Further, such a person should be someone of sound and stable mind who will protect and care for others and you in the work place for the sake of the task ahead and the "project" at hand. After all, who would want to work with a raving lunatic who would destroy life and properties?

Overall, it would appear that this person must be an individual who can *agree* on what to do and how to do it for the best results. This is a selection process after all and you are in charge of that selective process called "choice". It is the choice, as you may have seen, that you only will have to make. You have to make the choice of the person who will work with you in your journey through this world.

This is the same kind of choice that people managing various real life organisations such as New York Stock Exchange will have to make. That seems to be what is happening in Wall Street and on the high streets of London, the shops in Bangalore, the factories in Paris, through the broad streets in France, the oil rigs in Nigeria, the gold mines in South Africa and the many human endeavours in South America --- competent, trustworthy, supportive and cooperative individuals are sought, at the least, to do the required job. Again, who wants to be associated with a layabout? Connections must be with people who can share the same vision and support each other.

It is required that the person must of necessity be able to deputise for the other(s) when they are either absent or weakened by overwork. This relationship hinges on one thing: Ability of the person(s) involved to share and spend time with others if they are to share the vision and the rewards of hard work, for a long time.

Also, for balance, these two individuals, at least, involved in a relationship must share their issues and views and arrive at an *agreement* for the sake of stability after a period of *give and take* or *negotiations*. (For the reader who may not have paid attention, we have just crossed a landmark point in our discussion: *give and take* or *negotiations*). If not so, things may become lop-sided, intentions may fail and desire may falter. The need for *equilibrium* calls for the condition that these two individuals should have *opposite views* and differing opinions and conflicting biological structures. It means that the chemicals that will control these individuals should be dissimilar.

The world, at any rate, will be very dull if everything were the same. Legitimate diversities and moral varieties of the highest decency rule our world. Human beings after all are not zombies.

If the characteristics of the individuals are as stated, it would appear that, as a *further reward* for their cooperation or agreement, and for the need to continue the work on the "project", they could be blessed with something they both cherish, something so invaluable that it's beyond the reach of money or a single individual. Despite the current technology, it will still require the efforts of two individuals no matter how distant or the method of their contribution, before they achieve their set objectives.. Such a *blessing* may be children coming from their *intimacy*. It is a blessing, because, no one can lay an entitlement to having children. No one can predestine that he or she must have children. There are millions the world over who wish to but can't. Therefore, it remains a blessing.
 (Please remember we are discussing sexual relationships and marriages). It may also be a *reward* in form of money: A reward for their labour. Should the reward be children, these children would continue the work and or may further contribute to the work/project at hand, though this is not by any means certain.

***

The overall name for all this sharing of time, vision, mission, body, energy, work, life, finances, failure, success, pain, ease etc, is called *companionship* and it is the bedrock of all marriages and all forms of legitimate sexual relationships. It is the principal reason why marriage exists. It is the pivotal reason why marriage was instituted. Regardless of the variant, this is what co-habitation and "common law" partnerships are seeking to achieve: Companionship. True companionship is the foundation of all genuinely successful marriages and not just marriages that "patches on" by reason of social and political standing in the public. Once again, for the benefit of the reader, we have just arrived at a significant eternal point: companionship.

It, companionship, is unique to marriage, which could be defined as the inseparable *union* of two adults and individuals of opposite gender. This is the very basis of the *"help meet"* principle that underlies all marriages. We saw how this "help meet" business came about in an earlier chapter. So that I don't bore you the reader with ecclesiastical analysis, I will not repeat it here, though it might be worth reading the previous chapter again.

***

You might ask, is this unique to one woman and one woman marriage alone? The answer is no. Any variant of matrimony or departure from a monogamous marriage, such as multiplication of "marriage" as in some cultures (polygamy) must as a necessity converge towards this *companionship* principle. If not, then there is little wonder why the *"institution"* is said to be failing --- a clear exit from the *rules* that set the institution up in the first instance. Human beings, as we shall see, are very shrewd and manipulative of rules and laws; this underlies the main reason why the divorce rate is going up and it is becoming too difficult to live with one another. As I will explain later, whenever a relationship of whatever kind fails, someone must have broken the rules of the relationship. It is over and over again an unwritten contract that binds a relationship and can get broken. Whenever the words "compatibility" and "companionship" are not well-blended in a relationship, it may fail and the purpose of marriage may therefore be defeated. Let me conclude with the insight of Homer: *"There is nothing nobler or more admirable than when two people who see eye to eye keep house as man and wife, confounding their enemies and delighting their friends".* Did you notice the phrase "eye to eye"? It means the same thing as compatibility, which is a forerunner for companionship, for you can only spend your time with someone with whom you are in agreement. Or would you want to spend your time being in constant disputes? The answer is up to you.

However, my aim in this book is to lay bare the snares in human relationships and examine why associating with others can so painfully end in failure. It is up to you the reader to make up your mind. And making up your mind requires that you are aware of how you do so under a very powerful tool that is commonly called *free will* with its sister component, *choice.* The major challenge that confronts anyone who is looking for a relationship is actually how to get the right one and get it right first time. Still, this is the crossroad of choices at which you will need to make a decision.

If you, the reader, are ever to fail or succeed in any endeavour, not least finding a partner or spouse, this will depend on how you exercise your free will and the choice that you may make under the natural laws, moral codes and laws of the land that you reside in. The choice is yours. The choice has nothing to do with God. God does not choose spouses or partners for people. He did so once and human beings failed the trust.

CHAPTER FOUR
The Choice of Spouse and Partner:
Free Will and the Choices that We Make

"The will of a man is his happiness."
- Schiller, Wallenstein's Lager (VII, 25)

You may be pardoned for thinking that relationships of whatever shape and nature are a natural process in which two minds meet and that once there is chemical interaction/"chemistry" between them, a deal is made and a new relationship is born. Well, you are probably correct if you have been following R&B and Pop songs. Sadly, you will also note the high turnover rate of relationships amongst artistes which I have mentioned.

If you are however looking for a lasting relationship beyond the virtual world of fame and if you are looking for somebody who will be at you side, standing with you, backing you in the days when things are either sour or sweet, then the deciding factor which you should consider certainly goes beyond, chemical interaction / "chemistry".

On the other hand, if you are looking for a "one night stand", or an "affair", you may skip this chapter. Even at that, you may still read this chapter since, unless you make the right choice for your "affair"; you may end up with a kind of medical disorder that you never really bargained for. I should not be misunderstood at all; I am not advocating an "affair" neither am I in support of "one night stands" for the results of these acts may go beyond what you the reader could have ever intended as anyone working with abandoned children, mentally unwell individuals and people with sexually transmitted diseases will tell you.

If we then turn the plate over, if you are serious about your peace of mind and about avoiding the trouble that has plagued so many relationships before you or are afflicting on-going relationships, then take my advice: read this chapter for you need this tool to navigate the intricate nature of human conduct and relationships. You need the ability to differentiate and look in-depth at what is presented before you, including that partner that you are thinking of. Human beings are covered so graciously by beauty (skin, muscles, and appearances) so much that the true person (the intention within) is concealed inside, encased in an almost impenetrable fortress that is called the mind. But with dogged determination, skill and the ability to select under the power of free will, you can reach the heart of men and women with relative ease. That is what I present here.

***

I suppose that the best place to continue a book of this kind is to look at how we all got here in the first instance. By 'got here' I do not mean the debate on creation or evolution. I shall leave that subject to the various leading characters in the debate. The important thing, however, is that we are all here, including you, the reader. By 'here', I mean your present position, be it the current status of your health, finances, education, or general well-being. It means the effects and influence of our past on our present circumstances. Since we are on a journey into the future, our present and past will determine our future circumstances. The very idea that you are reading this book, for example, implies that you got here and are now reading this book by the choice you have made. You could have decided not to read this book. You could have done something differently. Nevertheless, you chose amongst many options that were presented to you, to read a book at this moment. You were not coerced into it. An exception does apply: if your boss coerced you or your instructor or teacher coerced you into reading the book at this moment. Then you can claim that you have no choice but to read the book. It is in that respect that I wish to introduce the concept of *free will*.

***

First, what does free will mean? I asked my eight year old son this question. He answered that it means, "You do what you will do." A fine definition but it required some expansion. I will extend this definition to mean: "The *uninhibited freedom* to choose and to do as you wish". Free will means that we can choose to either do the 'right thing' or to do the 'wrong thing'. By extension, it means that to be creative is to have free will – defined as 'one does according to one's *accord* or *will*'.

Legally, concerning coercion, in this case you have not exercised your free will to choose what you want to do. If you are coerced into doing things, you are merely carrying out the desires and intentions of people or a person who are coercing you. Nonetheless, once you have freely exercised what you want to do, you are held responsible for your actions. You can not blame anyone else. In that regard, choosing a partner, you may be surprised to know, or cohabitants and a spouse are no different. Did I just see you underline that fundamental truth? You are directly responsible.

Now, I should explain what the 'right thing' or the 'wrong thing', as stated above, means. I need to clarify that these two phrases refer to two relative points, or reference points. It is to those two points that our conduct, moral and physical actions or thoughts, are compared. If we are on the good side of the reference points then we are doing the right thing. To be on the good side means we do what we think is good in keeping with our morality, culture and our laws. We will not be at fault or cause offence or fall foul of any rule. We are as free as a bird. It means we do not depart from what our moral decency is required of us. It means we do what is expected of us, that which will promote our welfare and the well-being of others without causing offence.

If we are on the bad side of the reference points then we are doing the wrong thing. It means we are departing from the norms or rules that our family, our society and our country expect from us. It means we are harming someone and are causing offence to the larger society, or ourselves in many ways than one.

If there are no such reference points, there will be no standard of behaviour, expectations, competitions, achievements, successes, hopes and failures. These reference points will also determine our happiness depending on if we are on the wrong or right side of the reference points. What does it mean to do the 'right thing' or the 'wrong thing'? Despite the *'uninhibited'* nature of free will, it will amount to total chaos if every one of us is allowed in the larger society to do what we wish. Then we would be living in lawlessness. For this not to happen, we need to put some limitations on the way we think, what we choose, where we go, despite the free will that we possess. Similarly, families and countries put boundaries in place to contain the exercise of free will of its members. God, under the various legal enactments, such as the Ten Commandments, also put in place legal boundaries to contain human thoughts and actions. If these limitations are not in their places then human beings, in particular, (and to a lesser extent the animals) will behave in such a manner that there would be no society as we know it today. There would be chaos on the streets as one individual exercising his free will would behave in such a manner as to interfere and cause conflict with the freedom and free will of others. All these in the course of exercising his own free will!

* * *

To forestall this kind of behaviour it is necessary, as it happens, that certain restrictions, in the form of laws, rules and regulations, should be put in place to limit or to control the exercise of an individual's (our) free will. This is how society is regulated, and hence the very basis of our existence as a community. Imagine the *freedom of expression* that is made available to us by our own laws even though this is supposed to be a natural right *(which includes freedom of speech,* anyway*)*. Unless human beings are controlled by legal boundaries which are in place and are enforced, some individuals or groups will push the boundaries of this freedom to such an extent and they will exercise their free will to such a degree that they will commit offences, such as indecent exposure, incitement of anarchy and many others.

Besides the laws made by our governments, and according to which side of the debate you belong, there is a *natural* limitation as to how far we can put our free will into effect. This limitation is set by what scientists have called *nature*.

Example: Collectively, or as individuals, we human beings cannot exercise our free will to shift the axis on which the earth rotates around the Sun. Neither can we decide to grow wings or feathers like the birds of the air, no matter how much we may wish to do so. It does mean that exercise of our free will is limited, firstly by the overall control that is put in place by *nature* and then by the restraint under the law made by man (our *governments*). In both cases, however, these controls are laws – a breach of which will lead to, or be interpreted as, doing the '*wrong thing*' and then being on the wrong side of the reference points which I referred to earlier.

* * *

On the other hand, a compliance with either or both sets of controls will be termed as doing the '*right thing*'. It is within these sets of limitations that we all, or should all, exercise our free will (see my explanation below, on determinism). These limitations, therefore, largely define our freedoms - either given by man-made laws or derived automatically from nature. These simple explanations about right and wrong are turning points in our decision making process to choosing whom we want to be associated with, so I shall urge the reader, as we go along, to take it as one of the tools we will need in order to work on our choice, happiness and success.

An example of the freedom that is derived from nature will be the free will and freedom to breathe, speak, walk, sleep, eat and live and choose whom you want to befriend or marry among many others. This free will can be limited by the *choices* of the individual, be extinguished by man-made laws, or simply be taken away by nature if these laws are not complied with. I hope the reader noted that I have mentioned the word *choices*. What have choices got to do with happiness, success or failure? As we shall find out, no one opens the gate in the entrance to the home of happiness without having the element called *choices*. To do otherwise could be perilous. Marriage and forming of relationships are not different.

I have mentioned earlier that Adam did not choose his wife and Eve did not choose her husband. They were imposed on each other. It was God's will; not Adam's or Eve's. They were more or less coerced into the relationship. Today, except in some Asian, Middle East, and African cultures and some religions, that is rarely ever the case. Today, the determination of who are going to be our spouses and partners is firmly within our grip in our choices operating under our free will. Why is God not "coercing" individuals to marry a certain person? The short answer is as we shall see what becomes of our relationships is the result of our choice — either we chose directly or we are passive in the choice making process. The fact is that our spouses and partners were selected by choice. That is an undeniable truth. I am aware that some might argue the position of and influence of determinism in our choice-making process. For those readers who may be wondering what determinism means, it's the philosophical doctrine that every state of affairs, including every human event, act, and decision is the inevitable consequence of antecedent states of affairs. The issue to remember is that it's within the limit of laws that guide nature and human conducts that we have and operate our choices. We, human are not helpless on-lookers.

The logic in all these explanations is that, you select your partner or cohabitants solely on the choice which you have made or which someone made for you. After all, you can not blame anyone for a choice which you made consciously.

***

The aim of this book, you will remember, is to help you avoid the pitfalls and the unseen traps that litter the relationship making process, the idea being that we can make credible and valid choices that will contribute positively to our health and happiness. Any wrong choice can be devastating indeed. This is because, as the ancients would have put it, if you are wise, you are wise for yourself and if you are not so wise, you make bad decisions; the rewards lay ahead for you. Your relationship may simply be added to the existing numbers of failed or successful statistics. Only you can decide what you ultimately settle for: just you and no one else. My job is, simply put, to help you along the way. When you are done, I will have been long gone. After all, that is the power of free will.

(Note: Anyone who is interested in how we make choices should read my earlier book: *The Road and the Key to Happiness*).

CHAPTER FIVE
Why Marriages and Relationships Fail or Succeed.

"The meeting of two personalities is like the contact of two chemical substances. If there is any reaction, both are transformed."
Carl Gustav Jung (1875-1961)

By now, you have understood or, at least, you have read how we came about marrying each other and how the duty for us to choose who would be our partner is propelled into our hands. By now you are aware of the reasons and purposes why we have to enter into such relationships in the first instance. I have mentioned in the introduction and in subsequent chapters that you can either choose to be on your own, despite the perils of doing so, or you can enter into an alliance, or to put it in common language, a relationship, with another person. I have, similarly, mentioned and explained the various relationships that exist.

Now the big question is: what makes a relationship fail or succeed? Answering this question certainly calls for one to take an all-round view of things and events around us. Let me begin from the experience that I have garnered over these years.

I have had many enquiries from individuals asking me why some marriages fail or succeed. I have, sometimes, wondered aloud myself if only for the reason of rhetorical questioning. Marriages fail. Unions of two people do get dissolved. It has puzzled and plagued mankind for millennia. The new trend is that there is speedy dissolution and a racing or some competitiveness to it. The race to get a relationship dissolved has aptly been termed: "quickie divorce," to imply a less protracted dissolution.

If the reader has paid attention to the previous chapters, it would have been clearer why some marriages fail and why some are successful. However, there are some salient issues that either needs to be discussed or added to existing truths, as stated previously. Even if a marriage is established on solid ground of *companionship,* it is not guaranteed that there will be no slip-ups by someone in the union. There is no cast iron assurance that there will be no treachery. Partners, spouses, and cohabitants are human beings. Human beings change and can be persuaded to change. Human minds are not made of cast iron. Even cast iron can be broken down. Yet the human mind is a most formidable site of a fortress to conceal and to defend intentions and desires. A decision to remain firm and steadfast is in human mind. Why then do relationships fail?

Spouses, cohabitants and partners, can receive or be part of threats to the marriage. The first known human marriage and relationship, which we saw earlier, so nearly collapsed even under divine guidance. Great was the threat and the storm that befell that first relationship. Human beings are just too risky to be trusted with such delicate things as marriage.
To examine and find out why some marriages succeed and some fail, we need to determine what makes relationships, such as marriages, succeed.

***

How does marriage survive on a daily basis?
Frankly, marriage in many cultures used to transpire as a business, in which there was an exchange of one family member, often the female, as goodwill. Alternatively, it may be to cement a relationship between one family and the other. It still occurs in some cultures. For the moment, let us assume, as I believe it is, that marriage is a business that needs to be planned for, with strategic vision, mission statements in place and nurtured. Let us assume it is business as in any government or company. Let us take for granted that it is, as in all walks of life, something that requires planning and vigilance. Marriage will only survive if:

    a) All *acts and words* expressed by the two in the *union* are *genuinely* expressed in support of and in defence of the common purpose of the marriage (that is, in defence of the continued existence of the *companionship*). Words change things. Our actions and conduct begin with the formation of words. What we say, the way we say it and the circumstances under which it was said can either bring peace or cause inflammation. Words are creative. They can make well or can cause serious damage to individuals and the relationship.

b) That all intentions, desires and acts so expressed genuinely are communicated clearly and appropriately in time and place to the other person. Note that *communication* implies *exchange* of useful and constructive data that is called information, between at least two people. Communication can be by verbal expression, written notes and by signalling/body language. Silence is also a way to communicate if appropriate. The most speedily powerful of them all is when words are expressed in verbal means though all three forms above are very effective. Commonly in relationships, the means by which couples communicate is by verbal expressions. Unguarded verbal expressions can be lethal. In modern times, communication has been made relatively easy and accessible by electronic means. For example: common experience of anyone who uses the internet or mobile phone, shows that expressions of love and affection, as well as separation, threat of divorce and any information that impacts on the union can be sent or can take place over the internet (be it by email or video etc), cellular/mobile phone media or texts.

The important thing is to let the other party receive your intention in expressed words. Ideally, in a marriage that is civil, two people speak, one at a time while the other listens with rapt attention. However, we know from experience, that this idealised situation is far from reality. A lot of relationships have come to untimely ends simply because of either the misuse of bad words in communication (the content of the communication is terribly discouraging, abusive, threatening and unhelpful) or there is no communication at all. Silence in this case may not mean consent.

The important thing, however, is that any uttered word or conduct that does not support the *union or promote* the welfare of the other party/spouse is most likely to end the association. Did you take note of the words *"promote the welfare of the other party/spouse"*? It is a pearl in any relationship. That is, words in communication can either build or destroy the union. Therefore, if the union is to survive, it should be supported with encouraging and motivational words for legitimate goals that will both promote the union and advance the cause of its members. Again, the word "legitimate" is important for any relationship that threatens the common good of the larger society may fail, especially if cracks develop in the *union*.

***

Some reasons, some would claim, why they, the partners or spouses go into a relationship or marriage.

I have mentioned that what could potentially end a given relationship and, not least, a marriage, is often external to the relationship. Sometimes, this is what actually cements the relationship. Sometimes, these "cementing" or external matters can become the stumbling block for the couple, except when due care is taken and the danger is recognised very early so that preventive action can be put in place. The following lists represent some reasons for some marriages

1) *Money and prosperity:* Some individuals do consider the reason for their relationship as the financial gain to be derived from the relationship. Even if this is not cited, outsiders to the relationship can easily see that this is the reason for its existence. Again, this is a matter of choice for the person as he or she has the free will to make the decision.

   Perhaps one can say that a relationship that survives on subsistence hardly ends compared to a relationship that is comfortable. Money can be both a sword and a shield. This is probably why there are clearly more divorces in developed world: America (50%), UK (30%), Japan (27%) Australia (40%) and Europe, than anywhere else in the world. Religious similarities or differences can not be a sole factor in stemming or increasing divorce. This is because there are many claims that "couples that pray together stay together". The data proves otherwise. This is not to say the opposite is true. If you relate to somebody with whom you have divergent opinions on religious issues, it may lead to conflict and sometimes crisis. If there are couples who are together but have different religious views, then, it means there is something they agree on that overrides their religious differences. There are situations where couples share similar dominant religious perspectives, yet the rate of divorce is staggering. Here are some examples: 80% or so of USA residents attend or commit themselves to Christianity of one denomination or the other, yet they have a 50% divorce rate in the USA, with the majority being church goers. In the UK, 70% of people claim to be "Christians" though only 10% actually attend a church, yet the divorce rate is about 33%. Therefore, on that account, money is a sword against the relationship and the effect of religion is probably nil. In some traditional societies, marriages in Africa and Asia (Note: Cohabitation for practical pursoses is unknown in most of these areas) survive even in the absence of any real income other than farm produce, some subsistence market sales and the support of the larger extended family members. Note should be taken that in most societies in Africa or Asia these is absence of formal social welfare support. Yet in wealthy societies, the opposite is true. The pressure for material acquisition and the pursuit of money to support this material acquisition is tearing relationships apart (intimate or platonic).

What about the shield? Needless to say that scarcity of finances can put unbearable pressure on couples in a relationship as they struggle to pay the bills and meet the daily challenges. Some couples that I have met described their ensuing arguments following financial difficulty as "World War III". Plenty of money may, just, may prevent this "war," but not guarantee to shield the marriage or relationship if it's failing in other areas.

As I will discuss under the legal and financial implications of marriage, money could be a stronger shield if the couple pool resources in *agreement*. *(That word –agreement—again)*. The reality though is that this is not the usual case. We face a selfish and challenging world. Sadly, money has ended many marriages with plenty of wealth to spare.

Unfortunately, there are reports which cite couples as giving the aspiration of acquiring money as the primary purpose for their marriage. Well, what happens when you have it in abundance when this desire is satisfied? Obviously, that signals the end of the relationship. The lesson--- money should not be the primary purpose for a marriage, not even of any relationship, outside a formal business arrangement (see later under business relationships).

2) *Children:* This is often cited as the reason for marriage. Wrong. Children are not even close to the primary purpose. If having children were to be the primary purpose, then *voluntarily* childless couples have failed in their mission. Besides, the story relating to "help meet" would certainly defeat this aim. Nonetheless, having children is a blessing in a marriage which should be valued and not abused, though a lot of people do. However, a relationship that sets its mission as either having children or nothing in a marriage will certainly end up in divorce. In truth though, I have seen the distress that childlessness can cause to a relationship and

it should not be taken for granted in the planning process for a marriage. As I will discuss later, this crucial desire should be investigated before vows are ever exchanged. Once again, it should be emphasised that marriage based on companionship is not likely to end in childlessness, except when the couple takes their eyes off the ball. I have asked many people to tell me why they had children. Not a single person could give a reason for having children. They had no plan; they proposed no purpose and had no idea what to do with the children when they had them. To a rational mind, this is why there is so much child abuse in the world today. Children therefore are blessings. A kind of blessing by which, by our actions, we can either impair their emergence to the earth or impair their continued existence on earth.

3) *Sex:* I will deal more extensively with matters that relate to sex under a different chapter. However, I am very puzzled that some individuals would go into a marriage or intimate relationship for the mere sake of sex. The billion dollar question is what next, now that we have sex, or shall we call it "love", as the song goes? Some individuals think this is the primary purpose for a meaningful relationship. It may well be a *"one night stand"* or *"affair"*, but as I explained in the introduction, this does not count as a serious strategic relationship that is meant to yield a great result. I have seen the products (children) of a single night stand in my clinical practice. Some are depressed, some suicidal, most are unwanted, unplanned and rejected human beings who often no longer have serious links with their parents nor a future that they can defend.

Marriage and relationships that set out with the aim of its destination being sexual intercourse are heading for the rocks. Lust and indiscretion do not last long before they fizzle out, as the word goes.

What happens when sexual desire is satisfied? Often, people will look for another "variety". A series of *affairs* sets in. Treachery occurs. Third parties come in. The union fractures and gravitates towards its unfortunate end.

Sex, if I may say so, in a prelude to the chapter on intercourse, is the "icing on the cake" of marriage. No cake, no icing. As we all know, you can only have a valid and legal sex if two people cooperate, in union and/or in *companionship* to achieve sexual activity. For anything outside consent and cooperation, sex becomes a problem and illegal as in rape cases.

***

There is another common reason why people enter into a "relationship". Here the people and the various governments are acting like cat and mouse when it comes to talking about this kind of relationships. The people need to survive and the government needs the people. Neither is prepared to rock the boat. This type of relationship affects millions of people, especially in the Western world and to some extent in other countries that experience high inward migration of people. The target: biological and economic survival.

How is it done? The law is truly an ass in this regard. Just make use of it, ride it and dump it, it seems. If you are an immigrant and you are facing immigration trouble, why worry when you can marry someone who is resident in the country. People do so, even when there is no "love" and no affection, just a plain old self-preservation instinct is the driving force. The next step: satisfy the requirements of the law and what next? Divorce or maintain the relationship at your peril, especially if there are now children from the relationship.

The consequence is that it adds to the divorce rates. Alternatively, it adds to the number of unhappy people who have ended up with what they did not actually want in the first place. The way out: plan well as the relationship may in fact become permanent.

***

Why some marriages succeed and some fail: the key reasons

I have heard people say that love hurts (see chapter on why love hurts). Love neither hurts nor fails. It is human instability and unpredictability that hurts or fails. Let us see some of the reasons why relationships sink.

1) *Wrong Foundation*: Clearly, the most obvious reason is when a union or marriage is based on the wrong foundations. As I have explained in preceding sections, some relationships, I am afraid, are based on such things as property. Some individuals may calculate the potential of another individual and then come to the conclusion that, if they can form a relationship with that person, their lot in material terms is likely to be better---property wise. Well, it may really be successful in this objective but it will ultimately fail when the objective is satisfied. When it comes to self-preservation and survival, human beings will use all the techniques in the world to ensure their security. Therefore, it should not be surprising that men and women employ this method in marriage, or any relationships, too. Of course, it would have perhaps been preferable, if this kind of relationship had been based on a business relationship. Therefore, a marriage will fail if it is based on the *benefits that may flow from marriage*, rather than the benefits coming from the *foundation* of the relationship. On this point, one can recall the wisdom of Anthony Robbins, that *"Some of the biggest challenges in relationships come from the fact that most people enter a relationship in order to get something. They're trying to find someone who's going to make them feel good. In reality, the only way a relationship will last is if you see your relationship as a place that you go to give, and not a place that you go to take"*.

2) *Abuse/Misuses of Tools*: Whenever anything is created or manufactured in our factories, there will be conditions and terms of use to allow for maximal benefits. If you fail to follow the manual of use or the product is subjected to wrong conditions, the product will suffer

damage. The same thing goes for any relationship. There are certain things that hold the relationship in place. A marriage will fail or succeed depending on whether the tools that hold it in existence continue to hold. A crucial example of such tools is "love". Whilst "love" will be further explored later, it is sufficient to say that love simply means "do not cause harm" to another person--- intentionally or not. From this, we can see that, if a marriage is ever going to fail or succeed, it will depend on whether at least one of the *people (the couple, in-laws etc)* in the relationship is causing harm to the others.

Harm begins with words. Words, if *misused,* can cause psychological injury and pain, which is also recognised in law. That said, words that cause anger, unhappiness and psychological injury are rarely ever taken into account in legal process that may follow marriage problems; yet this tool, words, is the most lethal instrument to kill, cause damage or, on the other hand, heal. A marriage is bound for failure in the absence of good, loving, encouraging, motivating *words and an action that causes no harm* in an environment that should have been perfumed with kind words. A marriage is also more likely to be successful in an atmosphere of honest concern, true motivational words and encouraging acts.

Further, if you have abused your biological assets (your body and mind) such as having an early unplanned pregnancy and unwanted baby, it may end your relationship with this particular partner. This is because, the tension, the pull of the need to care for the baby and to balance your own life, might just be too much for you before you realise the consequences of your actions.

3) *Communication:* I have dealt with this above. Suffice to say that marriage and indeed any relationship, intimate or not, will either fail or succeed depending on whether the exchange of good quality, true and constructive information is either present or absent between the

couple. Words change things. Where there are no words, there is no way. A marriage that exists on hurtful words and acts, or one that tries to survive on pretensions and false façades, is doomed.

***

Conditions that make success or failure a possibility:

a) *Interference from third parties:* Marriage never fails, save for the occurrence of one of the following. The first marriage was shaken because of misdirection and bad advice from a third party. What happened between three individuals so many years ago is still happening today. The third party in the Garden of Eden was a snake, but in our modern world, this snake has taken the shape of a creature with two legs, arms and a brain, and all the configuration of human beings. This third party can be your in-laws. It can be enemies who pretended to be friends of the family. So long as one party allows the words and acts of others from outside the union to negatively influence their decisions, views or opinions of either of the companions, then the end is nigh for the relationship. These outside opinions may also be views expressed on TV soaps, news and womens' or mens' magazines.

b) *Shift in focus:* Every relationship and marriage should have something that binds them together. Ideally, this should be the common purpose of providing companionship to the other as *"help meet"*. As I have described above, it may be based on sex, enhancement of career, finances and so on. If either of the couple shifts sights from the common purpose of companionship, in particular, the couple will soon become intolerant of each other. This can be due to financial pressure, career, selfish interest, and extra-marital affairs or just about anything, including illnesses. In sum, once the sight of a common destination becomes blurred or darkened, it will be difficult for the couple and everyone involved in the relationship to see eye to eye. No one can see in darkness, after all.

***

CHAPTER SIX
Adolescent Relationship: The Turbulent Years

"When love is not madness, it is not love".
Pedro Calderon de la Barca

For a lot of adults, the foundation of our future relationships and indeed the partners that we may ultimately be with in the long term could be traceable to our early years in adolescence. Yet, adolescent years are a time when so many mistakes can be made because the mind of the teen is so much under different influences and uncertainties. Besides, it is, except with proper guidance, a time of wavering commitments and for others, a time of resolute attachment to others outside the home.

The danger is that, failure can be very serious and may have a long lasting impact on the psychology of the young man and woman. In spite of this, this volatile period is not escapable for every one of us as we have to grow into adulthood and must as a necessity pass through this phase.

The risk is also clear: if you grow into an adult too fast, you risk being burdened with a lot of challenges of life that adults carry on their shoulders. In contrast, if you grow too slowly and are not catching up socially with your peers even if you are well biologically, there is the risk of being called inconvenient names. There is therefore a need for balance in order to avoid the risks and the dangers which I mentioned above.

There is no doubt that that the years of the adolescent are years of flaming passion. Sometimes, it is so for the right reason. Sometimes it is not so. Who can stop a teen who is giving all his or her heart to another in trust? A teen who is escaping into a temporary euphoria, who believes in another world beyond the earth where one, can spend eternity in bliss whilst still in human flesh and blood?

The adolescent gets into different types of relationships and it is the most vulnerable period in a young person's life. In general, what holds for adult relationships is in large part true for the young person except that they, teens, are easily led and easily misled by the cunning ones of their age group as well as adults. For sake of definition, a teen or adolescent is someone who is under 18 years of age. Broadly, the types of relationships that teens get into can be divided into two: non-intimate/non-sexual on the one hand and intimate/sexual relationships on the other. As I explained in earlier parts of this book, the first type are called platonic relationships.

Whatever the type, the main issue with teen relationships is that they are based on trust. Teens can also express such strong trust and dependency in a relationship that if the relationship fails, it may hurt them very badly. Failure or hurt in a relationship of either type may leave a permanent impression on the teen and may therefore affect how he or she relates in the future. The adolescent mind is unstable despite the strong emotions involved in their relationships: they, the adolescents, can also change with relative ease as the case study below will show.

(The reader should note that at some points in this chapter, I have chosen to directly address the adolescent who may be reading this book. The change in style is aimed at driving my points home to the minds of the teen and to enable them appreciate the issues that I have raised here. To the more adult reader, I have not taken you for granted and if you feel that I have done so, please accept my apologies).

***

Let me start with the non-intimate, platonic relationship.
A non-intimate relationship is one consisting of ordinary friendship. It may be between schools mates of either gender or it may be a casual friendship with the neighbour.

It may be safe though not sexual. It may not be safe in other security areas, for example, an unsupervised relationship may be exploited, such as use in forced labour. The teen may also receive bad advice and so may be misled.

A typical young person who is just emerging from the cover and protection of his or her parents may not be aware of the dangers that lay in wait outside. I will use this opportunity to advise the young ones and to advise the parents that there are dangers out there and caution is advised regarding who they choose as friends.

Need for caution on all fronts.
The adolescent years usually mark a turning point in a person's life. If anything is going to go wrong in the person, it will go wrong now. If things go right, the foundations will be laid now. A child who is emerging into young adulthood has received some basic training (good or/and bad) from the parents or guardians whilst at home. He or she, who is now gradually stepping into the larger society, must in the past, have had some childhood friendships which may continue through adolescence into adulthood. Such relationships may continue to influence those involved for the rest of their lives.

***

Now to the adolescent
Teens could also have relationships which may also be friends which were made in school. Such friendships may continue for good or for bad, for a short while or for the rest of your lives.

However in the majority of cases and for almost everyone, you will meet new friends on the street, in new schools, through the internet and in many other new environments. They will influence you and either allow you into their own world or you allow them into your own world. There is no neutral point.

You can not have a friend or relationship without any influence.

Some will call the previous training or upbringing which you may have received in childhood as rubbish and urge that you should abandon your background and embrace theirs. They will attempt to teach you new ways—their ways which may not be the way you know or the way that is right for you.

***

Why adolescents behave they way they do.
Adolescence is where young minds must exercise caution, sit back and consider their friends, very carefully. Since, they, the young person, is going as a "green" person into the world where there will be strange things and challenges ahead.

Because adolescents are also not yet in full grasp of reality, they tend to be confused and not really happy with what is going on around them. This is why they may become rebellious towards rules at home and in public for they want to change things in their own image. Also, they sometimes think they are above the law (false perception as they are no longer children. Note that the age of criminal responsibility for children in the England and Wales, for example, is from 10 yeas of age and 8 years in Scotland) and in so doing they may get into trouble with the law.

***

How do I know I have the right person to associate with?
The golden rule is that adolescent or teens should be wary of what will *cause harm to their mental and physical health.*

To the teen who is reading this book
An associate or person in a sexual or platonic relationship is likely to introduce something to you to make you "feel good". Anything that will make you feel good or give you "happiness" or be described as a "happy pill" is a dangerous thing and should be resisted.

The problem of shyness
Another issue is that a lot of adolescents are shy at the start of their young life. This is a problem in boys who may want to approach girls for the first time. Shyness and the right words to use might pose a problem for boys. Shyness in girls is a biological issue rather than social as in boys and is a matter that is commonly seen in women. A friend might advise: "try alcohol

to help with your shyness or help the timidity". The truth is that might be the start of a bigger problem and slide into alcohol abuse and then damage to their mental health, brain and liver as well as end to their future career, my clinical experience have shown. Here is evidence from British Medical Journal (BMJ):

"Misuse of alcohol, tobacco, inhalants, and other drugs is now widespread among adolescents internationally and causes substantial health problems in this group.

Alcohol and tobacco are by far the most commonly used substances by young people and result in 95% of morbidity and mortality related to substance misuse in this age group. Despite the public and political concerns about use of illicit drugs, such drugs are much less commonly used than alcohol and tobacco, although they may pose more serious immediate health risks. The "gateway" theory about drugs (that tobacco and alcohol may lead on to use of illicit drugs) does not always hold in adolescence. Although it is true that almost all users of illicit drugs have used tobacco and alcohol, most adolescents who regularly use tobacco and alcohol do not progress to using illicit drugs".

Therefore, the advice is to stay away from anything that is promoted as morale booster, feel-good substances and "shyness-remover". The advice is to stay firm and develop natural personal confidence.

***

What adolescents are at risk of:
My experience as a clinician while interacting with many adolescents is that few if any, have ever got into problems *except* through the relationship that they keep. No one, for example, goes out of his way diligently searching for cocaine except if he has been told about it by somebody somewhere who he /she is associated with. In all, the advice or instruction must have been passed on from another say in a movie, films or books! It's still a relationship, albeit virtual and distant! Ghosts don't make movies and books. Behind them are other human

beings that indirectly influence our affairs. The same statements as above, goes for speed, ecstasy, LSD, cannabis, mushrooms, pain-killers heroin and many other strange preparations.

Main problem areas:
 1) Crime

Teens, out of naivety and ignorance, conspire with other "mates" or act alone, to commit crimes. Such crimes can be petty, such as stealing from home or in local shops. Parents are sometimes surprised at this and such behaviour may be described as being "out of character" for the young man or young woman. By this time, it may have become too late and the law may have taken its course. Once again, while territories differ, the age of criminal responsibility in much of the UK is 10 years. You, as a reader, if you are a teen, will be held responsible for your actions if you are 10 years old or over. Sad but true. Law does not know who is a "child". If you commit a crime, you do the time in young offenders' centres! Ignorance is no defence either.

 2) Lack of understanding about the on-going biological processes.

"This one is for you. I used it before..."

The rapid biological change that takes place in a typical adolescent is a challenge for everyone and not least you the young person. The changes in breasts and private areas and growth of hairs and pimples can be puzzling. This is the time when "mates and friends" advise all sorts of remedies and experimentation. My advice is to seek genuine guidance from trained professionals—nurses and doctors for example.

Do not take any preparations that are described as "good for you". Your mates may not know better and he or she could be misleading you.

 3) Drugs

I have not seen anything that is more destructive to the lives of teens than drugs and alcohol. I have listed some of the drugs above. Almost always, it is your mate who will introduce it and ask you to try it. Do not. It can kill or damage your health and seriously too, at that.

4) Sex and early parenthood

One thing is clear from experience: You can only have sex if you have been *lured* into it by an associate or "in order to belong" to your friends who are trying it. You may also want to experiment with it. The truth is, it might in the end, just be too early for you and it may therefore not be right for you. Besides, the risk of catching a disease is likely and that may cause damage to your future ability to have children of your own. In addition, you may also get killed by some deadly diseases such as AIDS. Finally, if you become a dad at 15 or before you are ready, life may become difficult afterwards, as you will now as a parent, have to look after 3 people (you, wife/husband/partner and child). There is time for everything. The bottom line is that, hold on until you are a proper mature adult when you will be able to sustain a family.

5) Career and Future

Through relationships or associates or "mates", your future can either be good or bad, it all depends on the friends you hang around with.

***

Intimate Relationships in Adolescence Years

As I mentioned earlier, adolescent relationships fall into two categories. I have discussed the first one. Now let me look at the second which is in fact a very serious type of relationship: sexual/intimate relationship.

Going by the law in most reasonable world territories, sex with a child who is under sixteen is illegal and it is a form of sexual abuse. I am not deluded by the fact that there are lands where these facts are dismissed for religious reasons. In countries where sex with a child who is under sixteen is prohibited, if it occurs, it carries serious penalties. The problem is what happens when two teens form an intimate sexual relationship? I shall leave that to you to think about.

This author is not a judge and I will not assume to be one here. My mission is to lay bare balanced information so that you the reader can make up your own mind.

That said, sexual and intimate relationships in adolescence, especially if it is the first relationship outside the parental/family care, can be taken very seriously.

Teens dream of non-realistic bliss. They have dreams that are out of touch with this world. They tend to live this fantastic relationship as if no challenge exists around them. They are consumed by it. It is a flame in their mind. Emotions run high. They envision it to the point of delusion. They spend time thinking about it. This is their life: joy and freedom at last. They may hide it from parents or in open homes where there is free information exchange, they may tell. Alternatively, they, the teen, regardless of whether they tell their parents/guardian, they will certainly have friends who will for the time being be their "counsellor" and "adviser"---day and night. Often, it is their "mate". Sometimes, it may be an adult.

The sad truth is that, such advisers and counsellors may mislead the innocent young souls.

When failure in a relationship such as this occurs, trust is betrayed and hearts are broken; it can take a very serious turn indeed.

***

Let me illustrate my claim by citing two stories as illustration of how turbulent and vulnerable an adolescent who is in a relationship is.

I am not going to talk about Romeo and Juliet. Forget it. That is too common knowledge. However, my stories are similar.

First, a young male---16 years old--- deeply in "love" with a girl of similar age. I was called to see him because he had wanted to die. Reason? The girl had told him that she is no longer interested in him. No specific reason was given to him. She was not going to go out with any other person. She just didn't want to continue anymore.

Second story: A boy of about 17 years old. He was in a relationship with a girl of about the same age. He thought she loved him. But the girl had different ideas. She told him she was going to go out with another boy. The rejected boy, who was by now in crisis, could just not accept that it was all over.

What about girls? The stories are similar. I was asked to see a 17 year old girl. She was very pretty by all measure of it. She thought the boy was in love with her but he jilted the girl. The girl took an overdose and ended up in hospital. She could not accept failure and rejection. After all, in fairness, the girl was beautiful. "Why can't I have the boy?" she wondered. The boy was now not going to come back. Sad but true. Reality had just dawned on the girl, the hard way.

While these stories are true and are from real life, they are by no means isolated incidents. These stories are true in Asia, Europe, Africa and America. They are true for teenagers everywhere. Their mental and physical susceptibilities expose them to events such as these. Their minds, innocence, trust and naivety make them too fragile.

The advice is that there is time for everything.

The relationships you form now will influence you for the rest of your life. Therefore, it might just be wise to properly ask wise adults for help, though some adults are in need of help themselves and are worse than the teens! The alternative is to tread with due care.

Why are they so susceptible?

The truth is that teens are still children and their mental and physical development is not yet mature enough to handle what is being expected of them by society and the law. They too are not aware of this basic truth. Just because the law says children are adults at 18 years of age, does not mean they can handle adult issues. Though some may be able to, the majority can not. Teens are more likely to be exploited by adults or "mates" with whom they may form a relationship.

Being children, they are gullible through trusting everything and trusting adults even the dangerous ones. Hence they can be misled by shrewd adults. This is the reason for the dangers that underlie bad relationships in teens. It also poses great risks to the innocent young minds.

***

Advantages of Sexual Relationships in Teens
The sad truth is that there is none. Let us consider some possibilities:

1) That said, there is some teenage "love" that has lasted a lifetime.
2) Another possible advantage is that if this kind of stability is certain and they have children early, they may have grand- and great grand-children sooner than most of those have relationships later in life.
3) Also, if the relationship is stable and happy, they will form a couple that knows each other through and through as they can grow together.

Disadvantages of Sexual Relationships in Teens
1) It is a form of child/sexual abuse and exploitation
   This is because the teen may not be in a position to weigh up the pros and cons of her/his actions. He or she may not have "seen" enough of life to help her make informed decision. She/he acts in ignorance. Decisions and agreements that a teen makes may not be valid legally.
2) It is illegal in most reasonable territories to have sex with a person who is under 16 (UK) and in some countries this age is 18 years.
3) Early parenthood may damage the future career of the teen. It may impair schooling and work.
4) She/he may contact sexually transmitted disease (Chlamydia, gonorrhoea, HIV etc) and therefore future

child-bearing may be impaired. The human papiloma virus may also cause penile cancer in men.
5) She may enter into a relationship which is wrong in personality type and in all other areas. That is, the partner/spouse may not actually be right for him/her.
6) She may, in the wrong hands, be "recruited" into prostitution and drugs.
7) She may be damaged psychologically when she realises the abuse and may subsequently develop mental health problems, guilt and regrets.
8) If the relationship fails, some take it very badly and may develop depression or some adjustment problems about the failure. It may be tough trusting and trying again. In spite of that, the majority of us will go through this "baptism of fire" (did you just smile or laugh at that?)
9) Early pregnancy, if it occurs in the teen years, may lead to unwanted babies and disrupted relationships. That is to say that, this is one of the causes of divorces as the teens may not have thought through their actions before entering into the relationship.
10) There is a recent report by the BBC and British Journal of Urology that a high sex drive in early years, in boys, may lead to cancer of the prostate later in life.

In the end, there is truth in the statement that every action has its consequence or reaction.

***

CHAPTER SEVEN
Is this Love or Deceit? Why Does *"Love"*
Hurt so Badly?

"Love never dies a natural death. It dies because we don't know how to replenish its source. It dies of blindness and errors and betrayals. It dies of illness and wounds; it dies of weariness, of withering, of tarnishing." Anais Nin

Imagine this: you see a still picture of someone for the first time over the internet, a person whom you have never met. You do not know what the person looks like in real life but after a little chat; the person declares that he or she loves you. Similarly, let us assume, you are in a party and you meet someone who speaks well with you in a casual talking session. You had no background knowledge of the person. After a little discussion, the person tells you that he/she loves you. You are surprised at this. You ask: Can this be love? Will this be love? The question lingers on in your mind. Now, let us assume this "love", whatever its meaning, lasted for the next one hour. After that, the person who supposedly loved you makes you upset. You got angry. You left the room and slammed the door after you. Think again: Where is this love going? Do you still think this is love? You began to ask critical questions. So far, your questions and bewilderment remain unanswered. Perhaps, you got a flicker of an answer. You nevertheless remain confused.

***

Whatever your answer is, let us further examine the subject of "love" and "hate" as it impacts on your relationship. What I have just explained are the experiences of many adolescents who are in impassioned "love". These scenarios are real life events which have happened to many adults. To so many, "love", without thoughts, comes and goes like a fume. To some, the word is meaningless. To millions, though, the word conjures pain and emotional hurt which is succinctly explained like this in the words of Aaron: *"They say loving you gives pains and is full of sacrifices. But I'll rather take pains and lots of sacrifices than not to be loved by you"*. They are prepared to go though with it in spite of the pain.

Yet to millions of people across the word, it is a word that connotes a session and life of bliss and euphoria. On the contrary, love can be transient like the morning dew or it can have the permanence of the Sun. Please sit comfortably as we enter into an explosive yet lively and unpredictable phase of human character.

Much has been made of the subject of "love" in a relationship. Some have asserted that it forms the basis of their relationship. Some have said it should form the foundation of any relationship: the driving force, perhaps, of every personal relationship. Is this a delusional idea?
However, a look at what is on record by listening to and reading research works shows that "love" means different things to different people. Meanwhile, few buzz words can generate so many emotions or could bring about so much unrestrained expression as the subject of love. Yet no one has been able to define what it means accurately.
The issue as stake here is whether love is important to a relationship? If so, why do we witness murders and harmful acts between individuals that are supposedly in "love"?

***

Therefore, it is the aim of this chapter to explore the true meaning of "love". The chapter would then continue with a discussion of the purpose of love and why its failings hurt so badly in relationships, marriages, and other inter-personal relationships, such as father-son, father-daughter, mother-son, daughter-husband relationships, as well as between platonic friends.

I do intend not to bother the reader with complexities of love, the history and evolution of it. I shall leave those for the academics in our midst. My true intention is to explore how best to apply love in our relationships.

Before I give my definition, let me consider the various languages or the intention to give "love". Here are some of the common phrases that people all over the world use on different occasions to express their love. Examples: "I love you", "I love my cat", "I love my wife", "I love my husband", "I love my country", "For God so love the world...", "God's love", "...unconditional love", "love is blind", "love from the heart" and of course, so many other ways of expressing "love".

What is love?

We should note the various phrases which I have quoted above about love. Therefore for love to be valid and manifested, it must be expressed as words or acts which can be rendered in a variety of ways. The methods of doing this are as varied as the culture and languages of expression and that is why love means different things to different people in so many different cultures.

Similarly, "love" can be expressed by means of spoken word, written word (say poetry, letters) and by acts such as intimate ones (kissing, platonic or otherwise). The other routes of expressing "love" include: music, SMS/texts and emails. Nevertheless, one area or perhaps, an act where love is so manifestly expressed is during sex in the case of intimate and legitimate relationships. In this occasion, one might hear in the peak of the act "I love you". The question remains: Is this really true? We shall see the true nature of the human mind in a while.

Viewed from the legal angle, at least in English common law (please permit my academic diversion), the word "duty of care" has been well developed (*Donoghue (or M'Alister) v Stevenson* ([1932] A.C. 562, 1932 S.C. (H.L.) 31, [1932] All ER Rep 1).

If we therefore consider the various synonyms associated with "love" in many languages and cultures, we would see that there is an association with "care", as well as affection, defence, security, fondness, warmth, protection, intimacy, attachment, among others.

With this analysis in mind, we proceed to defining what *love* means.

***

Simply put, love, means *do not, intentionally or negligently or mistakenly, cause harm*. We would see that this is a negative definition. It means you *should take all (legal, moral, cultural, social and religious measures etc) due diligence or care not to cause any harm*.

Examples: Practice and Applications

Admittedly, there are various forms of expressing "love" without sexual intimacy. One example is in platonic relationships which involve intense care and protection, as in father-son-daughter-mother-siblings. Others are doctor-patient, care giver-care receiver, government-people-public or friend-friend relationships. In all of these, the trust and expectations among the different people would be that none would cause the other any harm. Yet in practice, the contrary may happen, as in child abuse or cases of husband-wife abuse.

***

During the time I was writing this chapter, a colleague of mine asked me, what about people who "love another so much and could kill in the name of love, for example, family members who kill their severely ill members by euthanasia?" Alternatively, he asked, what about deeply religious individuals who could die for their religion or their loved ones, as we have seen in terrorism acts. Dying for a "loved" cause such as political views is also a possibility where *love* can achieve a spectacular display of emotional actions. The perplexing question is whether this is love?

The short and long answer is that first, these acts are more likely to be illegal and second, these acts by and large cause more harm than good. Therefore, the people who cause such harm would most likely not do so, if they have an alternative and valid or achievable means with deeper *knowledge and wisdom on how to address their frustrations and challenges*. As I will point out in the chapter on anger, these acts are the clearest indication of anger, leading to unhappiness and hostility. A so-called "love" would therefore lead to harm in the absence of insights on how to address pain, anger and frustrations that occur during a "loving phase". It does mean that when love comes in contact with obstacles, the love may momentarily give rise to reactions that causes harm.

It goes back to my original definition that *harm will arise in the absence of love*. Harm will also arise when desire and intentions are defeated or obstructed. This is why there is so much harm in so many so-called relationships in cohabitation, marriages, and father-son-daughter-mother relationships.

What about "love" that involve intercourse? Let us put the definition into practical use. This physical act of expression (intercourse) demonstrates, during the act, intimacy, care, protection, warmth and attachment. Above all, this is the period when the couple should ideally "cause no harm". Therefore, one should expect that during this period or after it, couples would refrain from causing harm. Yet much information in published data reveals that the opposite is the case. Ironically, couples and individuals in relationships kill and harm each other in everyday news. By and large, it's no longer news that harm is committed everyday by individuals who are apparently in "love"!

Such harm could be caused during pre-intercourse, during sex, or after coitus. It could include physical harm to the other person. This kind of "love" is an abnormality and is not love but abuse of the process (acts) as well as abuse of the intention to love. This is so, because, it does not conform with: *"take all (legal, moral etc) due diligence not to cause harm"*.

All in all, whatever the relationship, the basic character of "love" is not to cause harm, verbally or physically. Did you realise that I said *verbally*? You should do, for it is noteworthy.

***

Is "love blind"?
This is a common saying, sadly. Love is not blind. It's the human beings in "love" who choose to be blind to the obvious and what is so clear to others who are outside the relationship.

This popular saying implies that you are, permit my words, unwise enough to overlook the gross and clear deficiencies or inadequacies, diseases, impairment and trouble in the other person in spite of the trouble that you may undergo because of these imperfections.

Often, this "blindness" will be opened by reality much later as the relationship rolls on. Commonly, the "blindness" comes because of desire for sex /lust/money/security and intimacy of the moment or intimacy and security for a short while. It may also be a snare for the unwary which presents itself in the form of love. "Blindness" in love is, truly, found in a person who is not seeing deeper than the surface of things or of the relationship. When the specific desire that attracted the "love" is satisfied, the reality dawns and, "the eyes of love will be opened". By this time, it may have been too late to undo what has been done. Marriage or birth of children or other commitments may have taken place.

Love will subsist so long as you can tolerate and care for the person, who despite the imperfections, you can continue to "love" the person. Remember, it's your choice.

***

Does your relationship need love to survive?
This question might appear needless, but fairness however requires that I should consider it. Relationships can survive without love but no relationship can blossom without love. There are relationships which can be described as "loveless". This implies that parties to the relationship are neither causing harm nor adding value to each other. A loveless relationship is a form of relationship that has stagnated. It is at a standstill until

something gives. However, such a relationship may continue to hold for the sake of say, the children, or to protect the social, economic or political status of the couple. In future, things may change for the worse or for the better. Divorce may follow or the spouses may change their minds and mend fences.

On the contrary, relationships can only blossom in the atmosphere of love when the individuals make concerted efforts to ensure that no inside or outside elements harm the relationship. Such individuals may go to any length to protect their partner from any harm no matter how trivial the harm may be.

***

Failed or Faked "Love" (When love is absent)
What if I say "I love my son" or even if I say "I love a child"? Or someone says "I love God", "I love the earth?", or "I love my husband". In all these, it implies: "Whatever happens, I will cause no harm (with intention)". Yet, people profess to all these and cause harm anyway. The electronic media, the internet and the newspapers are filled with stories of failed love or love that came across a difficulty. This is certainly a misuse of terms and a failure of intention. At least, love in these circumstances becomes a fake concept.
***

Harm in the Name of Love.
How does one knowingly or intentionally cause harm? The harm that can be caused could include great harm with words, which often includes psychological injuries (like a boyfriend saying to his girlfriend: "You are a beast" which would not be consistent with the principle of care or love). Other examples are physical injuries to children, such as sexual abuse and physical abuse (great harm indeed). Rape in whatever form, character assassination of and by spouses and friends, deviation from God's law will not be a love for God for example, criminal activities against another or even against the earth or the government /people are all instances of harm in the name of love.

***

Why "Love" Hurts So Badly
Love, no matter how we look at it, is a trusting relationship. It is a trusting bond in which one relies on, trusts in and depends on the other for care, defence, protection and security. Children can and do love in the belief that the adult or his peer and sibling will not let him or her down in difficult times. Children love in the anticipation that parents and adults, whatever happens, will be there to protect and to care for him or her. Women do love in anticipation that the man will always be there to give support and to offer security to her.

Man does love in the hope that when his pride and courage are battered the woman will be there as an encourager and as strengtheners. In the same way, citizens love their country sheltered in the sense that he or she can count on the country and other citizens in times of harsh conditions as well as in times of serious risk to life. Therefore, couples are in relationships and in love in the optimism that no harm will come from the other partner, be it direct harm or via conspiracy.

Couples and friends implicitly agree to form a relationship in the anticipation that they can trust and rely on each other against the threats that may befall them. Two bonds they say are not easily broken.

Sadly these beliefs may not happen. Man and woman do disappoint. Children are let down. Children also let adults down. A country is run by a group of men and women. Forces of life do come against individuals in relationships, sometimes beyond which they can cope, by their personality make up. In some others, revenge---"getting my pound of flesh back"---is the reason for letting down in love. In others, letting down the other person may be a reason that is beyond ordinary human comprehension and may on some occasions, not be deliberate.

When these expectations or desires fail, then unhappiness sets in. The results are hate, anger, hostility, anxiety, lack of trust, malice and all forms of belligerence. It is hate because, the person who was left disappointed may not have expected such behaviour. It is anger because; there is obstruction in the course of the person's expectation. It is hostility because of anger which is now getting out of the confines of control. Since desire failed, unhappiness will set in its place. This is the basis for why "love" hurts so badly. In truth love does not hurt but failed love and the absence of love hurts greatly.

***

CHAPTER EIGHT
Advantages and Disadvantages of Marriage and Partnership/Co-habitation Relationships

"One advantage of marriage it seems to me is that when you fall out of love with him or he falls out of love with you it keeps you together until maybe you fall in again."
Judith Viorst

In many of the previous sections and chapters, I have mentioned that we can take the view that a relationship of whatever form is a business which must necessarily be productive. While in mainstream businesses, the principal aim is money making, in intimate relationship, primarily, it is not so. While the productivity in intimate relationships does not have to be a physical product like say a bar of soap, a car or a pencil, the relationship may be productive emotionally by filling the gaps that may be clearly obvious to the partners if the relationship were not there. On the other hand, the most visible form of productivity in any intimate relationship in which those involved choose to have this product, but not exclusively so, is children. Other products can be encouraging support or to provide emotional balance for the other. Alternatively, it may be financial or sexual. In the main, it must be productive; short of this, the relationship is a waste of both time and energy.

***

I have mentioned earlier that, some people go into a relationship without a clue as to what they are to expect from it. Some individuals also get into relationships with a mind set of what they are certain of. Some may have also made up their mind regardless of what may subsequently come their way. In the latter group, they do not care what follows so long as a specific need is met. For example, this need, in most women, is undoubtedly security. This may be financial security. It may be physical defensive security. It may be security in property. For example, some would want to acquire property with their partner. Some will go into a relationship which they never wanted in the first place but found themselves permanently in because of some missteps.

For men, the aim might be to meet the needs of intercourse, or to find a deputy and a helper. Often, men have a global view of how they would "conquer" the world in financial term as well as having geographical domination. Women, to them, are helpers in the process of the conquest. Power, in the main, is the ultimate pursuit of most men. Yet, as for women, a lot of men would go into a potentially long term relationship in error, having been driven by the need to satisfy some short term desires. In the latter case, most men would not have given consideration to critical issues that may ultimately affect the relationship they may have unwittingly entered into. Pitiable as this may seem, it happens everyday in every land in everywhere in the world.

In order to help you avoid falling into terrible things or pits that we never desired, I have taken the effort to point out here the major advantages and disadvantages of intimate relationships. If you like, you can call it the benefits and non-benefits. You will not be wrong in doing so. We shall look at this from the standpoint of medical, psychological, legal, financial/economic, religious and social views. I have gone to this extent so that no stone will be left unturned. By the end of this chapter, you would have read and be aware of probably all that you need to know about intimate relationships and their variants of cohabitation, "common law" relationships or partnerships. When you have read these ideas, you will be in a position to decide what type of relationship is right for you. It is your choice. Remember, the objective of this book which I urge you to bear in mind is to allow you to make good decisions with credible information at your disposal. As for me, by these acts, I have done my job as a writer: to keep you well informed.

***

These benefits or advantages and their corresponding opposites of disadvantages are the coalition of research work and clinical experiences as well as personal observations. Caution is required though. Even though I have focused on matrimony in these sections, I have also looked into other forms of relationships vis-à-vis, cohabitation, being single and "common law" relationships. Now let us look at the benefits of marriage.

Advantages of Matrimony

1. *Extended life.* To some who might be going through stressful marriage difficulties, this might seem ironic. They might wonder that in spite of the stress-related risk in their troubled marital circumstances, how it could be said that marriage leads to long life. The issue is that there are also many risks that single individuals may undertake that will pose serious risks to his or her life or in fact curtail such life notwithstanding marriage. In marriage, such risk-taking may be minimised simply because of consideration for the spouse.

Therefore, regardless of current personal circumstances, marriage does prolong life. This may work through good nutrition and less risk taking. Although a lot of members of the general public are almost certainly not conscious of it, there is now some agreement among researchers that you can lengthen your life by marrying. Marriage, it has been discovered, keeps the individuals who are in it alive for about three extra years, on average, in comparison with those who are not married. Most married couples do not realise it: probably because of challenges in their lives which could cloud their awareness of this great benefit.

***

2. *Shield against mental health problems.* In general, stressful life conditions can give rise to mental health as can any other life situations that overwhelm us. In matrimony, unlike for those who are single or individuals who are living a separate lives without clear commitment to each other, married individuals are less likely to experience or suffer from all types of mental illness or be in need of treatment for mental disorders. The key word here is less likely. It does not imply that they, married people, do not suffer mental illess. I, for one can confirm that they do. Men and women who are married, it has been claimed, have the smallest possible levels of schizophrenia and the lowest possible rates of depression compared to the singles. The reason for this

may be found in the common sharing of problems by the couple, with both individuals thinking of the long term, in comparison with cohabitation which may be aborted at any time if the heat gets too much. The reader should note that in the eyes of the law, cohabiting couple are living their individual lives. Cohabiting couples on the other hand are five times more probable to be depressed and those who are broken up are four times more likely to be depressed. It would appear that by nature of marriage couples may get involved in the partner's problem and thus reduce the burden.

The up–to-date observations in the pattern of disease development which are published in medical journals shows that being married confers some advantages on mental health. It is believed that it works all the way through some kind of shielding effect against developing mental health problems. It reduces pressure and worry – most probably because of the fact that the couple share worries, in keeping with the saying that a trouble shared is a trouble halved, just as custom says. To a certain extent, too, married people smoke less and eat in good healthy diets. As will be seen below, misuse of alcohol which is seen more in singles, may in some cases lead to mental health problems.

***

3. *Source of Happiness:* There are many examples of research in which people were asked what the reason for their happiness is. Many cited their matrimony (see my earlier book: The Key and the Road to Happiness, on the subject). Looking closer at this, one can come to the conclusion that when couples are married and fulfilling their heart's desire, it leads to happiness. The other possibility is that going through life alone causes loneliness which may lead to isolation and depression, as observations in widows and widowers have shown. Thus being in the company of the person whom you like (desire to or wish) to spend your time with generates happiness. Thus, marriage also helps to shape psychological health and happiness. Thus, marriage greatly reduces the likelihood of hopelessness and despair in later life.

Even at a point when the person experiences the loss of one's spouse, it is the loss that causes unhappiness rather than the marriage. Notably, the worth or the value that is attached to the marriage appears to be the best forecaster of overall mental health in later years. This can be considered in terms of the benefits that it brings to the stability of emotions and may be due to the proper and emotional support that married couples give to each other. This mental health stability may be due to the relief conferred by the sharing of likes and dislikes, as I mentioned above.

***

4. In *stress terms,* studies have shown that married men and women have an inclination to deal with stress and anxiety better than unmarried or co-habiting people. The reason may be found in the fact that couples are likely to discuss their difficulties together. Has it not been commonly said that two heads are better than one? Having a spouse who depends on you and vice versa can be a powerful inspiration to do well in work and to keep trying to be better, even though the work may appear difficult. Spouses provide poignant support and back-up for each other, and they help provide a sense of balance in life. In contrast to singles, this support is evidently absent. It should however be noted that "marriage" by words must be backed up by actions and commitments for this benefit to work its way through.

***

5. *Suicide rate is less amongst married couples.* Loneliness, being alone, isolation, all leads to unhappiness. Unhappiness leads to depression. Depression may lead to suicide, especially with alcohol, drugs and no one to talk to. Due perhaps to the supporting effect and positively encouraging impact of the couples on each other, many research studies have discovered that married men and women have lower rates of suicide when compared to unmarried men and women. This is probably due to a significant relationship effect that gives people a sense of

personal value and a feeling of dependability and responsibility to others. Caution is more likely to be exercised when a spouse realises that committing suicide may cause harm to the rest of the family. Indeed, this realisation is, in my personal experience, is one of the influences that sometimes stops people from committing suicide, i.e. realising that harm may be caused to the rest of the family. I have asked some of my suicidal clients why they would not carry through their wish to commit suicide. In a lot of cases, they cited the likely harm that their action will cause their spouse and family.

***

6. *Physical health benefits.* Good nutrition, less risky enterprises, good and relaxing sleep, problems shared and less stress are some of the reasons why there is better physical health in matrimony than in singles. Also, because a spouse may observe deterioration in the health of his or her partner, it may cause action to be taken more quickly than in singles. This may promote prevention of injuries and diseases. The sum of these may lead to improvements in the physical health of the individuals. Unlike singles, especially those that live alone, a quick response to calls for medical attention and support may help married couples to cope better in terms of their physical health challenges.

When a spouse is in denial of any deterioration in his or her health, the partner may exert some pressure on the other to seek medical help and to pay attention to the illness. It has also been discovered by researchers that bachelors or singles have much higher blood pressure than those who are married. This may be due to the stress that they carry alone or in addition to poor nutrition. There is plenty of British proof for these claims. The body of evidence in this regard is convincing. According to research on this matter, in the late 1960s, 20,000 middle–aged male civil servants had medical tests and were then followed for the next twenty years. At the end of that period, 14 out of every 1000 married men had died, compared to 21 for widowers, 17 for those single and unattached, and 21 for those who had separated. Unmarried men had much higher blood pressure. Thus, as the figures show, it has been much settled.

***

7. In respect of other *infirmities and accidents*. Persons who are married are less likely to die from all causes, including heart disease, stroke, cancer and car accidents. The reasons are not far-fetched. A good home environment, concern for the effects of the environment on their children, good nutrition and the tendency to take fewer risks out of concern for the welfare of their spouse or for the family in general, are some of the reasons. Further, there is even proof that social support between couples boosts the immune defensive system, making married people less likely to catch a common cold, researchers say.

***

8. *Misuse of alcohol is less in men.* Single and lonely men may resort to alcohol to cope with their loneliness. They may also use alcohol especially if they have friends who also drink or if they have used alcohol for a while. Researchers have found that married men have much lower rates of alcohol misuse or abuse than their unmarried or single counterparts. Women detest men who use alcohol to gain sexual advantage. One of my female clients once told me: "I hate him when he comes home smelling of alcohol and he wants to have sex with me". Women dislike spouses who use alcohol as a means to cope in the face of difficulties which the couple may be going through elsewhere, as this is seen as irresponsible behaviour. Heavy drinkers are also seen as bad role models by women for the young children in the family and may therefore discourage their husband from going down that route. Therefore, married men are more likely to take note of these issues especially if the men are conscious that misuse of alcohol can end their cherished relationships

Men who are single are more than three times as likely to be at risk as married men and to die of cirrhosis of the liver --- an alcohol-related disease. Researchers are of the opinion that wives offer encouragement, support, and protection from daily challenges that could otherwise push men towards alcohol misuse.

Psychological and medical disadvantages of marriage

As the reader would have noted, the above benefits are outlined so that the medical disadvantages can also be compared appropriately. These medical and psychological disadvantages are discussed below.

1. *Marriage requires a lot of time*, emotion, and energy from both the woman and the man to make it work. This can be exhausting and may lead to stress, frustrations and anger in some individuals. This may indeed lead to depression in some marriages, especially if the couples have irreconcilable views about how to move the relationship forward. If I may cite Indonesia as an example of irreconcilable differences, one of the reasons for the rise in divorce in the Country is when couples of different political persuations marry each other. Thus in general, it takes time for a couple to understand each other. They may have to go through trial and error, giving and taking. All this can take years and even decades before they reach marital maturity. Sadly though, this is the point ---*time required*----when a lot of matrimony undergoes strain and then falters.

2. *Domestic violence*---without necessarily quoting complicated figures---and *isolation* do increase in unhappy marriages. Domestic violence (or DV for short) is an expression of resentment or ill-feeling towards another. This is so often a result of unhappiness, anger and frustration. It is a sign of conflict and it is the clearest evidence of crisis in the relationship (see chapter on crisis later). In spite of the much publicised benefits of marriage, critics argue that only marriages with low levels of hostility reap any of its health benefits. The implication of this is that provided there are well laid out foundations for marriages and the couple has from the outset passed the compatibility test, the chance of domestic violence occurring is unlikely or at least, reduced.

3. Someone humorously put the advantage of marriage as *"you see the same person everyday and every time"* and as for the disadvantage---wait for it, *"you see the same person everyday and every time"*. This means that marriage can be boring and monotonous since you constantly see the same person. This may sometimes lead to friction and devaluation of the person with whom you spend your time--- most of the time.

***

Social Advantages:

1. Married people tend to, unlike the unmarried, have a *larger social network* of friends and relatives which protects against suicide (see also the psychological benefits above). Looking at this from a global perspective, this social benefit should not be surprising at all. Even if you marry a local man or woman, it means you have joined your family with another family. This benefit becomes even bigger when the marriage is across international boundaries and a mere marriage can link two countries and may also be a saving grace in difficult times for the two nations, not to mention the two families, involved. Compare the scenarios with someone who remains single.

2. *Loneliness and being alone* is reduced in marriage. Being with someone whom you love and with whom you share your time with, is a clear means of reducing loneliness and sense of isolation. Further, this advantage also reduces unhappiness and depression as couples can share joy and sadness together.

3. *Balanced Children*. If the marriage is blessed with children, then there is also the benefit of raising the children in a balanced and secured environment that comes with *stable marriage, secure home* and relationships. Children who are raised in a stable marital environment behave better and progress well in life as well as being less likely to end up in prison or mental health institutions (see the chapter on the effect of divorce of children).

***

Social Disadvantages

1. *Social ties.* Marriage takes away from community in some societies in the Western world, social connections. This may be seen as removing a specific spouse into another geographical location. For example: A girl from Germany who marries into a family in Turkey is more or less removed from her social connections in Germany. This scenario can be a man from Japan who happens to marry a girl from South Africa. The couple may disconnect completely from their respective origins. This claim however is not totally true in the Third World where this stated disadvantage may indeed strengthen social connections with the community settings. The reader may recall that, as it was in ancient times, some communities' main purpose for marrying their children to another family is indeed to strengthen the connections between the two families. On the other hand, the union between the two even in the modern world may be to continue to gain certain favours. However in the Western World, surveys show that married men and women have fewer ties to their kin than unmarried people.

2. *Childlessness and Social Detachment.* Married couples, in some cultures (this is not a global phenomenon but it is true in the West) also detach themselves from neighbours and the surrounding community. This observation is truer with childless men and women, though. This is due to the isolation of married couples from their own flesh and blood and community as a result of what some have labelled the "greediness of marriage". The childless couple may now concentrate on each other to the exclusion of others in their community, some research have shown.

3. *Lack of freedom.* Lack of individual freedom may arise in a union of two. This is because; marriage by definition is a union between two opposite adult genders. Their freedoms are dissolved in the union and ideally any decision by the two should be a joint decision. This creates a sense of loss of liberty to choose, by the individuals. This is akin to losing one's

independence thereby leading to a sense of deprivation in either one of the couple.

4. *Loss of aspirations.* In marriage and indeed in any relationship, responsibilities are created and there may be increasing feelings for individuals in the relationship that they have lost their dreams and aspirations as a result of the marriage. In some, especially in full time housewives, they may give up their career in order to concentrate on the care of their homes. I once looked after a woman in her fifties. She initially set out to be a lawyer. But due to the needs of her marriage, she had to give up her career in order to join her husband in his Post Office business which they now run together. The marriage may therefore suffer except if the couple face up to their responsibilities.

***

Financial Advantages

Let us face it: existing or potential wealth could attract a person into matrimony. Money can sometimes buy "love" though it may not be real love. The prospect of lots of money and financial stability is sometimes a factor in relationships. Unfortunately, money, even lots of it, may not prolong a dead relationship. That said, plenty of couples and individuals in reality, will throw their lots into matrimony, or if you like, relationship if wealth will be within their reach. Of course, who wants to live in poverty? But as they say, money may be a fatal attraction. In spite of this, regardless of the source of their wealth, there are huge financial benefits to married couples which are not available to cohabiting individuals, common-law partners or single men and women.

Perspectives from the world
There are some findings that marriage could make you richer. In studies that have been done across many countries, workers who are married were found to earn between ten and twenty per cent more than those who are living individual lives, such as singles

or people in cohabitation. One possible reason for this is that there is healthy "competition" between the two individuals to earn more and to work hard to support the relationship. Also, in a marriage, there may be many mouths to feed and many individuals to care for such as for children, in-laws and the couples themselves. Therefore, couples are more likely to work harder in order to make ends meet.

Let us put this in perspective in the USA. For example, in post mid-1990's (1997) the U.S. average earnings of married couples were roughly $47,000. For single men, the average income was $26,000 in comparison to single women who earnt $16,000. The amount that an individual man and single woman earns, if added ($26,000 +16,000), is less ($42,000) than the combined earning for the married persons ($47,000). This may be because of the need to meet the domestic financial challenges that married couples worked more. Of course, it should be realised that there are financial incentives which are available to them but not to the single men and women.

Men tend to work more while women look after the children at home. At least, that is the traditional role of couples. However the role of the wife is increasingly gaining recognition, for they contribute to the home income as well as supporting their husband. This latter point had been a knotty but now resolved issue in British Courts, just for the sake of regional comparison.

Here is another set of benefits that may accrue to the woman. As long as a woman stays married, researchers say, though, whether as a mother or not, she enjoys the benefits of her husband's increased income. There is a financial spill over to her. On the other hand, if the woman is the wealthier, the husband also shares in the financial largesse of his wife. Further, married couples also benefit financially because they are able to save more money considering their joint efforts in tackling the same or similar needs, such as paying for the same utility usage, mortgages/rent TV, power usage, car, and many others. In this way, spouses have the opportunity to combine their strengths, opportunities, and reduction in their financial weaknesses.

The financial benefits of marriage become even clearer when contrasted with cost of divorce and the living standard of divorced persons. Now, let us compare the two forms. Two households are far more expensive than one. Two individuals who are living a separate life are more expensive than one. It seems logical to me. On the other hand, after a divorce, the standard of living of the family drops by 25% (see chapter on divorce).

Cohabiting couples: Unlike married couples, cohabiting couples appear to live separate lives and so keep their finances separate. Thus they miss out on the benefit of synergy that a marriage union brings which I have stated above.

UK and the Commonwealth Perspectives

The financial implications in the UK are in general similar to what is obtainable in the USA and it is similar to most other Commonweath countries (Canada, New Zealand, and Australia) where couples operate jointly save where culture, disregard for law and religion have blunted this effect (such as in Nigeria, much of Africa as well as Southern Asia). In practically all places though, the law of the land usually and primarily support marriages. Now let us look at the financial advantages first.

Advantages

There are some issues that require clarification. From a legal standpoint, a couple is either married or are two entirely separate individuals. A "common law" couple is therefore a co-habiting couple. As such, they are living different lives. It is important that you keep this crucial difference in mind. I suppose, I have discussed this important fact earlier in the book.

Planning for Tax

Married couples enjoy a major advantage over unmarried couples when it comes to taxation matters. Married couples can transfer shares and investment property to one another without incurring capital gains tax (CGT). This is intra-spousal transfer. If unmarried couples do this, then CGT could be due when an asset is transferred. Example, if Mr and Mrs AB own properties in joint names, Mrs AB could transfer to Mr AB her shares without incurring the liability to pay tax on that transfer. Put simply, CGT, which is a tax on the profits made when you dispose of an asset, does not apply to people's home, the family home or home which is referred to as a matrimonial home. Unmarried persons who are in "common law" relationships or who are in co-habitation do not have these benefits as they are in effect, individuals. Nevertheless, a new law has allowed individuals in civil partnerships the rights that are accorded married couples.

Benefits and Pensions

Married couples can inherit part of their spouse's second state pension according to the UK Pension Service. This was formerly called the state earnings related pension or SERPS. It ran from 6 April 1978 to 5 April 2002, when it was reformed by the State Second Pension. A person who was in employment may have paid into SERPS.

SERPS is paid from State Pension age to a person who has contributed to the scheme.

Once married, the state expects that couples will support each other financially. The state believes that this "support" should be carried on even when the other spouse dies so that the living partner can receive the second state pension.

Unmarried couples, even if they live together, do not have to deal with similar complications. Unless there is a legal agreement in place, things may become difficult when the relationship goes sour. Thus, sharing of your life and home with someone, even for a long time, does not leave you with many of the rights to property and pensions which you might expect as in marriage. For instance, a woman who lives with her partner and raises their children for 25 years cannot expect maintenance for herself on separation, except if the children are still under 18 years. Nor is she owed a share of the house, unless she has paid towards it herself. Note though that this is not the case regarding civil partnership situations.

***
Certainty: Death and taxes
Two things are certain in life: death and taxes, they say. By marrying, you are saying that your spouse will have the right to most of your estate when you die, unless otherwise stated in a will. This can include joint bank accounts, shares in joint names and properties that are held in joint names. In fact, any asset that is held in joint names falls into this class of distribution, when you die.

They can also inherit your estate free of inheritance tax; this can result in a substantial tax saving for the living person. That said, cohabiting or "common law" couples can outwit the inheritance tax jigzaw to some extent, if they own their home or any property on a joint tenancy basis. That means that joint tenancy will operate as if you were joined in marriage in the first instance.

This is when *both* parties own one hundred percent of the property together and upon the death of one, the asset is transferred into the survivor's sole name. It may also be that they own part of a property in joint names.

That said, the better advice is that the common law couples or co-habiting couples should either own their own property outright or own it with the partner under what is called a tenancy in common arrangement. In that case, you as the owner can decide on the person to whom you wish to transfer the property.

On death however, even with a will in place, the living partner may be required to compulsorily sell the property in order to offset the inheritance tax liability since the property must have been transferred to you under tenancy in common. You will need to carefully think about these issues.

Financial and Property Disadvantages
1) The financial and property acquisitions during the life of the marriage may be seen by the court as "marital assets" and the couples *may* actually not own anything individually. This may become an issue at divorce and separation. Example, if the

assets which you acquire during your marriage become an issue during divorce and you fail to agree on how they should be shared before it gets to the court, upon judgement, the court may decide as it sees fit the way to re-distribute the assets.

2) Separately but similarly, properties and accounts in joint names may in fact be no one's property, but rather joint property. While either of the individuals may use the accounts and property as he or she sees fit during the life of the marriage, in reality this may be a huge cause of friction between the two and may actually end the relationship (see chapter on broken marriages). On the other hand, during divorce, the court may have to re-distribute the assets, including your pension and savings.

3) The freedom to deal with what one perceives as one's "own" property may be limited by the action and views of the other partner. So freedom to deal with what you consider as yours exclusively may actually be lost.

***

Religious Advantages of a marriage

Contrary to many views and orthodoxy, considering the biblical account, there is nowhere in the entire Bible whereby child bearing by individuals and married couples is "a must be done duty". If anything, you can not have children or have intercourse with anyone without having a relationship with the person, no matter how short that relationship may be. This reinforces my view that the first link between one individual and the other, as the biblical account shows, is the establishment of a relationship which is based on the foundation of companionship.
Therefore, to the disappointment of many, the basis of marriage is not child bearing, for this very act of bearing children is a follow up to an existing relationship.

In nowhere in the entire Bible, (or in any other religion to the best of my knowledge) is there any advice whereby marriage is made compulsory as an act made a must by God. That is, you can either marry by *choice* or remain decently single, and in all forms and interpretation of the term, sexless, as we shall see below.

Also, nowhere save the disappointing marriage between Adam and Eve, is God involved in the choosing of a marriage partner. The act of marriage remains under the free will of the individual: your free will. A wrong choice can have dire consequences though. In a similar manner, there is no ecclesiastical evidence that having children is compulsory. You do not have to have children. However, if you decide to have children, the evidence is that it must be under the umbrella of marriage. Both marriage and child bearing are under the control of choice: your choice.

Once these two (marriage, child-bearing) events occur, they become your personal responsibilities. You chose them and you have to stick with them, the rules seem to be saying. Further, going by Christ's discussion on this matter, you are only advised to marry if you can not, if I may put it this way: "hold your own". This is because marriage is not for everyone. He said --- some were made "eunuchs from birth" or "by men" or by their own choosing. This means, some people will be unable to have children (they can still marry and adopt though, if they want).

The latter view emphasises the element of choice in a relationship as well as in marriage. It did not encourage any other form of intimate relationship though. In the main, let us consider the benefits of marriage from Christian perspectives.

***

1) *Sexual Stability.*
If you are unmarried, you may be open to the temptation of sex outside marriage. The married couple may therefore not "burn with passion" unlike possibly the unmarried. This will prevent the individual from doing *wrong* since the married person has a consistent spouse to rely on–sexually.

2) *Lack of marriage may tend towards sexual immorality.*
Because of the temptation to sexual immorality, it is good to marry especially if the individual can not exercise self-control. Sexual immorality from the look of things is a cardinal wrong.

3) The couple are under the doctrine of *"help meet"*, to each other. They are helpers and supporters until death separates them. This appears to be the first reason for the relationship in the first place. The help mate/meet idea is not limited to a particular area as we have seen in the other advantages. It could be sexual; it could be connected to finance, property, words of encouragement, and many other areas.

***

Religious Disadvantages

1) *Trouble in the flesh*
Trouble in the flesh implies many things. It means such trouble as the need to have sexual satisfaction may be an inhibition to the proper pursuit of a faithful and spiritual path. Also, the need to satisfy daily needs, such as caring for the family, children, mortgage, maintaining a car loan, running after jobs and contracts in order to satisfy the needs of family/marriage, will all constitute a diversion from the spiritual path.. Similarly, the anxieties that are associated with caring for the spouse and children will exist in a married relationship.

2) Here is a quote from the Bible: *But he (and she) who is married cares about the things of the world – how he (she) may please his wife (or husband)*. The "she" had been added by myself.
If you are married, you may discover that your desire (as opposed to material satisfaction) or your heart is drawn towards your spouse. This desire is always to please the spouse and not to cause offence even if you are not happy with your decision or the joint decision that you may both make. The desire for things of this world which are material, such as property or the daily struggle to make ends meet and the search for the "glory of men" will pre-occupy the married person.

3) *Marriage is a distraction from serving the Lord.*
The need to satisfy the wife, children, maintain property and provide some security for the family and have enough money to keep many individuals is a "distraction" which unmarried or

single individuals do not have to contend with. Thus, the sorrow that follows failures and the pursuit of possessions are clear distractions which married people have to consider and experience. The single person doesn't have this burden of sorrow in failures, which have obviously driven many wealthy individuals to the point of suicide or depression. Thus the married man is anxious about worldly things, how to please his wife and how his interests are divided.

4) The union of married people remain until death:
A wife is bound by God's law as long as her husband lives and vice versa; but if her husband dies, she is at liberty to be married to whom she wishes, *only in the Lord*. This is a restriction on your choice if you happen to marry. However, except in one or two instances, once married, you remain married even if you do not like the spouse anymore. These exceptions are proven adultery and instances where the pursuit of the Kingdom of God by the individual takes precedence over all and everything else, whereby even if "your eyes" or "your hand" will not allow you to enter the Kingdom, you must "cut it off". For readers who may be surprised at the use of language here, the "cut-off" means, to "do without". The "eye" thereby represents a most precious and important thing in your life. Remember that, if you did "cut it off", you are still bound to your spouse until one of you dies a natural death. This crucial rule is broken so recklessly that it has caused the divorce rate to go up even in the so-called "Bible Belt" areas of USA.

***

Legal Advantages of Marriage

"Love", when it comes to the legal impact on relationship, can truly be said to "be blind". This is because the legal implication of a relationship is often not sought nor does it become relevant until there is a problem in the relationship. At this point in which the problem has developed into e.g. conflict and crisis, "the eyes that love had blinded" often regain their sight. At this point things may have gone so bad, that rescuing the relationship and marriage becomes a major challenge.

Usually, couples and partners of all shades are often too busy to consider the consequences of what they are getting themselves and each other into. The problem appears, for most people, to be the fact that no *visible* contracts are written or signed before the people commit themselves and each other into a covenant that has extensive legal consequences.

It is this unwritten but valid contract that individuals often find repulsive, at a time when it may have been too late or too expensive financially and socially to pull out of the "contract". In most societies, the only evidence of marriage is the marriage certificate and perhaps the few people that may have witnessed the ceremony. In fact, the value of the marriage certificate is to be evidence that a contract to be bonded to the other person truly exists and that the individuals are indeed bounded and bonded together.

The people are the witness to such a risky enterprise. Yet in all these situations, there may not have been a written and well negotiated contract beforehand. People don't realise that they are actually tying themselves into an intricate legal bond that has serious ramifications for their decision making, finance, property, and who has the final say in health matters and pensions.

This union or partnerships of two individuals have consequences for their children and even an impact on future generations. For example, it affects the children if there is ever a divorce. Take for instance: who gets custody of the children in case of divorce, when the children are less than 18 years old. This bond which may not have been well thought of outside the drive of "love," or shall we call it sex, may affect the mental health of the couples, the mental heath of the children in case of of separation and divorce.

Partners and couples who are considering entering into a long or short term relationship should pause for a moment and consider their actions. There is power in knowing. There are positive and negative implications. That is, there are legal advantages and disadvantages of marriages and also of other relationships. Now let us consider what these legal benefits are.

**

A look at the USA perspective

Advantages and Benefits

Inheritance and Survivorship: The rights of Surviving Spouses. In the USA but certainly in the State of New York and probably in the rest of the States, the widow of a married couple has certain rights to the assets and estate of her deceased husband, notwithstanding the existence of a will. As I mentioned under the British System and comparing the scenario to a situation of co-habitation, this right does not exist. Further, in situations in which there is no will (a condition called intestacy) and one spouse has died, the spouse who is alive (survivor) gets part of all the estate. If there are other family members, such as children, parents and other siblings, they also get a part of the estate. However, the important thing is that unlike in "common law" relationships, the spouse who is alive does inherit *a portion* of the dead partner'e estate. What if there are no children or descendants in the relationship? The picture gets more interesting. Here is the exciting part: the surviving spouse gets *everything*. Now, let us have a caution in respect of human desires. Giving these scenarios, is the reader surprised why some spouse will illegally attempt to eliminate the other person?

That said, this is not the only right that the spouse is entitled to when the other spouse dies. Right of survivorship extends to include *legal right* to many of the late spouse's benefits. I will simply list the others here. This includes Social Security pension and veteran's pensions. The list extends to indemnity compensation for service-connected deaths as well as medical care, and nursing home care. According to General Accounting Office, GAO the list and the right of the survivor extends to the right to be buried in veterans' cemeteries, educational assistance, housing survivor benefits for federal employees and survivor benefits for spouses of longshoremen. There are additional benefits to spouses of coal miners who die of black lung disease as well as $100,000 to spouses of any public safety officer killed in the line of duty. Further, the legal rights that are available to the spouses include continuation of employer-sponsored health benefits, renewal and termination rights to spouse's copyrights on death of spouse, continued water rights of spouse in some circumstances as well as payment of wages and workers compensation benefits after worker death.

Right to benefits while married: The spouses of military personnel who are separated by virtue of their postings enjoy some rights: employment assistance and transitional services for spouses of members being separated from military service; continued commissary privileges per diem payment to spouse for federal civil service employees when relocating and Indian Health Service care for spouses of Native Americans.

***

Larger benefits under some programmess if married including: *Joint and family-related rights*: joint filing of bankruptcy and permitted joint parenting rights. The rights also include access to children's school records. Family visitation rights for the spouse and non-biological children, for example, visit to a spouse in a hospital or prison. This extends to next-of-kin in case of emergency medical decisions.

Further, preferential hiring for spouses of veterans in government jobs, tax-free transfer of property between spouses (including on death) and exemption from "due-on-sale" clauses are some of the benefits.

Other rights: Please note that there are over 1400 rights that the spouses can enjoy. The lists below are mere abbreviations of the over 1400 items on the GAO list.

Threats against spouses of various federal employees are a federal crime.

Right to continue living on land purchased from spouse by National Park Service when easement granted to spouse

Domestic violence protection orders

Existing homestead lease continuation of rights

Funeral and bereavement leave

Joint adoption and foster care

Joint tax filing

Legal status with stepchildren

Making spousal medical decisions

Right of survivorship of custodial trust

Right to change surname upon marriage

Right to enter into prenuptial agreement

Right to inheritance of property

***

Legal Disadvantages of Marriage

Cohabitation and Common law couple
From the above we can figure out the following advantages for common law couples or co-habiting couples. Perhaps, the way to look at this is by the common adage that one man's meat is another person's meal. What are disadvantages to the married couples are what the singles and co-habiting couples could exploit to the fullest as benefits. On the other hand, to some extent, what the singles and common law partners found as disadvantages are clearly beneficial to the individuals and couples in matrimony.

Advantages
There is no binding *"contract"* as in marriage. So individuals can walk out of the relationship at any time. Either in real terms as a written contract or as invisible contract but sealed by marriage certificate, cohabiting couples as "free spirits" are not bothered by the existence of marital arrangements. There is no commitment except for the care of any children between them, which may require legal process or contract to deal with.

The independence and freedom of each person is maintained as there is no binding obligation on either person to the relationship. It is a loose arrangement after all.

Therefore, each person can:
Property: Deal with his or her property in any way he or she seems right. There is no right of survivorship; there is no automatic transfer in case of death without a will. The individual can transfer it by will provided it is not a property that is owned in joint names as joint owners.

Finance: In the same way as in the case of property, provided it is not in joint ownership, the individual can deal in any way he or she seems fit, with her finances and bank accounts.

If the cohabitantsrs have children between them, then they are responsible as parents of the children. The role of parents either as a married couple or cohabiting couple is basically the same. This includes the need to provide a conducive environment for the children to develop in, protection against dangers, and provision of necessary things, defending the children, educating, and advising the children.

Though co-habitation, the impact of separation on any children in the relationship will still be similar to the effects under separation of married couples on the children.

Disadvantages of cohabitation

1. The first thing to note is that cohabitation is clearly a selfish arrangement which means there is no commitment to it or to

each other, at least on the face of it, as well as legally. Strictly, the individuals in it can live a separate lifestyle. Having said this, cohabitation does not in any way prevent contractual arrangements whereby the two can contribute to maintaining, say, the flat that they share, or for the payment of electricity and phones. It does not in any way prevent them from owning property together as any citizen is free to do so, in legitimate terms.

2. The fate and custody of any children may become a long drawn-out legal battle if the parents could not agree on who should look after them or who can have access to them. Sadly, many of these issues are played out in the public domain with the press having a field day.

3. If one partner, in particular the mother, is bitter, she may decide that her children will not bear the name of their father as the surname. This means she may give any name she wishes to the children as their surname. This may look absurd, but that is realityand the law . Having said that, the man can make application to the relevant authority, to have his name included in the birth certificate for the child/children. This is not so in matrimony.

4. Except when there is a valid agreement in place, the benefits of transfer of property may not be available to cohabitants. If a partner of a cohabitant dies without a will, the living may not inherit the property of the dead as is the case under marriage.

5. The financial benefits that are available to married couples are not available to persons that the law views as living individual lives.

6. As we have noted, the physical and mental health or psychological benefits of marital life is not completely available to common law couples and cohabitantsrs. Examples: the low rates of depression, schizophrenia, unhappiness, suicide, alcohol misuse which are seen in married couples are not replicated in singles or in cohabitation. The reason may not be far-fetched. Commitment to one another in life, disease and until death is not

there in cohabitation. Therefore, the degree of urgency to handle medical issues may be absent in cohabitation, in absence of any psychological commitment to the cause of the relationship. It is an individual life after all.

In sum therefore, it is up to you the reader to decide what you may want in any relationship. It is also up to you to decide which type of relationship is right for you. The option is yours to choose.

**

Life as a Loner: The Single Person
One of my teachers in medical school once taught me a profound lesson when he said that: "In marriages, while many people want to rush in, many people want to rush out of them". This is where the single person who remains decently single escapes the encumbrances that are associated with intimate relationships---be it marriage or a "common law" relationship, co-habitation or partnership. He or she neither enjoys the advantages nor takes upon himself or herself the challenges which those in one form of relationship or the other faces. Being single, in this context means that the person is neither in a sexual nor in any non-platonic relationship. He or she may have platonic friends.

Let us review some of the merits and demerits of remaining graciously single.

Advantages:

1. Single-mindedness confers on the person an unobstructed ability and freedom to decide on any course of action without apprehension of what the partner will think, say or do. This freedom is not available in matrimony. It may also, depending on the depth of the relationship, be absent in cohabitation in which there is a contract of who contributes what to the cohabiting household.

2) The single person has the honour of being free from the need to share the financial burden of any other partner. Except when a contract to disclaim is available before you marry, you run the risk of inheriting the debt of your spouse which he or she acquired before marriage, should he or she die. This is nevertheless counter-balanced by the other benefits of marriage. The bottom line: Single persons, avoid these complexities.

3) The person who is single is not bothered about the medical worries of a partner. As married persons, the health and life, as well as safety, of a spouse is almost always on the mind of the other. The single person has no worry about this.

4).There is no interfering in-laws or friends of spouses to worry about. As most married couples will tell, one of the most feared foes of matrimony is the impact of the in-laws. For a single person, this is one less worry to contend with in his or her life.

5) There are no children to bother about. Expenses may be limited to the individual alone. For a married person, the cost of raising a child in terms of time, energy and financial investment is high, as well as being an additional burden on a budget that may have been tight on the couple. For the single, he or she does not have to worry about this.

6) Save for intercourse, platonic friends (see chapter on friendships) may provide most of the support that are available under co-habitation or marriage. The gains that a single person receives via the support of his close but non-sexual friends may wipe out the benefits that could have been due to him/her under marriage.

7) In individuals who are religiously minded, being single without sexual encumbrance may allow the individual to focus on religious duties or calling. He or she does not have to bother about satisfying a spouse materially or sexually and neither is he or she concerned about the energy drain that comes with sexual activities.

***

Disadvantages
While there is much to gain from being single in many respects, there are patent and huge disadvantages to leading a single life.

1) Loneliness can drive people into desperation, anxiety and depression. Isolation and being alone could cause anxiety as there is "no one to talk to". This in turn could be so frustrating that serious mental illness could develop; especially drug, and in particular, alcohol misuse could become a major problem.

2) No one is a desert island of self-sufficiency. There will be times to rely on someone who is close for private discussion or to relate and discuss confidential matters. A spouse is the nearest to another spouse. In single individuals, this association is lacking, needless to say.

3) In times of serious physical and mental vulnerability, such as in diseases, there may not be credible urgent support outside formal workers (who may also be strangers) to provide help. That is, a single person may either have to rely on strangers from outside or rely on members of the extended family for help.

4) Many lonely individuals, young and old, have died in their apartments without anyone being aware. Therefore, disease may grip and kill the person without anyone noticing.

5) Inheritance may come to a waste if there is no one to transfer the estate. On the other hand, the estate for which singles have worked so hard for may go to charities or the state. It is not unknown that such estates have gone to complete strangers in the past in circumstances like this.

6) Except for when the person is highly disciplined, he or she may "burn" as under the religious definition or desire for intercourse. Being single does not imply the condition of being sexless. If the single is not able to comply with his or her religious chastity, she or he may "burn" or lust after intercourse.

7) We have seen that marriage has a lowering effect on alcohol misuse. It does means that compared to individuals in matrimony, life as a loner increases alcohol misuse.

8). Heart disease from high blood pressure and stress, poor nutrition, cirrhosis of the liver due to misuse of alcohol, due to alcohol and loneliness, unhappiness and impaired mental health are known to occur more in the single people compared to people in matrimony. These illnesses tend to be especially higher in single men.

I have set out above, the benefits of marriage, the advantages of cohabitation, the luxury of being single as well as the downsides of each of these relationship types. It is up to you the reader to decide what you want out of your life. The important thing is that you now have the information to make your choice. The ball, as they say, is now in your court. Whatever you decide upon let me take you to the other side of the human character. All that glitters is not always gold. Relationships do have their dark sides too.

***

CHAPTER NINE
Causes of Broken Marriages, Broken Relationships, and Their Consequences

"Marriage is one long conversation, checkered with disputes."
Robert Louis Stevenson

Now we have covered the formation of relationships and what sustains them. We have also seen what love is---a central issue in relationships. I have also discussed what could tear relationships apart. We have equally seen in great detail, the advantages and disadvantages of marriage and other forms of intimate relationships, as well as single living. Let us now take a good look at when these relationships are wrecked or at the minimum, when they undergo stress and strain. Human beings, it may interest you, can change like the weather. Human beings behave like a metal when exposed to intense pressure; tending to show considerable stress.

In this chapter, I will be concerned with the consequences of broken relationships. As a result of the considerable impact that separation and broken relationships entail on the individuals and the children, I will look at this in the next few chapters. This is so because a lot of individuals and couples who are entering into relationships seem not to be aware of the potential adverse outcomes of what they are about to go into. Also, broken relationships can and do have dire consequences for the individual, the couple, the family and the society at large. Most importantly, strained relationships have serious consequences for the apparently innocent children that may be caught in between the couples.

***

As a basic rule, whenever you have more than one person together there is bound to be a conflict. To avoid complex psychological argument that you could have a conflict even within an individual (such as body-mind split or lack of coordination between the brain and the body of a person), I will stick with my basic rule. Therefore, the minimum is two people together. They could be focusing on the same task or different tasks. For example: two children who are playing together could end up having a disagreement even though they will make up soon. A manager and his employee could disagree and have conflicts. Whenever there is a relationship, there is bound to be conflicts. It could be about a thing that conflicts with an individual's interests, or it could be disagreement about how to achieve a target. In human relationships this simple principle holds even between the tongue and the teeth so close, yet the teeth can occasionally bite into the tongue as they say, when there is a disagreement, or if you like in medical terms, *"dis-co-ordination"* between the tongue and the teeth!

***

In marriage and in any relationship whatever its form or shape, there is a supposedly high level of trust between the couple, dependency on each other for security and financial support by the couple as well as the children in the relationship---all depending on one another for their overall well being---in an atmosphere of trust. In addition, there is a high level of expectation for the future by the children and the couples as well. They all want to live trouble-free, stress-free lives. No reasonable person likes trouble in any event. Hanging on this expectation, as we have seen, are happiness, mental stability of the couple or the individuals as well as the mental, physical and future stability of any children who may be involved. Similarly, the happiness of in-laws, who are secure in the knowledge that their children are in "love" and in stable relationships, may take a knock. Family members and friends may also be directly or indirectly affected by the break down of the marriage or relationship.

The larger society also depends on marriage for nurturing the next generation of individuals and to give effect to the mental as well as physical and social stability or cohesion to everyone that are involved in the marriage.

***

From these innocent dependencies, it is clear and predictable what the likely effects of marriage and relationship break ups would be. It is relatively easy to predict the likely impact of a broken relationship and broken homes. Thinking globally and biologically, regardless of any religious inclination, it appears that any home, family and couples, who keep, strictly, to their biologically assigned roles are less likely to have conflicts. That is man function as man and woman functions as woman. Why would a true male of XY gene want to usurp the female function to be pregnant?

Why would a male father fail to instruct, defend and secure his children and home when he is healthy, employed and able to do so? I am not unaware of the roles that the law or various legal systems have played in blurring the gender roles or supposed ill-feeling by men that the law has been used in emasculation of male capabilities, however, the more these biological roles are blurred, the more the likelihood of conflicts. This is perhaps the reason that in homes across the world and cultures where their roles are kept intact, there is less chance of conflicts.

That is to say, peace will endure in situations when men keep their biological roles where women feel safe, healthy and secure without oppression from the men. It should nevertheless be remembered that men are ultimately, in most homes, responsible for domestic provisions and security. That said, conflict will be less likely when women give support to the men without contempt, betrayal and embarrassments against the man This is especially so when things occasionally fail to measure up to expectations. In saying this, let me go into further real life details to explain what specific issues lead to conflict in human intimate relationships, for that is the crux of the matter, as the saying goes.

Origin of conflict in a relationship

The foundation of any conflict is when the desire and intention of, say, "A" is *opposed* by the desire and intention of a party or person called "B". Let me explain: If I desire to get out of my room, first I have to stand up, walk towards the door, open the door if closed and then leave the room. If "B" does not want me to get out, this will be his desire. He can choose to block the door by his body or use materials to prevent me from getting out. Alternatively, "B" could call for outside help to disallow me from acting on my intention to get out of the room.

In order to fulfil my intention and to overcome the obstruction in my way, I will try and remove the resistance. I could do so by negotiation with my opposition, I could call the police, I could call my lawyer if I have the means to so so or I could defend myself physically or if I am able to. Alternatively I could take the law into my own hands in spite of the dire consequences.

Just imagine it, if my desire to get out was about me getting to the bathroom or to catch a bus for a job interview or to escape a fire in the room. It could also be about petty things such as being shut down from talking or being prevented from taking steps that will advance my legitimate cause. It could also be about my innocent presence in another person's vicinity. In the latter case, bitterness against another person does not have to be expressed in action; it could be expressed by silence or inaction or in words!

***

Meanwhile, as in any other partnership or relationship, ironic as this may seem, two *opposite* genders go into a relationship on the basis that their desires and intentions would *merge as one* in the form of a union. This is far from what happens in marriage in real life. Often, the opposites truly oppose each other, with each person attempting to enforce her or his desire on the other, all to the disadvantage of the union and against the spirit of companionship.

As we shall see in business relationships, two persons or companies form a relationship on the basis that their intentions and desires will come together as one. It is what happens between organizations too, especially when the result being expected is greater than the sum of their individual efforts or capabilities. This is otherwise called *synergy*. Therefore the foundation of synergy lies in human intimate relationships.

Practical experience has shown that in relationships of all sorts, this beautiful scenario called *synergy* is far from what happens in reality. Desires and intentions, and even acts, do conflict. Conflict may also arise amongst people who are truly working together, as in for example what the military referred to as "friendly fire". This means even when there is a united front in any relationship, conflict of intention can still occur. You may accidentally harm your partner. This kind of friendly fire is not what I am concerned with in this chapter.

***

Nevertheless, the major cause of conflict which is, as I mentioned above, fundamentally anything that will *threaten* the survival of or the *influence* of the person (morally, legally, financially, healthily and materially) or *impair* his/her enjoyment of life. Nations go into war when their way of life is threatened. Families will defend their positions and property against the intentions of a violent burglar.

The question is, how do we apply this great insight into relationships or, put in another way, how does this come into relationships? To get an understanding of how this affects relationships, first let us look at the major causes of conflict in intimate relationships, of which marriage plays a central role. Therefore, the clear causes of conflict in relationships or marriages are:

Financial issues including properties:
I have mentioned elsewhere that money does support marriage and relationship. Of course it has to be said that some individuals do form a union with another person with the sole aim of getting rich. Such relationships, which are based on pecuniary advantage, can survive only by a thin thread. What happens when money is not forthcoming? Argument upon argument will ensue. The relationship may now be on the brink of collapse.

Therefore basically, money and what it can buy is a major cause of conflict in a relationship. It may be that one of the individuals is not making enough money or the other person is spending too much to the detriment of the spouse. It may also be about reckless spending on frivolous things by either individual in the relationship. When there is no agreement, verbal or written, on how and when to spend the money that belongs to the matrimony, then arguments about money will not only be as hot as burning sulphur, they may never end. That may be the start of the end of the relationship.

***

Sexual matters.
Men love sex: that truth has to be admitted. It gives them a sense of dominance and satisfaction. Women, in general pursue sex less so and are more laid back, though some women are more sexually active than a lot of men (see chapter on gender and individual differences). However, the important thing to note is that conflict is inevitable when a person in a relationship desires sex, but such desires conflict with the other person's existing interest. Except when there is negotiation between the two individuals, conflict is sure to occur.

The "negotiation" does not need to be verbal. It may be by signs or by spoken expressions, good verbal words and legitimate physical acts. It may be by an enabling physical or mental health conditions that promotes sexual intercourse. Except if these conditions are there and are "agreed" to by persuasion or spontaneously by the couple, quarrelling is certain. Except for couples who provide a favourable environment for intercourse, conflict is sure. Some men, I am told, for example, would approach their spouse under the influence of alcohol. Yet, I am told, a lot of women loathe this approach. Sadly, some men have not taken note and this leads to reluctant and difficult sex.

Over time, these acts accumulate and could explode into crisis in in the future, against the man. Sexual matters relating to style, frequency, intensity, location as well as enthusiasm during the acts, are all areas of differences in relationship intercourse. Lack of sex between the couples could lead to frustration, bitterness and crisis. I have seen a few cases in my career where couples who are neither divorced nor separated and are living under the same roof refused to have intercourse together.

Some even went for as long as ten years while they were still in their prime years. Not surprisingly, when they consulted me, they could hardly see eye to eye in my clinic. The conclusion to draw from these instances is that, sexual matters, be it lack of sex, over-sex, distorted methodology, long duration, short duration, lack of agreement, could all lead to serious conflict and broken homes.

Matters that affect children
Children are a third party to any marital relationship. Note that a relationship must have been formed between two people before children, either of their own or adopted, ever join them. I don't know of anyone who is attempting to form a relationship by inviting children into the initial "negotiation". They are an outside influence, though indispensable and a crucial balance of power in some cases.

The views of the individuals in a relationship on how to raise the children, the number of children to bear, the morality or discipline to impose on them, the school to attend, the friends to keep and so many other issues that surround children, are major causes of conflict and crisis in a relationship. Very often, in my clinical experience, the father may want to impose some boundaries and the mother/wife may oppose it. In other cases, the father may keep "silent" whilst everything else goes wrong in the home to the disgusts of the wife/mother. I have seen a situation where the man just kept his "peace" whilst his child was busy smoking cannabis. Helpless, the woman became depressed and directed her anger against the man.

Children themselves can constitute a challenge to the spouses, due to, say, problems of birth, diseases, and when parents have to make life-death decisions. Sometimes, one parent may agree with a medical procedure and another parent may disagree. Eventually, if not managed properly, it may lead to serious conflict in the family. It may also be the behaviour of the children, such as issues concerning illegal drugs, where one parent may agree with its use and the other parent may disagree. Such examples can become a major source of conflict to the individuals in a relationship. It may split the marriage or relationship.

***

In-laws
Few, if any outside elements, influence a relationship and marriage as much as the in-laws. Sadly, in-laws (mother, father, brother, sister etc) are notoriously cited to be a factor in ending some otherwise stable marriages, due to the conflicts that they may cause through bad and divisive advice and actions.

Other causes of conflicts are religion
Practising different religions and differences in modes of worship may harm your relationship. It can cause untold hardship and conflict in relationships. Imagine if your spouse shares the opinion of his religion that it is right to kill others in the name of one's faith. Imagine if you do not share that view. How do you cope? How do you express yourself without serious repercussions?

Imagine if you call on different gods in the same home! It is like someone putting one foot in a boat and the other on the shore. When there is a wave, he may certainly not remain standing. Even in homes or marriages where the *mode* of worship of the same God is different, say: Catholic and Baptist, conflict may even flare up here in spite of the sameness of *Authority* they call upon. It is clear that human beings just do not like opposition to their intentions! My advice; only enter into a relationship with someone who reflects your view and shares what you share or values what you value. This is, once again, called *compatibility*. It is so true in any relationship even if individuals suppress their intentions, they may not act sincerely in the course of daily interactions. The basis of this is that, someone's desire is going unfulfilled.

***

Career/work
If there is a competition for time, prestige and money in the context that one person develops his career or her career in the relationship, especially if one individual humiliates the other, then conflict is a certainty. Ascendancy to power may annoy the less powerful spouse against "power that is". Envy, jealousy against the "throne of power" may develop, which may lead to serious treachery.

Health
I know for sure for I have seen it so many times, even in legal case laws. Mental health illness can arise as a result of frustrations or in other words when intentions are defeated. This is commonly called failure. Mental health problem can develop due to failure which may or may not have been related to the relationship. It may also arise due to other reasons such as drug misuse, genetics or inheritance from parents etc. However, how can we apply this principle in relationship? Here is an example. If one partner is mentally unwell, the other partner may see the illness as a shame or something that she can not cope with. She or he may decide to end the relationship. This sometimes leads to divorce or at least, separation. The cause of this may be exhaustion from caring for the other person who is ill, or general unhappiness about the association with someone with mental heath problem.

This statement is also true for physical illness. That said, health issues being the cause of conflict is more of a problem, as in HIV and other sexually transmitted diseases, where the cause can be attributed to an individual as the source of the infection and may therefore lead to a conflict in the relationship.

Culture and politics
No two human beings are the same. Even twins behave differently though they may have been raised in similar ways. Now consider individuals in a matrimonial union who are raised in different homes, different communities, nations and beliefs. Except when they *agree*, their *ways of doing things* may be poles apart from each other. Conflict and crisis may rule the relationship until, perhaps, it comes to an end. In recent times,

the principal cause of broken marriages in Indonesia has been linked to political differences. Thus, anything such as politics or beliefs in which the couple failed to have an agreement is a potential threat to the marriage.

With these in mind, therefore, let us look at some of the devastating impacts of conflict when it leads to separation and/or divorce.

***

Effects of Divorce / Separation (see also the advantages and disadvantages of marriage)

Financial Implications:

Short term

On the woman: Though the role of who is the "the breadwinner" in a family is changing, and in some places, the man is no longer the breadwinner, there is evidence that in a lot of families, the woman still depends on the man to provide some assistance. In fact, socially, regardless of how much the woman may be earning, even if she is earning much more than the husband, she still seems to expect at least some token support from the man. This is given an added urgency when one considers that children are more likely to be in the care of the woman than the man, in any event. This adds to the extra requirements for financial support for the woman. Thus, one of the first and most devastating impacts of marriage failure is financial difficulties for the woman, considering a break up in the relationship may create "single parent" status in some cases. This is especially so if she had depended on the man for much of the marriage. Also, it is worse if she is in the age bracket whereby she can no longer re-train in a vocation or career. Note however, that marriage separation or divorce may not be by legal routes alone. Divorce and separation, tragically as it may seem, may also occur by death.

***

For the man: Given the traditional role of the man as the one who the family, including the wife, depends on for support, the financial impact of marriage failure may not be as pronounced for men as for women, but that does not erase the adverse effect on the man. In some homes, of course, the female spouse may be the breadwinner, but that does not remove the perceived role of the man. In any case, a home where this role is reversed, except for when the man is disabled, is likely to be an unstable relationship. Women, we know, are likely to taunt the man to the point where he may call it quits.

As I was pointing out earlier, the impact of separation and divorce on the man may become more apparent if the couple have similar earnings and contribute close to or equally to their living. This *synergy,* you may remember, may have allowed the couple to live a life that is far beyond the earnings of a single individual. That is to say, the impact could also be felt more significantly by the man, if they maintain a high standard of living which is only sustainable by the combined income of the couple. The man could also suffer badly if his business - the source of his income - is in ruin as a result of the break up. The reason could be that the wife was a major business partner. It could also be that he may have spent considerably on the divorce so much so that he is left with little or no resources to run his business.

The man's situation can be made equally worse if he becomes unemployed or he becomes physically or /and mentally disabled. At this point of disability or employment, when his standard of living has taken a hit, financial help may not be readily available. Yet he is obliged by nature and law to continue to fulfil his "recurrent expenditure" of food, energy and security needs. At this point, pleasure and luxury may be the least of his worries. If all this could happen to a man who was earning before the divorce, then imagine the plight of the man who was neither employed nor had ever worked during the life of the relationship. If the raw, fresh and perhaps green living tree could be inflamed, imagine the predicament of the dead and dry wood.

Nevertheless, as in the case of the woman, the man may come off worse, if he can no longer re-train for a vocation or career in terms of his age of disability. In all these, he will need, or could have benefited from, the support of his wife.

All hope is not lost; the reverse of what I have stated above could also happen. The man and the woman may become well off, financially, following divorce. Consider a situation in which a pauper was married to a rich person. Upon divorce when their estate is redistributed, the pauper may be significantly better off than the point he or she entered the marriage.

***

Impact on property and assets

In some cases, as is often the case, either or both of the couple could lose their cherished matrimonial home, savings and pensions to the other, or the home could be sold entirely as part of the settlement. The implication is that each or both may have to re-start property acquisition all over again, if at all possible.

If the marriage break-up proceeds to court or even settlement in the hands of lawyers, it could cost both individuals very highly which would in itself be a drain on the pocket of the couple. All these things could happen irrespective of who is to blame for the divorce.

***

Long term

If you had hoped to live a life of freedom from financial worries in your retirement, you had better think again if you are having problems in your marriage. Think well before you get into sealing a relationship with someone which down the line may ruin your financial hopes. Be forewarned that few, if any, human beings can be relied upon. Think well, before you start your divorce for you may become poor in the days of your sunset, at a time when you should ideally recline in your back garden to enjoy the summer evenings. You may become bitter and poor at a time when your energy has waned, when your eyes are dimming; at a time when going up the house stairs becomes a challenge and when your teeth have become few. This could seriously affect your ability to go around the world sailing in a yacht or enjoying your dream holiday in an idyllic island somewhere in the Pacific Ocean. Your long term ambition to give to your children and your children's children could potentially be in ruins with your divorce. Your pension could disappear overnight, unless you calculate very well, now. You may end up in a benefit line if you happen to live in countries where there is social security. If you live where there is no social security, may God help you as you struggle to feed and clothe yourself. Do you want my advice? Plan now.

Your pension could be split up between the two of you or your pension could be transferred outright to either one of the couple. Therefore, depending on the arrangement, one person of the two may not have a pension in the end. Savings could also be split up or be transferred either way. You could end up the poorer or the richer. We live in a dangerous world, where the law could back those who oppose you with the intention of stripping away your hard-earned assets.

In the end, one or both spouses could be poorer or richer for the divorce

Medical Impacts of Divorce and Separation

Mental Health and Psychological Effects of Divorce /Separation

The first and immediate impact of divorce or separation is seen in your mental heath. You simply can not accept the reality of what you are experiencing. In the immediate aftermath, you become anxious, restless and "confused". You become confused because your concentration is impaired. You can not recall what was said to you or what you said in the last minute. Let us look at some detailed consequences that you may experience, irrespective of where you may be on earth. Divorce is no respecter of persons. Mental health problem does not discriminate when the condition for it is right, as in separation and divorce. You could at this point behave very irrationally. To put it mildly, in the eyes of others, your behaviour becomes "out of character". In the extreme, if care is not taken and you fail to control your emotions, you could be a target for the Police as they fear for your security, the security of your spouse and children and of property. You may be lucky if your spouse has not already reported you before now. If he/she has done so, then, your future is no longer in your own hands but in the hands of strangers who may determine where you end up, even if you are not at fault. In the short term, at this level, you may end up in a police cell or on a mental health ward. You are simply too risky to be left on your own. If you are in doubt of my words, do your own bit of research. You will be convinced. In the main, let us look at some individual issues.

***

Defeated expectation: In any break-up, the first casualty is (a defeated) expectation: an expectation to be married and remain married in bliss. Your characteristic temperament and associated behaviour can take a serious hit. This includes the expectation to be happy as well as the expectation to have the support of loved ones, spouses, in-laws and children. The defeat of this desire leaves a vacuum which often leads to unhappiness and low self esteem. In your own eyes, so to speak, your hope vaporises. This is why separation and divorce is so upsetting. The upset may be mild, if it has been long coming. It may be too much to take if you were not expecting it.

Unhappiness: Any violation of trust by either person in a marriage is a clear evidence of a crushed desire and intention to have a peaceful co-existence in the relationship. Clearly, this is a form of disenchantment. A disappointment leads to unhappiness. The chain continues as unhappiness leading to bitterness. The bitterness leads to hate against the other person. The hate may however be mutual.

If unchecked, the unhappiness continues as anger, acute anxiety (marked by heightened expectations, sleep deprivation, restlessness, agitation, aggression, easy irritation, sweating, loss of energy and so forth), and depression (manifesting as early waking, loss of energy, loss of appetite, changes in weight, life becoming gloomy, tearfulness, loss of interests, self neglect, lacking in motivation and you may become suicidal or bloodthirsty against any of the persons involved, such as in-laws, children and spouse or an adulterine third party).

Are we not living witness to many murders that are committed by spouses and ex-spouses against one another? Do I need to prove these points? Just listen to the news or do a bit of internet reading. Are we not helpless onlookers to the daily suicides and murders in the name of love, the world over? All these experiences could come in the early phase of the separation and then continue until one resolution or the other. Sometimes, it could end well. In other times, it may end up in tragedy. Whichever, bitterness is not so easily cured.

In some who are at risk, *depression* may be combined with a persistent false belief held in the face of strong contradictory evidence, and unrealistic suspicion of others, which is summed up as *psychotic depression* or "real madness" to use common language. Unrealistic expectations and flamboyant ideas may also feature in some as *mania/hypomania*. It should be remembered that each of these is an indication of a disease. Other disorders may become full blown diseases in their own right. They may be resolved in a short time in a way similar to sadness *that is seen in bereavement* or they may become a long-lasting event. The biggest problem is *bitterness* that often does not get resolved. (Please see also the chapter on the impact of divorce on children below). Resentment has a funny way of not going away. It takes a lot of counselling upon counselling to resolve this.

***

Physical issues Due to unresolved anxieties, especially in some women, self harm is a real possibility. Suicide is also known in men to occur following divorce or even separation. Have I not mentioned murder? This is part of it. Also, unresolved anxieties may lead to *peptic ulcers* and bleeding internally. Avoidance of food or even poor nutrition, loss of weight and its consequences may now occur. Similarly, anxiety could lead to *high blood pressure* thus causing angina, *heart attack and stroke.* People can easily conclude that all is not well with you. Some people even do not recover.

A vicious cycle could set in, involving financial difficulties and mental health problems. In severe cases or in the final analysis, he or she could end up in mental health hospital with all the attendant consequences: cultural taboo, employers and the pubic become wary of you too. These developments can and do occur in either parties, regardless of who is at fault for the divorce. You may say, well, these are extreme situations. Note though that these events could occur in mild or in severe forms. It depends on how individuals are able to handle disappointments. It may take time before the now ex-spouses could pick up the pieces.

Who comes out worse off between the couple? A most recent research has concluded that women are more affected than men when it comes to the adverse impact of separation and divorce on the couple.

Legal Implications of Divorce and Separation
Legally, divorce and or separation mean that a bond is being broken. If this is the wish of the couple, despite the obvious implications, the law will grant their wish even if it will cause them to be unhappy as a result.

These implications include:
a) The spouses are no longer legally recognised as one, or as two people in a union. Whatever they hold jointly, such as properties, bank accounts etc. will no longer operate as under matrimonial law, especially once such ownership is split during divorce. Thus, one partner may become poorer at the expense of

the other as pensions, matrimonial home, cars, savings may be re-distributed.

b) Along the same thinking, benefits, such as tax free financial transfers between the spouses, end upon divorce. Similarly, inheritances that in some cases may be due to the surviving spouses upon the death of the other will no longer operate.

c) Depending on circumstances, the courts may limit access to any children involved or even limit access to the other spouse or create conditions for accessing the children. This is often acrimonious in modern times.

Regardless of these very painful conclusions, divorce does not preclude a future re-marriage between the two parties nor does it prohibit the development of friendship between the two (see also chapter on friendship).

***

Advantages of Divorce and Separation
Note: The view taken here is one in which there is determined intention on the part of at least one person or individual in the relationship, to end the marital union. That is, one of the spouses may just decide against the wish of the other to end the marriage.

Separation by death
Though death is a form of marital and often painful separation, no reasonable person ever wishes to separate in this way. That said, this form of separation does have a more painful element to it, though the surviving spouse can and does adjust to the new and hopefully natural development, in most cases. If clinical experience is anything to go by, the adjustment can be tough on the surviving spouse and the children who are left behind (see advantages of marriage in previous chapter).

This is not the same thing as legal separation. Legal separation is an initial intention to live a separate life, even if the couple are living under the same roof. The consequences are that in time it will lead to divorce. Continuous living of this nature by the couple will gradually amount to the sum of months (24 months in some cases) which may ultimately lead to granting of divorce by the courts. This could happen in the UK at least.

In separation by death, except for when the surviving spouse or an individual manages the situation with good insight, there is a huge risk that the family which is left behind by the dead, will be affected in the same way as the family that underwent legal separation. This includes the emotional impacts which I discussed above.

Nevertheless, there are rare situations when legal separation, in spite of the distress, may bring some "benefits". We should bear in mind, however, the common saying during a marriage ceremony: "for better or for worse" which tends to suggest that whatever comes, the two people will be bound together until death separates them---no matter the circumstances.

I have seen devastating events impairing marriages and relationships, even up to threats of death and public disgrace, yet the various couples stuck together, and found common ground to continue the relationship (see later chapters on case studies).

Some "benefits" and justification for divorce

Divorce may be justified and it is usually is, on legal and religious grounds, if there is proven adultery. This is perhaps the only ground where law and religion agree on divorce. On such occasions, each party can begin *afresh* with the benefits of experience and freedom that comes with such divorce. The severe consequences outlined above should be balanced against this *newfound freedom*.

Temporary separation, on the other hand, may give the couple time to reflect on and re-evaluate the gravity of their situation, adjust and correct or address any pressing issues. This may be a life-saving breathing space in some cases. It may also allow room for counselling and other interventions.

What of marriages in which severe physical injuries are inflicted on each other? Do they end in divorce? What of situations in which police have been involved and the career of either person is on the line, or in situations where there are severe devastations? The answer is to be found in practical examples which I stated above. In that case, the spouse will have to weigh the advantages of divorce against the advantages and disadvantages of marriage.

If divorce and separation can have such devastating impact on the adult couples, what about the vulnerable young children that may be involved? Let us see.

***

CHAPTER TEN
Broken Marriages, Broken Relationships: Effects on Children

"The best way to keep children home is to make the home atmosphere pleasant – and let the air out of the tires".
Dorothy Parker

Let us deal with first things first. What are the benefits of marriage on children? I mean the benefits that are conferred on children when the parents are functioning and not merely when they are present? This is important as parents can be present with children yet be considerably damaging to their health, as for example when children are abused by their own parents.

Let us look at the main benefits that children in a marriage and in other relationships, be it single or cohabiting, enjoy. The reader should note that there are distinct advantages and benefits of a functioning father, such as providing enforcement of rules and discipline, providing direction, defence and security. In combined efforts with the father, mothers provide comfort, reassurance, encouragement, defence and general provisions. The functions which I have listed above can occur in any functioning relationship, be it cohabiting or marital, so long as they perform these duties as parents. In fact, these functions occur wherever parents function as a reasonable parent should.

***

Academic performance does get better: Children who are living with two parents, either in marriage or not, perform better in school and are less likely to drop out of school. Similarly, they tend to do better later in life as measured by income earning and their ability in retention of employment. This claim is in comparison with situations whereby the child lives with single parents. These benefits to the children living with their two parents exist probably because they have a stable foundation from the outset of their lives.

Criminal conduct and behaviour is lower:
In communities with disproportionate number of single parents (usually mothers), such communities have higher offence rates than areas where there are two-parent families, probably because fathers are more able to manage and control boys' behaviour (see the rule enforcement which I stated above about fathers). Children of married parents are less likely to turn to gangs and crime for social support than children of single parents.

Lower rate of before-marriage sex in girls: One study found that girls from two-parent homes are less likely to experiment with premarital sex than girls from single-parent homes. In the meantime, the issue with premarital sex is not just about liberation, there are serious issues with infection, early parenthood and impaired careers, as well as others which I discussed in Chapter under: Adolescent Relationship.

Better parent-child psychological bonds. Psychological ties between parents and children are stronger in married homes compared to single homes, researchers have claimed. This is probably because parents are protective and take special interest in the progress of their children. In single parent homes, the lone parent is possibly too busy juggling too many things at the same time. This reduces the bonds between her/him and the children. Children work harder when they thrive within an environment of a two-parent relationship, not just marriage, research works have claimed.

Wellness: Unlike divorced parents, children in marital homes are better supervised by both parents and are therefore likely to identify danger and dangerous conduct early. Is it not a global acceptance that two heads are better than one? This clearly applies to supervision of children by both parents in relationships. Thus they can and do prevent damage in their children to a greater extent than single parents or divorced parents who may be too busy and too tired to bother about even minor things in the child.

Child-abuse: That mothers and wives or women in general have a "softening effect" on men is a socially undeniable fact. Men exercise caution in the presence of their wives. This simple truth has huge benefits on our health and that of children. When men (and women) get angry they can take it out on their innocent children who may in fact know nothing about the cause of the incident. When men and women are together, the chances of this happening are less. This is because of the need to protect the children and one parent is more likely to be cautious in the presence of the other. Need I show evidence that women to a large extent, with some exceptions, are better at reducing---by their placid nature---tense or volatile scenarios? In those exceptions though, the women may serve as inflammable substance on a raging fire. Thus, the saying: *"Hell hath no fury like a woman scorned"* is true after all.

Poverty: Since both parents may work or alternatively at least one parent may be working while the other looks after the home, the children of married parents rather than single parents are less likely to suffer poverty as compared to children of single or divorced parents. This appears logical to me and does not require in-depth imagination to see the reasons why this is so.

***

The devastating effects of divorce on children

It is sad enough that children are involved or find themselves unwittingly and vulnerably in marital or parental break-ups. They never choose those situations. That is the reality and the truth regardless of the age of such children. The devastating impacts of divorce and separation are more pronounced in children under 20 years old. They bear the brunt of the break-up. Sadly, few couples ever stop to consider such devastating impact on the children. Put simply, when a marriage comes to an end by any means (death, legal, custom, religion etc), the children suffer considerable consequences. I list below some of these tragic outcomes. I have seen some single parents who deny these events which are well supported by scientific evidence. Perhaps, a cautionary note should be sounded here. The fact that some isolated single parents out of many of other single parents has done well and the children have done well does not remove the reality that there are remaining majority whose lives are blighted by divorce and mismanagement. Many child-carers and psychiatrists are living evidence to the devastations on children's mental health that divorce causes. This is also supported by the UK's government data on the subject.

The reason for such devastating impact stems from the simple reason that children have an expectation to have two supportive parents within whose realm they enjoy security, provisions of necessities, defence, direction and discipline. Therefore, when a relationship comes to an end, there are major consequences. All of these of course result from a child's perspective and from a failed expectation/desire to have a fulfilling and happy life.

***

1. *In the short term (pre-adolescence)*

In the short and possibly in the medium term, the child would wonder what is going on. He or she could not understand why his or her parents are going their separate ways. The child may ask questions or the child may suppress the questions. He may not be bold enough and the questions may therefore be subdued. This suppression will in some ways, be it in bad behaviour or in mental health, manifest itself later. Alternatively, it may just remain as bitterness which may fuel attitudes towards life and others as life goes on.

Anxiety and depression: Except when properly managed, the child could become withdrawn, confused and depressed as well as anxious. The child could become sleepless, lose weight, refuse to eat properly and academic work could suffer considerably as a result of the acute phase of confusion, anxiety and depression.

Growth may be stunted. Due to poor nutrition, sleeplessness and anxiety, growth may become arrested.

If his peers in school are aware of the situation, he may be taunted. From here, the child may start to react in an unusual way, such as with violence and/or withdraw further into his inner world. There are reports that in some cases, the child could blame himself or herself, (which may be true or false) as the cause of the break-up.

2) *In the medium term (adolescence)*

Gangs, violence, drugs and abuse: depending on circumstances and the age, especially if there is no parental support (such as honest paternal guidance for boys, genuine maternal support for girls and vice versa), the child could end up in the wrong company outside the home, due largely to isolation and parental neglect. The child could begin to receive improper and damaging advice from wrong "counsellors". This advice will obviously be harmful to the child. The results may be an end to a quality productive life.

Prostitution and early sex, violence and drugs: the result of poor advice and bad guidance would be exploitation, possibly in prostitution, especially in girls. If you are in doubt, read the news about children who are in prostitution in the UK. No children from good supportive homes will end up in such circumstances.

This phase could also mark the introduction to illegal drugs (which goes hand in hand with early sex). Few, if any people doing illegal drugs can be described as peaceful. Therefore violence to persons, the community at large and criminal damage are probable outcomes. They could begin to steal in order to feed the craving for drugs. The vicious cycle can only lead to one of two places, prison or mental health institution. The evidence for these is staggering.

Damaging effects in the medium term:

The outcome of all these are: early pregnancy or premature parenthood, criminal activities, such as, gang behaviour, gun running, possession of drugs, physical and mental health injuries. In the final analysis, the future becomes very bleak. Early death may occur, if the child does not end up in prison or a mental health institution. The foundation for prosperous longer term future would now be sent into the abyss.

Further adolescents' years
Teens also experience anger, fear, loneliness, depression and guilt. Some feel pushed into adulthood if they must take responsibility for many new chores or care of siblings. Teens may respond to parents' low energy and high stress levels by trying to take control over the family. Others feel a loss of parental support in handling emerging sexual feelings. Teens, because of this effect, may doubt their own ability to get married or to stay married.

***

3. Longer term.

Vicious Cycle: In the longer term the bitterness of having come from a broken home lingers on. It may carry on to adulthood as well as into the child's own marriage later in life, if any. His/her marriage may suffer the same fate. Thus a vicious cycle is firmly established. It will take a determined effort to break this cycle.

Bitterness: There is also the likelihood of bitterness and disappointment leading to anger and unstable relationships in the future.

Sexual orientation: There are some reports that aberration of sexual orientation in teens and adults may occur as a result of parental divorce. This will not be surprising given the vulnerability of children in divorces, the lack of proper guidance from home and being exposed to opinions from outside the parental sources or from outside "counsellors" who are out to exploit and mislead them. The author has also seen a scenario where the change in sexual orientation was a rebellious reaction. The basis of this being bitterness and hate for the perceived gender of the parent that is allegedly at fault for ending the marriage.

4) *Mental health, criminality and imprisonment*: In the writer's personal clinical experience, children, especially but not exclusively boys from fragmented homes, tend to suffer from Attention Deficit Disorder (ADHD) early on and Personality Disorder (PD) later in life.

Life on poor achievement and poor productivity

At the end of the child's life cycle, looking back, he may have spent the quality part of his life achieving no tangible things. His life may have been marked by one kind of turbulence to another and from one containment institution to another: a life that is full of failures, diseases and bitterness. Often, these children end up having their own children who reflect their own life unless there is a fortunate turnaround in the brutal cycle.

Here is how the *Journal of Psychological Medicine* concluded their research on the matter:

"Divorce and separation were associated with increased anxiety and depression, and increased risk of alcohol abuse. This was the case after adjusting for educational attainment, age at first marriage, parental divorce, childhood aggression and neuroticism, and current financial hardship, lack of a confidante and frequency of social contact with friends or family. The association between divorce and risk of alcohol abuse became non-significant when the latter variable was controlled for. Associations between divorce and psychopathology were observed even though half of those separated or divorced were re-married or reunited with their spouses at the time of the analysis. There was, furthermore, no association between these mental health measures and time since first separation or divorce".

That said, there are single parent families who did not come to that position by their own accord, and parents with considerable insight who manage their challenges properly with good outcomes for their children. Therefore, there are many children from divorced homes, who, as I said, do well in life. Though, I will advise that wise readers should not contemplate this as a credible option. These exceptions are as rare as, say, one in a several broken homes.

***

Does divorce confer any benefits on the children?

Once in a blue moon one can say divorce confers some benefits on the children in the family. This is the case considering the children's biological and financial needs, defence, security and general guidance requirements. This is in addition to the overall sense of cohesion and unity in the family which gives a balance to the child/children.

In some occasions, constant wrangling by the parents is more likely than not to have an impact on the mental health of the child. Also sexual harm, physical/verbal injuries, denial of proper guidance, introduction to drugs and alcohol or general irresponsible behaviour etc. by either or both of the parents would obviously cause greater harm than the benefits of protection and defence which I stated above. This has to be put into a scale to consider which one is of greater harm. Would divorce confer greater benefits than removing the offending parent(s) or the child?

The best option is usually to remove the child from the source of mental and physical injuries rather than proceed with divorce by the parents/spouses. If both of the parents or are not bold enough to remove the child from harms way, then the government will have to do it through the social services. If not, the entire nation will have failed the child. Indeed, the whole world has failed the innocents.

The effect of this option is that the child will know for sure that his/her parents did not divorce and may therefore avoid the dire results of divorce on his/her own mental health and life which I discussed previously. Divorce, it can not be over-emphasized, has a devastating impact on the children.

As an end note, divorce in a relationship that exists without children, is in some ways, more tolerable considering the damage that family fragmentation does to these vulnerable children who are caught up in family feuds.

One can therefore find no other ground leading to benefits from divorce, for the demoralizing and damaging effects of divorce are too colossal to be toyed with. Rather than divorcing or separating, anyone contemplating marriage should assess his/her marital or relationship proposal critically, before jumping into it. Ask: Is this right for me? Am I made for marriage or an intimate relationship? Should I have children? For what reason do I want children? What is the purpose of children? Of course, that is the purpose of this book. On balance, one may opine, to be decently single is by far better than the futility of failed marriage. Again, that is a choice that you may have to consider.

***

CHAPTER ELEVEN
Broken Marriages/Partnerships: Effects on Relatives, Friends and In-laws

"Never rely on the glory of the morning or the smiles of your mother-in-law." Japanese Proverb

Obviously, at the time that a relationship is established, there are four different groups, formal and informal, who are involved. The first are the couples themselves. They represent the core of this relationship. Let me call them the first or "A" team. Imagine them as the core of four circular rings that surround each other. They, the couple, found each other and perceived that they will be good for one another.

They invited the remaining three groups to recognise and to join them together. The second group are the family and friends. They are the second ring and directly overlie the central core. They solidify the relationship and give some permission for it to proceed. In modern times, this permission may in fact not be required for the relationship to be established. Individuality---"I will do it my way, whatever you think, I am an adult, you know"--- tends to replace the age-long wisdom of the parents and friends.

The third group is the society at large for they sanction and applaud or boo the relationship depending on the *type*. They are the third from the core. In our days, there is subdued disapproval *for some* relationships but for fear, few can stick their heads out in the crowd. What do you say to a man of 60years marrying a girl of 18 or even under 16 years in some countries?

The fourth and last ring covering the outmost part of the entire unit is the law or the authority or the government. The law sanctions and gives teeth to any type of relationship it wishes to recognise. The law or government also positively and for the right reason, perhaps, discriminates between different types of relationships. Sadly, the government in many ways have made laws that may also cut a gulf through relationships. Often, the government are represented by the relationship registry, the police, the lawyers, the law makers, social services, Inland Revenue and others.

All these groups will in one way or another influence the outcome of the relationship and marriage that you are about to enter or that you have already entered into. On the other hand, when things go wrong, all these groups can not escape the consequences of the actions of the couple. They will either benefit or pay the full price.

Now, I shall call these groups that are outside the central "core" the relationship the "third parties". The couple themselves are the first set of parties. Strictly speaking, children are not party to the relationship for as the common English saying goes: "Nobody can choose their parents". Children, especially those who are under 18 years, are often helpless on-lookers in the whole drama, if ever they were born before the marriage. In most marriages though, children come later.

Presumably, these four groups that I have mentioned make their own contributions to the marriage. Interestingly enough, it can be for ill or for good. The decision for the good or ill of the relationship rests squarely with the couple in the relationship. If the central core can no longer hold, the peripheral rings will fall apart. Also, if the central core is too combustible and about to blow, the peripheal rings will be shattered following the "explosion". Thus, the couple is always the decisive factor.

If the couple allows the *third parties* to influence the relationship in a *bad* way, the marriage or partnership is doomed. If they disallow the adverse influence of the third parties and they *both* take the *good* influence, there is a good chance that the relationship may flourish and survive. The choice is yours.

Having said this therefore, let us take a look at the effects that broken relationships may have on the third parties themselves. Remember, we have already taken a detailed look at the effects of the central core and the children.

***

The in-laws
Well, there can only be in-laws in a marriage. There are, strictly speaking, no in-laws in co-habitation or with a "common law wife" or in "partnerships". But then, let us assume that the in-lawship principle applies also to partnerships. In-laws can be a snare or stumbling block to the success of the relationship. In-laws can also be a bedrock or fortress to lean on in times of trouble. It all depends on who is listening to whom. It depends on how you put the "counselling" that you have received from in-laws. This advice can sustain your relationship or it can send it into the abyss.

If in-laws have wished the relationship to succeed, the relationship may hold. If they want you to fail, like the "snake" that I talked about earlier, the relationship may come to a very devastating end indeed. In-laws means either mother or father or any of the siblings of the spouse. They will not go away and they will impact on your relationship. The earlier you take notice and deal with them appropriately the better. They all need special attention and care. Sometimes the care has to be containment or even curtailment. On the other hand, you will have to give them open access and a broad welcome into your heart for without them, you marriage may not survive for long. This latter group are however few. Going by the experience of many, the bad overweighs the good, it seems. Nonetheless, when challenges come, they, the in-laws will have their own share of it. Here are some impacts.

***

Case 1: Agnes (original name withheld) was in her late fifties. She had a daughter who was married to a financially successful man. They had a daughter. Agnes and her own husband had fully supported the marriage of her daughter, called Ann (original name withheld). For some reasons, the couple, Ann and her husband were to divorce. Agnes could just not take it. She developed anxiety, depression, sleepless nights, loss of appetite and weight loss. She considered that her social status would be tainted by the proposed divorce. For days, she wept. On the day when the divorce was to be granted, she was so anxious that she had to be sedated in hospital. Ultimately, the divorce went through. In time, she worsened but in the medium term, she recovered and carried on with her on life. However, Ann is left to nurse her wounds too.

Case 2:
John was a man in his mid seventies. He was a devout Christian. His son, who was in his late thirties and married for 10 years, had separated from his wife with a view to divorce in a short while. John, on hearing this, became withdrawn, bewildered, refused to eat and became depressed. He refused for some time to talk to his daughter-in-laws's family, believing that they caused the separation. John also considered the divorce a complete disgrace and aberration to his faith. Until he died, John had not got over his son's divorce.

On the other side of the coin, if any of the in-laws had wanted the relationship to end, it is obvious that the slightest attempt by the couple themselves to end the marriage or relationship would be a day of joy for the in-laws. Millions of such in-laws exist on earth---for good or for bad reasons! Look before you leap, therefore. Test the waters of your in-laws before you start to swim. Remember, human beings are capable of hiding their true colours or intentions for the sake of self-interest or being perceived to be doing good. My advice: cut through the shadows.

Friends of the family
Provided the friends have not harmfully contributed to the end of the relationship, the first reaction to hearing of attempts at separation or actual divorce is usually met with bewilderment, sheer disbelief and shock. This may be followed by a sense of loss and blame. If they have been active at ending the relationship, there may be a cynical "joy" while secretly mocking their friends whose marriage or relationship has failed. My advice: be careful whose advice you follow. It may do you good or it may ruin your happiness.

Note that the separation may not necessarily end friendships (see chapter on friendships), but it reduces cordiality and contact between all the friends. Bitterness and surprise may continue for a long time. However, depending on the depth of the friendships, the thoughts of the ordeal may linger on for a while, leading to sleeplessness and some anxieties.

Other Relatives
Brothers and sisters-in-laws do feel a sense of disappointment, emptiness and loss when couples separate or divorce. Sometimes, if there is business link, this may be damaged. Overall, separation and divorce does have far-reaching consequences for the relatives involved.

***

CHAPTER TWELVE
Broken Marriages: Effects on Society

"All progress is precarious, and the solution of one problem brings us face to face with another problem".
Martin Luther King, Jr.

I mentioned in previous chapters that there are witnesses to matrimonial relationships and not the least, one witness to any marriage is the society. You might wonder how the society is a witness. Well, pretty simple.

If you happen to live in the UK (just as in any other rule-obeying country), once you give notice to the government via the registry that you intend to marry someone, that notice is actually to the entire world and to your immediate society as well. It will be made public for a number of days in case there are any objections from, say, someone whom you have jilted or a moaner who doesn't like the relationship. If there are no objections, it is reasonable to conclude that the society has accepted your intention to be married. In that case, the society offers authority to the marriage by this acceptance.It makes it solid and real. Were it not so, anyone could have objected and thus throw a spanner in your smoothly operating engine.

The society at large also has the expectation that the marriage or relationship will, in turn, support the society by not breeding irresponsible children and that the couple will also contribute positively to the society. So the support is mutual between you and the society. These benefits and the rules are not coded and are not written anywhere.

This is the norm and the culture in every land in the world. Regardless of where you may be on earth or where you may be reading this book, societies do not like families and couples that give them trouble. This is not, in my opinion, difficult to understand. How can a society stand other than in chaos, if families and relationships within it frequently generate trouble? Short of this, such couples can be easily identified and may be isolated. The society or community is built on the expectation that the members of such society within it, will come from stable relationships, such as marriages. Again, this is common sense that is not written as law in any law book. It is just plain old common sense. That is to say, the family is the bedrock and the smallest functioning unit of any society---whatever your views on current debates about *normal* biological relationships may be. Meanwhile, a family is a *genetic man, genetic woman* and children. It is the children from such *genetic* relationships and the happiness that follows a successful marriage which ultimately sustain a society. Any society that fails to honour genuinely positive productive and reproductive associations between human beings will dwindle and will ultimately end. History has taught us this lesson. After all, it is human beings that make societies and indeed, the value of any place or land is directly a reflection of the value (or kind) of people who live there.

When relationships falter, the society and the country and the world pay a huge price for the decline, even if children are produced from other reproductive techniques (see chapter on "Is Sex Necessary?"). What therefore is to be expected from a society whose units---family, the smallest units--- are in disarray, albeit gradually, through divorce, separation and perhaps others means of disintegration or lack of integration? Here are the consequences of broken marriages and broken relationships and as the UK's Conservative Party leader David Cameron calls it, if I may quote British Broadcasting Corporation BBC, and the Daily Teleraph, "broken society/Britain". Follow me, therefore, as I take you through the prison institutions to the mental heath systems and a society living in fear.

***

Decline in order

A decline in the order of society is to be expected from broken relationships and marriages. This is so since surviving or functioning marriages and relationships ought to be a cohesive force in joint action against the potential bad behaviour of the children that may be produced by the couple in relationships or marriages.

The result of such broken cohesion is simply that children from such families are likely to take instructions from outsiders away from the home—often from peers whose parents may have broken up too. Remember, birds of the same feathers flock together. Remember also that there is power in *synergy*, which I discussed earlier. Therefore, once there children can find solace in their outside friends, they will follow the advice that these friends will offer them. After all, these children could no longer receive credible advice from parents who are now trying to patch their own lives following divorce or separation. This gradual formation of group may lead to formation of gangs whose aims and objectives are to pursue a given cause. This *cause* can never be a good one without these children being reformed. I have never seen or heard of an unreformed gang of delinquent children proposing to do anything credible and positive to society. All of these are to the disadvantage of the larger society. The societies have got to pay for their own failures to streamline marriages and child-bearing.

It is not just bad behaviour; but also the cohesive action of parents which forms and guides the overall behaviour of children. Therefore, a society will benefit if its young members are of good behaviour, for there will be fewer people going to prison and or getting killed in acts of violence. There will also be a lesser number of members of the society who are maimed or killed by badly behaving children from broken homes. When broken relationships are common, the world is a more dangerous place to live in. I know some readers will argue that the danger has been long coming or long recognised. Whatever your position, one thing is for sure, the world is less safe a place to live in because of innocent children that, due to the failure of adults, have been transformed into dangerous criminals.

***

Insecurity
Either as individuals or in the formation of gangs, chances are

that children from broken home, lacking the benefit of cohesive discipline, may begin to terrorise the local and larger communities. This often results in such crimes as robbery, stealing, harm to individuals and murders, which we hear about everyday in the news.

In local areas where such crimes may be occurring there is an all-encompassing feeling of insecurity. A sense that something is not right somewhere: An eerie feeling of paranoia, whereby you tend to suspect everyone unless a contrary intention is otherwise proven. Suddenly, the innocent kitchen knife becomes an object to loathe and to fear in daylight and at night. You really never know who is hiding a pointed, sharp metal object under his over-coat. In essence, guns, often held illegally, have attained a status of toys---something to possess by broken minds from broken homes--- who also fear for their own lives. Around the country in general, there a feeling of a break-down of law and order, which is caused by and traceable, ultimately, to homes where these perpetrators originate from.

So that I am not accused nor am guilty of making broken homes responsible for all the ills of societies, there are children who are well brought up who ignore proper instructions and instead follow those of his "mates" only to end up in mental health institutions or prisons. The impact of this is that such children not only shame the society, parents and family, they are as good as never having been well instructed in the first instance.

***

Cost of care

Mental Health

In discussing this issue, the assumption is not made by any stretch of the imagination that broken families are exclusively responsible for mental health deterioration in an individual. The hard truth though is that they are a material contribution.

Some, if not a lot of children from broken homes will end up in mental health institutions. This is well-proven and the reason is pretty obvious, since some will end up in gangland. At the minimum, under peer pressure, the gangland is likely to introduce them to drugs such as cannabis, speed, ecstasy, LSD etc. You only need a test dose of these substances to impair your thinking. If care is not taken and the individual continues to consume these substances, there are high chances they will impair their minds and thinking for a long time. Once your thinking and judgement is impaired, you are likely to do the "wrong things and be on the wrong side of the law" (see the chapter on freewill and choice"). This is the start of mental health problems. There are two consequences here:

The first is that, the presence of mental health individuals in society means they need to be cared for. If not, the larger society pays a terrible price in instances of maiming, killing and a host of other crimes. In welfare states like Britain, the question might be asked: Who is going to pay the cost for this care? The society will. How? The government one way or the other will have to look for the money to fund the healthcare system. One of the surest ways of doing this is to raise taxes. If the initial taxes are not enough, the government will simply raise more. One way or the other, we all pay. What about countries where the State does not pay? Well, you will have lunatics on the streets, in political power and as community terrorists.

The second issue is that, if the society fails to care for the mentally diseased, such society risks high levels of insecurity, harm and possibly alarming murders. These murders do not necessarily flow from being mentally unwell. It is a known fact too that some of the sad outcomes from separation and divorce are that couples who have broken up do kill and maim each other (see case studies in later chapters). The couples may also use proxies who act on their behalf. Following this, such individuals may embark on a killing spree, as we have seen in recent times and frequently too. If you the reader are surprised at these hard words and the tough facts which I present here, then you are probably from planet Mars or plainly playing the ostrich who hides its head in the sand believing that its problem do not exist or will go away.

The other closely related issue is the link between mental health and imprisonment and broken homes. Clearly, from the foregoing discussion, it would be clear that children from broken homes, who lack a cohesive and concerted upbringing, may receive, in order to fill the vacuum, instructions from their peers. Will these be good instructions? Will they be bad instructions? Only you can tell. For me this is not too difficult to imagine. From clinical evidence, the advice is usually bad, such as "try these" drugs.

I have noted that, such peers may also gang up to commit crimes. Well, if you commit crimes, there is one of two ways in which it can end, in a land that is ruled by law: the criminal may end up imprisoned or in mental health institutions. It follows that children from broken homes are likely to end up in prison. I know that there are doubters out there on the account that they had broken homes but their children did well. The hard truth is that theirs are exceptions to the rules.

***

Taxes for care

Someone somewhere will have to pay for the imprisonment of criminals in order to restore security to the community. Someone will have to pay for the mental heath care of the mentally ill. Your taxes will have to pay for it—either you like it, loathe it or be indifferent to it, you will pay. There is no escaping it. The higher the financial burden on the government to care for these people, the higher the likely chances that you, the reader, will pay higher taxes, even if you are not the cause of the problem! Yes, you pay. Annoying, isn't? If this annoys you, then take my advice: plan well for your relationship.

What about decreased productivity?

While not everyone from broken homes will end up in mental health institutions or in imprisonment or with drug misuse problems, there is a chance they just may. Children under 20 years of age are likely to be more vulnerable and to fall into the categories which I have described here. These people may have no crucial work-examples or credible role models (as we like to nicely paint it) to follow, and are most likely to depend on state benefit support in countries where this is available. Where social benefit support is not available, the roaming individuals who are hungry and angry may resort to illegal means to survive---at your cost. In the end, the society gains very little from them in terms of productivity.

In sum, the society, the country and indeed the world at large pays a huge price for these failings as well as for the fragmentation of these cohesive family units of the society. The cost in treatment of mental health disorders, care for the prisoners, increase in crimes, insecurity in communities, loss of productivity, death and agony are some of these effects, not to mention the subdued hostility or real hostility against marriage and general unhappiness that pervades the society as a result of broken hearts and hopes. Divorce or separation of couples, to be truthful, has no real benefits for the society. This is because divorce may promote, in the long term, bitter individuals, and especially in those who choose not to re-marry: loneliness, isolation and a sense of being alone in this world, particularly for those without children. Sad, but you are in charge.

***

CHAPTER THIRTEEN

Anger and Frustration: Causes, Prediction and Management in Relationships

"Anger is in the bosom of him or her who knows no harmless way of dealing with his failed desire and intentions"
Dr. Joel Akande

Personally, I do not know of any source of anger that developed in a person without another individual outside the person who is angry being involved. That is to say, there is always a relationship side to anger occurring. No matter what, the relationship may be short, or it may be long. The association may be near or in far flung distance from the person who is being annoyed. Interestingly, you may also be angry against a non-living object. For example, there was a case of a man in the USA in 2008 who was mowing his garden. For some reason, his mowing machine developed a fault and it started to give this man problems. The mowing was not going according to his desire and plan. Angry, the man took his gun and, can you believe it, shot his mowing machine. If you are puzzled at this anger, so were the police, who promptly arrested our man for consequences of his anger, his violent disturbance of his neighbours and illegal possession of a gun. Further, his action created fear in his community, the story went. Imagine for a moment, if this anger was between two human beings who are in a relationship. Let us examine this issue further. In writing this book, I have been asked if anger is in itself a crime. No, anger on its own is not a crime. Controlled anger, like all intentions without actions, is not a crime. It's the action from being angry that may be a crime. Such actions may endanger the life and property of others.

Much has been made, especially in modern times, of anger and its management. Many books have been written about it. There are also complicated attempts to explain the foundation of fury in biological terms. Celebrities of various shades colours, sizes and geographic locations, in both platonic, employment and/or intimate relationships, have been convicted in courts of law in the UK, USA and elsewhere in the world. They have been reprimanded for consequences of their anger and as such have been sent for anger management or in some cases given more severe punishment including community service as well as imprisonment. Those are the lucky ones. Has the reader not heard of rage at home leading to murders, rage leading to the public destruction of property, or anger leading to wars? For your information, there is no deliberate war, no intentional destruction of humans and property, no deliberate killing, no premeditated harm that ever occurs without anger underlying it. Take my word; anger is the root of all non-purposeful destruction. Anger can be demonstrably verbal (words), or by physical acts, or by, can you believe it, silence. In cultures where the ready expression of resentment and emotions is not permitted, anger can be subdued. In such a place, it is very hard to immediately know the true feelings of individuals who, apparently without you realising it, are annoyed with you.

Consequences and punishment for anger is not limited to celebrities alone. That will not be the end of it; it will continue to happen to the low and the high, to the rich and the poor, to the old and the young.

The importance of this chapter lies in the fact that you can only be *genuinely angry* and hope to have a *productive correction* with someone whom you have a relationship with. What I am saying here is that, if you are angry at something, it means you want some corrections that, in some way, may satisfy your desire. Otherwise, if you have anger with another person whom you can not reach nor be influenced by, then it is futile to be angry. Imagine being angry with the country's President while he is not even aware of it as you reside in a little village house in one remote part of the country. You may just be able to ruminate while you can not do anything concrete about it. Therefore, applying this principle to your relationship, except when your spouse or partner knows or you show that you are upset; he or she may not be able to do anything to remedy the situation. This is why communication is so important in relationships.

To be able to influence someone for good or ill means you have to be in a relationship with the person, or be about to have a relationship with the person, no matter how short that relationship is. The person must be receptive to your views, questions and opinions, or at least be willing to learn about the *cause* of your anger. This is as true in intimate relationships as it is in platonic ones. It is a matter of fact in business associations or in mere friendships.

Yet, at the core of all relationships which come to an end, there is either an unresolved anger which is pretentiously subdued, or anger may be acted out as in domestic violence (DV). DV you may have seen and as I will also explain later, is a common and quick cause of dissolution of relationships.

Demonstrated or not, the relationship comes to an end---except if there is a contract in place that says the relationship must come to an end on a given date--- because the defeated desire, and the resentment that follows it, linger gingerly unresolved. Therefore, if we can understand this and deal with the roots and causes of *failures,* then we can deal with relationships that may be undergoing stress and strain. As we go along, I shall deal with what leads to this devastating feeling of anger. However, I want you to remember that what you see, hear, smell, touch and do is sometimes, not necessarily always, within your ability to choose. On other occasions, you may be helpless. Let us say your country is going to war. You are angry at that idea, but you are not in position to influence the decision to go to war. What then is the purpose of your anger? It's fruitless after all. Here are some similar situations

***

In marriage, spouses could show their anger or keep mute and hope things get better. In cohabitation, and other friendships, the same rules apply. Individuals may become selectively mute in the face of irritation. In a business environment and because of the need to maintain decency and to earn a living, anger is often subdued, even if you loathe to death what the boss or client has done. It may well be that you just don't like the job or the job environment. What if the law of your country constrains you from taking action against your teenage daughter whose conduct is an embarrassment to you? In such scenarios as above, fury crawls underneath but it is kept in check---for if you act out, the losses might be greater than the gain. In the case of your child, you might lose your daughter to the social services, she might report you to the police, or she might precariously leave home if you act with high-handedness. Therefore, before you act on your frustration, you may need to carefully weigh up the potential losses against the potential gains. It's your choice but it's also a delicate world out there. With all this background now well in place, let us consider the anatomy of rage.

What is anger? According to experts, anger is a strong feeling of displeasure and belligerence aroused by a *wrong*. Mark it---a *wrong*. For me, this is a complicated definition but I will try my possible best to bring it to our understanding.

This explanation gives us the scope to explore what anger means and how we can deal with it. This piece of writing will depart from a lot of official or formal records about anger but will also make use of known facts about anger and its management. For a moment put aside all that you have ever known about anger for I want safely to lead you into the true nature of resentment. Forget, for a minute or two, all the complex theories and convoluted structure that you have been told generated anger. Try me, put these words of mine in this chapter to practical test and see if you will get any result or not. The reason is to avoid complicated psychological and biological arguments which, as it may turn out, may not be helpful to the readers.

With this in mind, let us look at the *root of anger* in general, putting the above definition into focus.

***

Causes of Anger and Frustration: The root and science of anger/frustration

Biological and Protective Anger (controlled or channelled anger): Without doubt, anger is a normal biological reaction to an unfavourable situation. You get angry perhaps simply because something did not go your way or go the way you wanted it to. Very simple, isn't it? It is unfavourable, because it threatens your survival, pleasure or peace. For example: Let us imagine that you are trying to work on your computer. Let us assume that you have tried a couple of times. On each trial, it freezes. You are in a hurry. You have to restart all over again on each occasion. You have limited time. You are starting to be anxious. Then you began to call the software companies all sorts of names and you direct your feelings of frustration and disappointment against the computer box in front of you. The computer is not responding despite your lack of progress. This condition is unfavourable to your desire. You get annoyed.

Take another example: You just came back from work and you intended to have a short sleep--- a kind of rest. You lay in your bed at about 6pm on a summer day. The teenage boys in your neighbourhood would not allow you to rest. They were screaming and running whilst paying soccer/football. Unable to sleep, you got up and called their attention to the fact they were disturbing you. They did not heed your request. You *failed* and they continued. You went back to bed. The noise became louder and louder. At last, the football was kicked violently. It broke through your windows and it landed on your belly in your bedroom with some of the broken window glass. You were enraged. Not only that, your intention had been frustrated miserably. Your sleep and peace were badly shattered. Your expectation to be in relative calm within the walls of your own home was terribly disturbed. You got angry.

These kind of scenarios call on the individual (or couple, society, state, company or even nation) to take protective action to preserve the person from irrational response. This type of irritation, on a larger scale, calls on a nation, as the case may be, to refrain from violently reacting to the frustrated intention. On the other hand, the person who is angry may take measures to protect himself/herself, or take measures to ensure that his or her desire and intention are realised. That is a biological reaction towards self-preservation. You simply take action to reduce your dissatisfaction.

***

Frustrated intention or defeated desire is of the same kind of feeling to having a *sense of rejection*. You want something you could not get because "you were not good enough" for some individuals or "authority" that had blocked you. It represents a failure of desire and this is why it is so painful to the person concerned, who is now angry. Often, the individual feels threatened. This is because his/her desire to enjoy life or derive certain benefits from the desire has been despondently defeated or thwarted.

In the majority of occasions and probably in the majority of people, anger passes without further action/manifestation on the part of the irate person. He may just take the disappointment in his stride, so to speak. An example of this is seen in many homes and in public places. It is also seen in many marriages and other relationships regardless of their form. Your spouse could annoy you tens of times in a day. Yet, you can not afford to be angry on all those occasions. You will have to allow a lot of them to pass. If you don't, you run the risk of mental illness or being labelled as such. Anger is seen amongst bosses in many businesses and it passes without destructive impact, in most cases. Imagine if your boss at work reacts angrily to all forms of dissatisfaction that his subordinates bring to him! Who on earth would be able to work with such a boss?

People don't react to every situation they are displeased about. They simply allow the feeling to pass. This is a type of anger that is called *controlled anger*. It is a *protective and normal biological anger*. Such a person (or people) is often not under *serious* threat and so may not react to remove the threat. Even if they do, they have a credible way out of it. If they are under serious threat, there would be a strategic way to overcome the frustration. Picture a situation in which you left the bathroom tap in your office on, and water from it filled your office, destroying confidential and security papers in the process. Just consider how irate the boss will be, yet he can not afford to be seen to be manically angry. That is biological anger.

***

Common causes of anger and frustration: Specifically, anger can arise from just about anything, including but not exclusive to financial issues, children matters, career, sexual frustration, failure in investment and property, general life concerns, health-related issues, general sense of inadequacy or persistent failures, persistent domestic opposition from spouses or lack of support from supposed loved ones (parents, spouses etc). The list goes on and on. A person who is readily coming into conflict with the law may be an angry person too, as his intended desire is frequently blocked by the law. These felons become hardened against the law and work hard against it in a way that is best described as a hard rock meeting an irresistible object. In the end though, in most cases, the law wins.

A death or disease in the family or the death of a friend may lead to anger in those who are bereaved, by reason of the loss for which they could not do a thing about. Therefore in general, any intention or expectation about anything that fails may lead to anger. In the public domain, anger may come due to perceived political problems. It may be due to a dislike for a government course of action or government economic policies. Some people just don't like the treatment they receive in life. They loathe life as a result. As we shall see later, hate is a result of anger. Some come to loathe the world and living--- for its challenges. Some hate the world and they just can't figure out why there are so many difficulties and apparent anarchy in the world. Clinically, sleep deprivation and poor quality of sleep can also cause a person to be angry because the intention to have good sleep is frustrated. Remember, anger is always due to frustration: a failed intention.

***

What is the end product of anger? Happiness comes upon us when our legitimate and valued desire becomes reality. Unhappiness results when our legitimate or illegitimate but valued desires are frustrated. Therefore, when our desire is defeated, regardless of how many times we may try, it results in frustration. Despite concerted efforts to overcome the frustration, if the valued desire fails, it results in unhappiness. It should, therefore, be noted that the end result of anger is unhappiness, whatever the cause of it.

***

Pathological Anger (destructive or uncontrolled anger)

Anger becomes a problem and pathological either on a single occasion or in multiple times when anger is accompanied by hostility and or any form of destruction (violence, war, beatings, destruction of property etc). In short, anger becomes pathological if the verbal and physical expression of the angry person now causes psychological or physical harm. Ironically, this harm may be self-harm or harm to other individuals. It may also be physical harm to properties that belong to other persons. This is called *uncontrollable anger*. This should not be confused with defensive and legitimate anger which may also be in some ways similar to, but different from, pathological anger. The latter type may be in response to a seriously threatening situation. If such a threat is not removed, it may cause greater damage. This is the main basis that most people will give good reason for their anger. They will say they are under threat and so they act in self defence. It is the same reason that nations justify their angry war reactions. In case of our personal relationship situations, it is the same reason that spouses and partners give for their reactions in domestic affairs: self-defence, which in most cases, is not even recognised in law. The bad news for the spouses is that such reactions often appear tenuous to the police and the law courts.

Scientists have said that uncontrollable anger can be due to genetics and a person's environment and so forth. These are not the issues here. The issues are that there is a connection between anger and your relationship to others. You can not get angry except when human beings or inanimate object defeat your intention. It is that simple. The problem is that most people do not know how to constructively overcome their mental, human and non-living obstacles, and that is what causes frustration and anger.

***

The chains of how anger develops are:

"A feeling of displeasure". This means not being pleased. The question then arises as: "Displeasure with (or about) what?" The answer is displeased with frustrated intention and desires.

The result of this displeasure is a "belligerence" which means first *unhappiness* then *hate* follows, leading to *violence and hostility,* and many other features, and finally, if unresolved, the unhappiness continues.

These outward behaviours of belligerence are in fact due to a "*wrong*" which is the intention that was defeated. What is a wrong then?

A wrong arises when a given intention established by, say, Mrs B, the person causing the "wrong", negatively influences or frustrates the desire and intention of another person, Mr B. The next thing is that Mr B will react in an angry manner to Mrs B. The event could then take a different life of its own from that point onward. Police could be involved. The couple, or one of them, may end up in hospital. This is exactly what happens in some spousal relationships.

Another example:

If Mr. X behaves knowingly such that his behaviour does not allow the intention of another person called Mr. B to be established, then Mr. B will be frustrated because of this. Then Mr B will get angry at Mr. X. Let us take a practical example: You are driving on a road, in a hurry to catch an important meeting. Then suddenly, another car, driven by Ms S, crosses your path so that you can not move or be on time for your meeting. Your desire and intention has been curtailed and frustrated. You get out of the car and react in some way to and against Ms S. But you know that, usually, such behaviour is not accepted in normal human relationships or in society, or even under God's laws.

Now what has happened is that you are angry at Ms S for the frustration of your desire and intention. This is the "wrong" that you are reacting to. Your reaction is called "belligerence" against a given wrong. And your reaction is called anger. It's pathological if you cause harm.

Another example: assuming that you asked your 13 year old daughter not to go out at night and told her that she should do her homework. She refused to listen. Either you reacted or did not, and it caused some resentment in you and you are angry. Equally, because your daughter's intention is also frustrated, she is angry against you too.

Similarly, if you intended, regardless of your age, that you (a) should not fall ill but you did, or (b) that your family or parents should not divorce, or (c) that none of your parents should die and they did, you will become unhappy and angry with any of these situations.

In marriage, assuming as you should, you are expecting ("expect" means a manifestation that follows desire and intention) to have a happy marriage and that your spouse should behave in a certain way. If this expectation is defeated by any of the means stated above, you will become deeply unhappy and angry. One can also be angry against the government for "failing to meet certain expectations". In a similar manner, many people are "angry" against God for apparently "failing" to do certain things for them. Some are even angry that God did not provide their ideal spouse for them. The thing to remember is God is not the decision maker here. You are. You saw your spouse and/or partner and decided that he or she is the person you want to be with. You are in charge here.

***

Who can be angry or frustrated? Anger can occur in *anyone (note also that dogs, sheep, hippos etc, could all display anger when frustrated!)* who is capable of forming a desire or intention. This includes children and teens who sometimes desire their own way in order to change society. They can become angry if they don't achieve this. This is the reason for the rebellion in them when they are frustrated.

Other people who can be angry are married couples, in-laws or anyone in *any* form of relationship–formal, informal, private, public, sexual, non-sexual, business etc. The root and dynamics of frustration is the same.

The bottom line: disappointment leads to anger. Anger leads to destruction.

Nevertheless, the angriest person is a person who is so unwise that he or she knows very little about what he or she ought to do, legally or morally, to bring about happiness without causing offence (harm), verbal or physical. Such a person will be very frustrated indeed, as well as very angry. Anger, you remember, is a sign of discontent.

***

Manifestations of Anger and Frustration

With these explanations, one can come to a profound conclusion that anger is the clearest manifestation of a frustrated intention. As I have said in the book, *The Road and the Key to Happiness*, a frustrated or defeated intention leads to unhappiness. Also, an intention, good or bad, that goes unhindered, gives happiness. And like depression, anxiety, bullying, threats, vengeance, selfishness, blaming, unpredictable behaviour and evasive action, they are all signs of unhappiness. Anger is one of the octopus-like manifestations of sadness.

How do you prevent anger?

The most important prevention tool is wisdom. You must have strategic foresight to forestall any attempt to disappoint your intentions. It is that simple.

See *The Road and the Key to Happiness* for details on how to get your desire established.

What fuels and influences anger?

Decision making processes are and should remain under our conscious control. The decision making process is central to happiness. Anger is also subject to decision making processes. However, except for when this process is removed from the individual, such as when one is under the rule of certain laws, as in military orders for example, or during, say, anaesthesia, the decision process is subject to our control.

Thus, drugs, illicit substances, alcohol and outside emotions such as humiliation by anyone either in public or private, may fuel anger. Ironically, if anger can not be controlled voluntarily, medication may be called for to subdue the hostility, but not the failed intentions. The main issue here is that drugs (cannabis, cocaine, alcohol etc) can *fuel* anger, even to criminal levels. Once again, I am conscious of the fact that all divorces or family conflicts can not be blamed on drugs or alcohol misuse. There are also people who may simply have other reasons for being angry. However, the influence of substances on human behaviour and criminality has been proven beyond reasonable doubt.

***

Anger management

Whilst it is important to prevent an event before it causes harm, what happens if the event has taken root? The short and long answers to this question are that anger must, in one way or another, be subdued or resolved/expressed. There is no running away from it, anger, to make it go away; it must be resolved. One way is to deal with the root of the problem. See *The Road and the Key to Happiness*. Other means include, counselling (see later) which operates through the power of expressed words, as explained in my other book: *The Secret and Supremacy of the Expressed Word*. Another means of dealing with anger is forgiveness; if this method has not already taken place then it should be advocated. I can not see any other means by which irretrievable wrong can be resolved other than by means of forgiveness. Amongst many, other means include honest tolerance, listening, poetry, music and writing---all are forms of *expressions of intentions.* In general, all forms of anger must be expressed, one way or the other, in keeping with the principles in the book, *The Secret and Supremacy of the Expressed Word.*

The outcome of anger

Except when you deal with or express the anger or obtain the result of the original desire that was frustrated, anger, if it was either subdued or not, will lead to offence. The first offence that anger will lead to is hate.

Secondly, hate will lead to offences against humans or man-made law. Hate or malice can lead to threats, conspiracy, and destruction of properties, self-harm, suicide, and homicide. At least, hate can cause the pulling out and use of the most severe weapon of all: bad words. Try it, make your spouse annoyed, and then experience the power in words as a result! I hope those in relationships are paying attention. Does this sound familiar? You are not alone after all.

In most cases, anyone who actually commits any of these offences listed in the preceding paragraph, is likely to either end up in the hands of the police, get harmed (self harm or being harmed via others), killed or disgraced and be disregarded. If there are children in the vicinity, children may learn and be induced into a vicious cycle which may become established later in life.

If any of these do not occur, hate and anger can lead to a diagnosis of poor mental health, even though the person may not be dangerously unwell, as in what we call *personality disorders.* However, this will depend on the culture, the law and the society in which such angry individuals reside. The outcome may include admission to a mental health hospital directly or through the prison system. The label following the diagnosis of mental health disorders is clear for everyone, with eyes, to see.

In conclusion, therefore, frustrating the intention and desire of your spouse or partner, who in turn gets angry at this, is the surest way to destroy a relationship. Further, uncontrolled anger will destroy relationships. Poorly expressed frustration in a relationship will lead to the failure of the relationship. Anger that is not properly channelled into productive use is most certainly going to ruin your relationship. So much can be said to the wise.

***

CHAPTER FOURTEEN

There is Power in Knowing: Talking Frankly with You.

"He/she who walks in ignorance or walks blind-folded will stumble." Dr Joel Akande

Marriage is not compulsory and an intimate relationship is not an obligation. Having children is not a necessity either. I have proved these issues in earlier chapters of this book and I hope they are settled. I hope that these declarations are clear enough. However, once you get yourself into it---marriage---, you have got yourself into a very serious business. You have, as your partner, the most complicated creature on earth--- a human being of the opposite gender. Know that for the truth. You are in the most complex association ever!

Now you want to get married or get into a relationship with someone. This is your plan. Let us call that Plan A. Once the decision has been made to get married, marriage becomes a supposedly one-way affair. Ideally, there is no turning back, although people sometimes do. Marriage is a union designed originally to be inseparable. Therefore, there are consequences for separation or divorce (See the chapter on broken marriage and broken relationships and consequences).

I want to give some pieces of advice here which I have distilled from years of personal and clinical experience.
For a start, let us assume that you do intend to purchase a landed property. For sure, you just don't see a property and then immediately decide that it is the right property for you. The reason is that you need to do some research. Is the seller, for example, the right owner, or does the seller has the power to sell as he or she claims? You will also look for comparative prices so that you don't get cheated. You will do your homework in ensuring that the property has no major problems hanging over it. You will need to ensure that once you begin living in it as a home, it will not collapse over you, so you need to know that it is well built--- by surveying it. Is there a hidden crack that may make it non-habitable? All of these things, if you intend to enjoy

your purchase and to ensure your investment is worth it, will have to be checked carefully.

***

Similarly, if you are buying a car, you will first decide what car you want, won't you? Is it automatic or manual? What price will you pay? If it is a new car, you need to have guarantees that it will work and in case it breaks down, that you can take it back to the garage for repair.
If it is an old car, you need to know if the owner is the true owner who is allowed to sell the car. Is there hidden corrosion? Is there false mileage? Does everything work as the seller claims? These are amongst many things that you will need to check carefully.

For a third example, if you are to be appointed as, say, President/Prime Minister or Secretary of State/Minister, for example, or to any public post for that matter in the USA/UK/France or in any rule-abiding country which values things and human beings, believe me, your background will be well-combed by the secret service and other government agents so that you do not become an embarrassment to the nation. The nation and these agents would want to know the true you--- inside and out. The reason is obvious: so that you are dependable, sound in mind and body, able to provide security and to defend the country in peace and war. That is, the nation and agents would want to know you.

This is similar to what happens in great businesses. They don't just appoint anyone to sensitive posts. They will check the person out.

Your relationship with your spouse and your relationship with anyone should be considered as a "sensitive post". No matter what, the particular relationship will affect you for either ill or good. The relationship could embarrass you or enhance your value.
What is pathetic about human beings though is that we do not consider our relationship as being crucial to our existence and when things go wrong, we say, "if I had known" in regret. You

should treat your relationships, especially true and intimate relationships, as if you are the Government of the USA, UK, Russia etc and you want to appoint your spouse as your Secretary of State. Investigate him or her through and through. Look for hidden cracks that are covered by the grace of beauty. Treat your potential spouse as a car that you want to purchase. Ask questions from the "seller" which in this case, is the spouse himself/herself, family members, friends and relatives. Treat your potential spouse as a "property" that you intend to purchase. Ask a "surveyor," which in this case are the doctors, friends etc., to give you confidential opinions via scientific investigations (see below and also chapter on Relationship Questionnaire).

***

If you fail to do your "homework" properly, you are laying the foundations for expensive repairs of the "cracks" that you ought to have discovered in the beginning. Think about it, if you are going for a job interview and you have little or no knowledge about the job and of your employer, do you think you will ever be successful in the job? The employer wants to know you and what you know about them. Prior to your interview, you need to investigate the employer with whom you are about to have a business relationship. If you walk blindly, you may fall over a cliff, into the deep blue, perhaps turbulent, sea!

Why would you want to treat your potential spouse differently? Again, let me sound it clearly, human beings hide things. Human beings are difficult and they like to hide their true intentions. But if you apply wisdom, you can see through the opaque human glass. If you shine the light of knowledge, you can overcome your unawareness about what you are about to get yourself into. Truly, the choice is yours and you can not blame anyone else if you exercise your free will freely!

1) *Plan ahead and well in advance/Have strategic foresight.* Look into any potential marriage or relationship or union as a business. As I mentioned above, consider it as if your life

depends on it. Take it very seriously, except if you are also a joker with no specific direction. In that case, *this book* is not for you. In that situation, as in any case, your life is in your hands, so long as you are not a *child* and you are neither mentally disabled nor live under duress of another person. If you are a child, you should read the chapter of this book under *child abuse* and also the chapter on *adolescent relationships*. If you are none of these people, then whatever you become is a result of your decision and plans.

That is the first rule. Frankly, marriage in the old days in some ancient cultures used to be seen as a business. It is no longer so in some cultures. Whilst one is not advocating *commodity trading* in marital process, marriage is truly a business between the spouses in modern times rather than between the in-laws as it used to be in the ancient days. Business---that is exactly what it is. You need to invest. Your investment resources are time, affection, trust, your body, words, and materials which include money. Note: Having mentioned money in this list, I should caution that in relationship, money is and should not be the first investment. Trust and promise not to cause harm are.

Step two: guard your investment jealously. Watch your marriage day and night. Do you remember my request at the Introduction when I said you should please be an "eagle" and "owl"? Now you need to be if you have not already been. Third parties are in the wings to disrupt your relationship. Be attentive to laws that may threaten your relationship. Under the Matrimonial Law, in some states in the USA and to some extent in the UK, you could divorce your spouse for no specific reason other than the fact that you simply no longer want him or her. It is that easy. Your reason is that you are fed up or you need a variety! Among other reasons, this is is called "quickie divorce". Guard against them if you value your health, your children and your spouse.

You need a business plan on how you will sustain the "business" and make it work. Remember you are entering into a covenant (some say "contract". See later chapters on relationship agreement). In truth, if you fail to plan, you have just planned to fail. There are serious questions that you should ask at the early stages and at every subsequent stage of your relationship. You need to keep things in focus.

Who is going to lead this union: for example, is questions that must be answered before you marry? You need to know and agree now. This is important as the relationship can not do without a leader. The leaders can not *be equal*. Even if the couple are "equal", the responsibilities are not equal. Do not allow yourself to be deceived by the pop culture. Don't deceive yourself. Remember, it is your life, so if you leave this question unanswered, and then you are postponing the day of reckoning. A ship with two captains sailing in opposite directions will sink! Also, a ship without a sailor is bound for bottom of the sea.

From the very start before you get serious and when there is a chance to get out of the relationship, do some forecasting (some will say, prophetic work). Have foresight as to where you might want to see your marriage/ relationship in 20, 40, 60 years time. There is a serious problem if you can not "see" this. If you could not see this, then you have nothing to protect. It means you have no vision of where you are going. This means you have mental blindness of where you are heading. You may just be like a reed that is being blown to and fro without direction.

Now start to ask important questions: What would you do if the other partner dies, becomes seriously ill, threatens to leave you or does something awful? Be realistic. You need the answers to these questions before you get your marital rings.

Most importantly, do your homework on the relevant laws that operate for and against marriage. (See the chapter on legal implications of relationships and marriage). There are two sets of such laws. God's laws and laws and moral codes made by your government(s) and your cultures. Be wise. Research widely. Avoid tears and regrets! Know for sure that human beings are very mercurial.

***

2) *Critically assess your spouse* in areas including compatibility in all areas, as well as medical issues/mental health,

companionship, temperament, role of in-laws (some in-laws can be deadly, so test the waters before you jump in) and decide with your spouse, the order that each of these (in-laws, your spouse, your children if any, friends etc) will be in the home when you settle down. Who will take precedence in your home? Leave no stone unturned. Check and double check your spouse, friends and family with due care.

Avoid regret later in life. Don't be carried away by the *"love is blind doctrine"*. Love and marriage is not what it seems or what you are made to accept. Be warned, there is more to it than meets the eyes. Avoid heart-ache. Ask crucial questions. Do the necessary tests---medical, mental etc (see assessment questionnaire). Is this person right for me? If there is any lingering doubt in your mind, take my advice: bail out now! Don't marry on the basis of showing mercy on the potential spouse. Don't waste your time. Hide nothing from yourself. "To yourself, be true" is an old adage and motto of my High School and it is no less true here. If you have no companionship and compatibility as primary themes for your marriage then take my advice: escape now! Marriage is not for everyone and it is not a joke.

3) *You are entering into partnership.* You need an agreement (see chapter on sample marital agreement provided in this book). You need at least, a basic written document on what you both agree or will in future agree on, such as children, care of children, financial provisions, properties, sex and its performance. Don't be shy. Plan now. Spell out severe penalties for any breaches of this agreement. Marriage or relationships are a serious and treacherous business that can be full of betrayals, chameleonic behavior, and snake-like deeds, back-stabbing, plotting, conspiracy, concealment, and dishonesty - all in the name of "love".

4) *Always have a Plan B.* Human beings change like weather. Have a plan of what you will do if any original plan (Plan A) fails. Be warned, there will be third party interference (deadly in-laws, friends etc) in the relationship. What will you do? Remember, the snake in the Garden of Eden that came

between Eve and Adam. You will have your share. Have a plan how you will deal with it. I will advise patience and in-depth wisdom. Conflict is inevitable (See the Chapter on conflict resolution). Have a "how" you will deal with it. Get sound constructive counsel and wisdom. Plan this with your spouse, if possible.

5) *Take into consideration how the product or children*, if any, in the marriage must be protected at all cost or at full price. Like it or not, you can not deny that you will also come to make such crucial decisions at some point in your married life. If you leave your children, your greatest "asset" ever, unprotected, and you fail to defend them, they may fall into the hands of abusers. Avoid unnecessary headaches. Act wisely now. Take wise counsel: Being decently single is better than a broken marriage.

Besides these important five questions, I have been inundated with other questions which I have answered here. One of them is, "What should I know about myself before I get married?" And another is, "When should I get married?" These, and many like these, are dealt with below. Let us start with, "What should I know about myself before I get married?"

"What should I know about myself before I get married?"
This is a very valid question in light of the fact that before you can accuse other person of wrongs, you should, at least examine yourself for your own uprightness. As they say in law, those who must come to equity must have a clean hand. This means, you can not point an accusing finger at others while you are in filth. Therefore, before you can ask your partner or spouse to undergo medical checks, you must at least prove that you have done the same thing or be seen to be doing similar investigation. "Physicians", they say, should "heal yourselves". This, in my opinion, is equally applicable to relationships.

First, ask yourself, "Who am I?" Then trace your parents. Where did they come from? This is important as some diseases are more or less limited to certain races and regions. Take for example cystic fibrosis, which is well know in people of European origin but rare amongst Africans. The reverse is true for sickle cell disease. If your parents are from either of these regions, you need to check if you are carrying any of these diseases. Are you carrying any other genetic diseases or infections? Check it out. Are any of your parents or yourself suffering from other rare genetic diseases even though you look healthy from the outside? You need to ask and do tests if you do not want to transmit diseases to your children. If you are a woman and you want to be pregnant, you need to know if there is any disease that may interfere with your pregnancy and children, such as high blood pressure, diabetes or problems with thyroid and many others. For a man and woman, you need to know if you have the temperament to live with another set of people (husband/wife and children). For a man, you need to know if you have the material means to support a wife. All the noise about "equality" between a man and woman will fizzle out in early marriage as the woman will look up to you to provide financial, moral and material support for her. "Equality" will show up later when you are both comfortable and no longer in the "rat race" of this life. Saying this, later, the woman may say she no longer needs you as a man when she is now "equal" to you as the man: at a time when both of you no longer have financial worries, property problems, have good jobs, you are both settled, and you have healthy children. Then the need for freedom and "equality" will surface. Remember though that this book is written so that you may know ahead. I am not unaware that the man may also at this time of relative comfort, seek his freedom as he now no longer "need" the woman having satisfied his life desires.

For the woman, what you need to know about yourself is even fuzzier. The most important question is, *"Have I got the right man"?* If this question is not answered appropriately, the marriage may become unstable. Are you rushing into this marriage? Do you need more time to consider issues? Are you truly ready to leave your parental home, in spirit and body, and unite with another (man)? For the woman, there must be no doubt in your mind as to where you are heading.

***

"When should I get married?"
People ask, "How do you know *when* (that is, the time) to get married?" The short answer is, you should not get married as a child. A child, by United Nations and International Law to which the USA, UK, France and other major powers are signatories, is someone who is under 18 years. Now in girls, the reproductive organs are not fully matured until about 20 years and above. Boys are practically ready as soon as they can produce sperm, from say 13-16 years of age! However, does this mean they are ready financially and mentally, as well as materially and socially? Here is where individual cultural background comes in. You are ready to be married when you are ready mentally, financially, socially and biologically. Ideally this should be between ages 22-28 biologically, when an individual's fertility and sexual activity are supposed to be at their peak. There is nothing wrong in getting married much later in life. So you can do it at the age of 30, 40, 50, and 60 and so on. They each carry distinct advantages and disadvantages. For example, if you marry and have children at 60, there are many drawbacks to this extreme. If you have children at 15 years, there are huge problems and very little advantages, if any (see chapter on adolescent relationships). In spite of the choice that people enjoy in the UK for example, there was much furore in recent time. It occured when a 13-year old boy allegedly fathered a baby. It later turned out that it was actually another 15-year old boy who is the real father of the baby that was carried by a 14-year old mother. This incident raised consternation amongst the major political parties and indeed the nation on question of right-wrong or morality of teenage parenthood. Only you know what suits you.

***

What should I not do before I get married?
This is a common question that I have been asked a couple of times. People enquire what they should not do prior to entering matrimony. The question appears really innocent but a closer look will reveal the trap in the question. You might wonder: *Should I have sex before marriage or not? Should I live together with my partner or spouse for a while? Should I have children before marriage? Should I buy property before I get married?*

These are some of the issues that you may need to address prior to your relationship becoming serious.

Let me answer some of them. I am conscious of the topical nature of some of these questions. Also, going by the current trends in the world, some of my answers may not resonate with some readers; let me put you on the alert. Take, for example, Should I buy property before I get married? Well, for men, this is almost a necessary question. You, as the breadwinner, need to have at least a rented place. If you can not buy, you should consider buying later with or without your spouse.

For women, owning a property before marriage may be intimidating for some men who see themselves as the breadwinner. If you have your own property into which you want to invite your man, he may feel insecure and become unstable. This is because, he will not be in control and of course men really love to be in control. That is the reality. I have witnessed situations whereby the woman had her property, but she promptly added the name of her husband as co-owner in order to protect her marriage. The downside to this arrangement is that should the marriage fail, then because he is now a joint owner of the property, he could claim a share of it. In any case, if he had contributed to it and he lives there during the marriage, it will be tough to remove him. This is because he will claim that the property is a matrimonial property. To avoid problems, you may think about this and incorporate it into your marital agreement (see chapter on marital agreement).

***

Sex and children: If you have sex, you should expect the result. The result is children. You may also contact a deadly infection, unless you have done your homework well. The question arises, if you do not intend to have children and you just had sex and you did have children, you have just committed yourself into a relationship that has legal and social implications. You will need to care for the children. If you run, Social Services will pursue you everywhere. If you do not intend to marry at all, then you have just transformed your relationship into a different category such as cohabitation or "common law" relationship. You may become unhappy for a long time. What about the children? Well, unless you value and care for them, they risk being abused!

Let us assume that you have an apple to eat at work. You took it from home. On your way, you had a bite. And you continue to eat until all that remains is a bit and the middle stalk. You still took the remaining bit and the stalk into work and hope to eat it. By the time you get to eat your apple for your lunch, I bet that the novelty would have worn off and you would be less likely to want the apple any more. What you are more likely to do is to throw the remnants away. If you have not kept the apple properly despite your bites, it may have started to go bad. This analogy fits well with the question of what *should not be done* before marriage in respect of sex. By the time you settle down to matrimony and you have so much "known" your partner, by then the novelty would have worn off. There is nothing new to discover. Similarly, there is no guarantee that the fiancée or fiancé would not have been "corrupted" by other potential suitors (apple going bad) as is the case of the apple. Therefore, the value of the partners would diminish and before long, separation and divorce may supervene.

I am not however deluded to the reality of this question. Sex before marriage happens all over the world. One advantage, one might claim in the least, is that you know for certain what your partner is capable of doing and you also know her reproductive capability. This argument can not be sustained though, in view of the pre-marital assessment questionnaire and investigations that I have outlined in this book.

What kind of sex do you have in mind and with whom? To answer this question you will need to take certain steps. The first step is that you should be certain that you are dealing with a gender that you desire via *genetic testing*. This is important since there are many appearances that go beyond what the eye can see in these modern days. Ever heard of a "man" getting pregnant?

This is not a joke. There was a case in Pakistan whereby wedlock was sealed between two individuals of apparently opposite genders. Little known to the families and the couple, there was a surprise in the offing. There was a discovery after the wedding, to the chagrin of the couple and their families, that the "spouses" were not the genetic genders that they had hoped for. Really, you need to know where you are going so that you can avoid falling into a ditch. This event ran, in truth, contrary to their intentions. If you act wisely, you will bear the fruit of your wisdom.

Yet another common question goes like: *"where can I meet my future spouse or girlfriend/boyfriend or partner?"*
By and large, this is a knotty question that has troubled many minds and families for ages. The basic advice is that most couples meet for the first time where people congregate. Many settled unions meet at their schools, parties, bus stops, hospitals, work places, wedding ceremonies, churches and places of worships, airports and so many other places. Couples could also meet within their own neighbourhood. As I mentioned before, marriage in many cultures used to be like a commodity exchange whereby a boy from "X" family shows interest in a girl in family "Y" or vice versa. The relationship is arranged and introduction is made between the potential couples and families. If they both agreed, it's a done deal. In Asia and in some African cultures as well as some major monarchies, this method is still the case. You may also find partner through your friend. That is a person who is a friend to your friend may actually become your partner or spouse.

Despite the huge risk that is associated with it, in modern times, internet dating is popular in many parts of the world. A safer bet is the traditional dating agency that will of course screen the respective individuals before the introduction to each other is made.

A couple of things need to be said for meeting your partner or spouse: The first is that you need to conquer your shyness if you are a man. You need the social skill and boldness to approach women who in most cases will pose a resistance. But perseverance conquers if you are determined and you have made the right choice. Do note that your approach may be painfully rejected by the women. This is natural.

The second thing is that your partner, spouse or character of the person you have chosen will in general reflect the circumstances by which you met each other. That is, if you meet someone in a party, chances are that, she or he is a party goer. If you met in a pub, he or she is likely to reflect that habit. If you meet at work, you both probably appreciate work. This is important as you may turn around in future to reject your situation if you no longer like the same habit under which you met but he or she continues in the old character under which you first set eyes upon one another. You need to know this now.

The third truth is that in a lot of ways, someone who will become your future wife or partner may at first sight offer help to you or you offer help to him or her. That may be the start of a bigger relationship that will lead to marriage!

What about the common question of, *Should I live together with him and get to know him?* Should I live together for a while with her and get to know her? The short answer is that if you do so, you may have just tacitly converted your relationship into "common law wife" or "cohabitation" or "partnership". None of these are recognised by law and none of these can derive the advantages that are available under the legal wedlock (see Chapter on Benefits of Marriage, Single, Cohabitation and their Disadvantages). One could understand the logic behind this thinking and of these questions that are being asked. It would appear that it makes perfect sense to live with someone with whom you may potentially spend the rest of your life with. It would seem that it's perfectly in order to "test the waters" and know the personality of the other person. Why rush a meal that is yours in any case? You may choke in the process of the rush!

The danger is that, you may end up with a relationship which you never liked nor intended. So many things could happen before you realise that you may not be able to get out of the relationship. One of these is, you may start having children and also buying or owning assets in joint names. This will become a legal minefield for you later. I have discussed elsewhere in the book, the distinct advantages and disadvantages of co-habitation or "common law" relationships. You should take note of them. A picture, the great Chineese people have proclaimed, is worth a thousand words. I guess my words should be fewer for the reader who is taking note of the picture that I have so painfully painted.

***

CHAPTER FIFTEEN
Relationship Questionnaire

"Every person, all the events of your life are there because you have drawn them there. What you choose to do with them is up to you." Richard Bach

Millions of individuals are looking for a quick fix to a potentially serious life project. So serious is relationship formation that it may affect your life permanently. It may affect it for good or for bad. There is no questionnaire that can substitute for keen interactive physical observations. There is no amount of detailed questionnaire that can replace first-hand practical experience and information that you gather in the real world about your partners/spouses. You need to make your own mind up about the likes and dislikes about the other person who you propose to commit your life to.

During the time of your practical assessment of the person, as well as the time you will spend on information gathering, you will need to be CIA, MI5 and FSB all combined into one, with the attention to detail of Agatha Christie or the caution and attention to every observation, like a scientist. My teachers used to tell us in medical school that you can not learn medicine by correspondence. Neither can you learn engineering by distance learning. In the same way, you can not understand your future and current partner by reading the person through questionnaires. This method of knowing your partner on paper or by correspondence has serious flaws.

Future human and indeed current human conduct can not accurately be predicted on mere questionnaires, psychologists will tell you. You need to see the person.

If questionnaires are helpful, they are helpful by reason of the fact that they are guides only. Even before the internet age and now being giving more energy by the World Wide Web, a lot of people have relied on questionnaires to determine who their partner could be. I am not at any rate surprised at what kind of different person had turned out at their homes even though the assessment questions say otherwise. If you doubt me, try internet dating. The cases that policemen and women in different countries have cracked indicate that at one end of a remote computer could be a 55 year-old man, who pretends to be a boy who is a teenager, and at the other end could be an innocent teenage girl who believes the 55-year old impostor to be her age mate.

On the other hand, a man in his 40s may pretend to be a woman of 25 years, to another innocent man in his late 20s. Just imagine when these two sets of people would meet. The predator meets the prey. You could unwittingly be dealing with a sex abuser. Human beings hide their true identity and only a proper due diligence test can reveal who they are. Just imagine the danger in these scenarios.

Imagine that because of your inattention, you got into the hands of a sex molester. Just as the lion and leopard do, human beings tend to lay in waiting for a vulnerable sexual prey that they can exploit. You will need to be very careful as there is no substitute for long term knowledge of your spouse with the extensive observational mind of a curious scientist. Similarly, a one-night sexual stand could land you in territory that you repulse for the rest of your life.

Only you could decide what you want in a relationship. "Here today and gone tomorrow" is another likely outcome of a flimsy relationship that is formed in hurry.

***

Having said this, a questionnaire can guide you to your intended destination. But you will need to be alert to your specific requirements. No two individuals are the same. No two families or couples are the same.

I have set out below a relationship questionnaire which I have developed as a result of my clinical experience, gathering facts and observing situations from my patients and personal observations. It incorporates my experience over the years. Further, I have inputted elements of the operation of the (UK) matrimonial law viewing it from my legal vantage position.

***

Finally, I have first hand knowledge of marriage too and I know the familiarity. I am therefore not standing at a distance and telling you what to do. I am part and parcel of the experience, as the saying goes.

These questions are not necessarily personality tests, which are asking you if you care about who are likely to spend, financially, the most in the relationship. These questions are not intended to test if you can speak well or kiss better or ask you if you care who does the after-dinner washing. Those are flimsy and are an aberration away from the substantial issues. If you base your marital questionnaire on which of the couple is likely to open the car door for the other, you may fail in your relationship, if you are a woman.

The reality of marriage implies that the social facades that are presented to the outside world are not a true test of the strength and value of relationships. If you base your future on a test that asks you if you care or are jealous if your spouse is advancing in his or her career, then you will be frustrated in the end, when your vulnerability is exploited at your most weak point in the life of the relationship.

Take my advice: fortify yourself, because marriage is a challenge, a kind of business that is tasking even to the shrewdest soul. Think about it, the royals with all the paraphernalia of power at their disposal, pastors with all their spiritual insight, reverends with all the respect they command, Hollywood's A-list with all the fame and money, country presidents with all the power, premiers with all the political aura and influence, great business minds with the euphoria of conquest, formidable scientists who think they know it all, the high and the low, the humble and the proud have all stumbled at the altar of marriage that is poorly made. Millions of people have fallen by the way-side of the marital journey. Ask now: what will be your own outcome?

These questions below are meant to help you reach your *long term goals* as they are not a mere superficial assessment.
Here is the guidance. There are thousands of variable answers to each of these questions. Only you can provide the answer that is most appropriate to you in the way you see things. It's your life, you know. I am only a helper. Now, no two individuals are physically, genetically and psychologically the same. You are who you uniquely are. Even twins who are raised the same way do have different views and behaviour. With these points in mind, let us look at the questions.

Please note that these questions are valid for pre-marital and also marital relationships. You will also find that the questionnaire had been formulated to suit assessment of ordinary friendships too.

***

Part A
1) Intended purpose of the relationship and not the pretentious "love" doctrine.

Everything in life and everything that is in existence has a purpose. Now for what reason(s), are you getting into this relationship?

Except when you have a purpose, your relationship is in danger as you have nothing to protect. If you allow so-called "love" to blind you, later when an established relationship occurs, your eyes will "open" to reality (See chapter on love above). You might call this the utilitarian principle. You can not and should not be blind-folded to walking into a cliff.
Examples of reasons might be:

a) Social acceptance.

b) To satisfy parents.

c) Monetary/financial reasons.

d) Immigration.

e) Companionship etc.

f) For security

2) Intention

Every act in life or anything that we see or know of begins with an intention. *Now, in respect of this relationship, is it your TRUE intention to enter into it or were you "recruited" or coerced into it?*
Examples of situations that could "recruit" you into a relationship, without your intention, are:

a) Family pressure.

b) Peer (friends') pressure.

c) To fulfil religious duties.

d) To satisfy work requirements e.g. high executive positions, politics etc.

e) Attempt "to belong" or "conform" to certain society norms

3) Expectation

Unless you are completely aimless, you should have an expectation of both your partner and what you intend to derive from the relationship; marriages fail and relationships end on the painful ground of failed expectations: "I *did not expect* him (or her) to behave like that" or "she did not meet my expectations," are common sayings following a disappointed relationship by individuals who may not have done their homework properly.

These are coded words for "I am not happy," or "I am not satisfied." This could be the beginning of the end. Watch out.

What are you expecting from this relationship?

Examples of expectations are:

a) Financial and/or business stability.

b) Career or business advancement.

c) Resolution of immigration matters.

d) Having children: What is the purpose for having children? Have you thought about it?

e) "Till death do us part" companionship. It should be noted that this is the only and primary purpose of a relationship or marriage.

f) Sexual satisfaction

4) **Person specification.**

In most questionnaires you will find with relationship counsellors, are based ONLY on this person specification bracket, regardless of the extensive nature of those questions. They often overlook the important issues that I have outlined here.

You are not the same as the next person or your spouse. You require someone who is nevertheless like you who can share what you share and value what you believe in.

In order for you to meet your purpose, intention and expectation, have you outlined, in detail, the kind of person you require with whom to reach fulfilment considering your personality, history, social standing, and your purpose?

If you fail in this, everything might just collapse and you may struggle in the end. This part is crucial because if you fail, it will be like a square peg in a round hole.

Examples of a kind of person to fulfil a given criteria are:

a) Does the person meet the career requirement?

b) Does the person have the temperament you need?

c) Does the person fulfil the financial standing you are looking for?

d) Does the person have an appearance or anatomy you *desired* as above?

5) **Have you thoroughly investigated the person before jumping in?**

If you jump into a stream or a river without first knowing how deep or shallow the stream is, you could end up with a broken skull or brain injuries. Relationships are not different. Human beings vary and can be dodgy. Unearth the true person under the cover of skin. Remember, the value of a place is the people living there. For a person, the truth as well as the value of a person, is what is in him or her (his or her words/intentions).

Have you investigated?

Examples of medical checks that could be carried out are:

a) **Medical/mental health investigation. Is the person carrying a disease not visible or known to you? (See below for samples of medical investigations)

(Don't be shy. Remember, you have an aim/purpose, intention and expectation. Prevent your expectations from being defeated. Otherwise, you will end up being unhappy).

b) It is never too late; ask friends and close relations about the

Partner's past. Have you done so?

c) Be a critical observer of the partner's behaviour.

d) Have you met the partner's friends and family? Are they Ok for you? Remember the adage, "Show me your friends, and I will tell who you are".

6) **Fit for Purpose/Job specification.**

Every corporate executive knows that unless they have the right person for a position, the company might fail. You are not different. Ultimately, a couple is a company or business in every sense.

Do you think your proposed partner or intended partner or existing partner is fit for intended purpose?

Examples of "fit for purpose":

a) Ambition: is the person ambitious in terms of job, education and career etc?

b) Is the person aiming for children or not? Is that your own purpose too?

c) In thin and thick, rain and sunshine, is the person able to stand by you for a lasting companionship? Only you know. Weed out the pretender now! Don't play with your future happiness.

7)   **Shared Vision**

You may have a vision of what the relationship should be, but that is you. The other may not share it or may share it for a while and then ignore the vision and mission. Companies, governments and homes as well as individuals would fail except if they have a vision of where they are going and how to get there. In addition, everyone working with them must share this vision if they are ever to succeed. The basic example of such "company" or "government" is a relationship between at least two people and ultimately their families.

Is your partner sharing your vision? A relationship may fail if, for example:

a) Each person has a different vision of where things are going or where things are supposed to go.

b) There is constant disagreement on the approach to the relationship. Energy is being wasted unnecessarily. It can be that either partner was/is pursuing a joint approach or mutually inclusive but different approaches.

c) There is interference by third parties without the agreement of all involved.

d) Is there a designated leader in place? Both individuals can not be leaders at *the same* time. Note that in respect of homes, there is a cultural, historical, religious and social designation of who a leader is in marital relationships or in any given relationship. Which one is yours?

8) Communication

Did you know that there is no change or progress in this world without a word being expressed? Company executives are fully aware of the importance of this element. When words are expressed and exchanged between at least two people, communication is said to take place. The moment you can no longer communicate with your partner, there is a problem. Communication can be either written, verbal or by signs (body language).

Are you having such difficulty?

Difficulty in communication is a sign of failings in your "purpose" and "intention".

Examples where such difficulties may occur are:

a) Betrayal of the other as in (f) below and thus an attempt to defeat the common objective of the union/relationship.

b) Intolerance of words and conduct of the other no matter how credible.

c) Physical and mental illnesses.

d) Inability to understand the aims, objectives and common purpose of the relationship.

e) Inability to share the same vision from the start or later.

f) Interference by third parties e.g. extra-marital, family and relations, or friends.

***

<u>Part B</u> (Did you or did you not find your ideal person from going through the above questions. Either way, please, continue here).

9) **Love**

Love is one of the most abused words in the world. Actually, love means, "cause no harm deliberately," to yourself and to others. It does not mean, behaving or condoning foolishness or illegality, but it implies overlooking/forgiving the weaknesses and frailty in others, hence the "cause no harm" principle.

Now, knowing that you, just as in others, have imperfection both in behaviour, intention, acts and physically, are you prepared to forgo your purpose or part of it as a trade-off for other expectations?

Examples of where love would work are:

a) A mutual realisation of human weaknesses.

b) A unilateral intention to forgive or "love" or "cause no harm" in the interest of everyone involved.

c) A fulfilment of religious obligation to "love" and "forgive," even in the face of injuries caused by your partner.

10) Ditch it or tolerate it.

Granted you did not find the person specified, you have made mistakes along the way, you have been betrayed, or your spouse/partner is no longer "fit for purpose": *Do you tolerate what you have or you just want to "move on":*

Examples of where you may run into conflicts are:
a) Family pressure.

b) Religious obligations.

c) Involvement of children.

d) Previous good memories together.

e) Social standing and pressure to maintain or reject the *status quo*.

f) Severe illnesses, for example mental illness, or any illness that brings a huge burden on the other.

11) Going wrong: implications

If things go wrong and the vision fails, the purpose could not be realised, children and families are involved or properties are involved, have you considered the implications of "ditching" your partner? That is divorcing? Have you considered the serious implications?

Examples of the effects of breaking up are:

a) Mental health problems in the children (depression, anxiety, social isolation, drugs, general life failings etc.).

b) Mental health problems (anxiety, depression etc) in both or either partners.

c) Anger, frustration, disappointment and anxiety in extended families involved.

d) Litigation (huge financial loss to either person, public display of private affairs, which is you wash your dirty linen in public).

e) End of family happiness and cohesion.

f) Spread of existing infection by one or both partners.

12) **Before things go wrong and after things have gone wrong and the vision has failed:** *What do you do?*

a) Have you sought counselling as soon as possible?

b) Have you made alternative plans for coping with the loss/new life? It can be challenging to adjust though.

It is my hope and firm belief that if you truly answer these questions without any deceit to yourself and you also have a session with your partner or spouse to go through these questions, then there is a likelihood that you will do well.

You will notice that I have not provided a rating scale here. I have not provided figures to determine if you have passed or failed. The reason is that human beings and their circumstances can not be crunched into a thin bottle or be reduced into simple figures. I urge you to go through these questions dutifully and carefully.

Religious people are just as susceptible to friction, frustration, and deep unhappiness in marriage as anyone else. In fact, according to one study, the rate of divorce in the so-called Bible Belt considerably exceeds the American national average (*New York Times*, May 21, 2001). Therefore, someone must be breaking the rule that is supposed to guide marriage and all other relationships.

**A note on medical tests and investigations*
Now let me write a bit about medical tests which I have referred earlier to as medical checks.

These tests are precautionary and testing them is not to say that other unseen and unknown factors or diseases that you did not test for may not emerge later in life. One thing is sure: at least you have made good attempts to clear the way for your future and to exclude common diseases. Despite the dangers that if any of the tests may show the presence of diseases, some couples may still press ahead selectively oblivious of the diseases. The beauty of these tests is that, they will help you to plan if you may pass the revealed diseases to your children. Also, the results will help you to decide if you want children or not. Also, there is power in knowing that, if you do decide to press on with the relationship and the illness is clearly present in your spouse, at least, you can calculate your life expectancy and the burden you may carry during the period. Similarly, if you happen to pass any of these diseases to the children, you can not blame anyone else, for you have made a decision based on vital information which is available to you. Think about it, why would you want to have children whose defects are preventable? Why do you want to be in a relationship whose trouble is foreseeable?

a) Genetic tests/chromosome disorders: test for the true identity of the gender that you desire. Is he XY or pretending to be something else? Is she XY or an assumed or manipulated make up? If you don't test, you may, to your disappointment, end up with the gender you never imagined. The world is changing. You may be surprised how far human beings have gone to do things differently. Do tests for Down's Syndrome (in all), sickle cell trait or sickle cell disease (people of African and Asian origin), cystic fibrosis (especially but not only people of European origin), Thalassemia (especially amongst but not only people of Mediterranean origin). These are the common ones; your doctor can add more if necessary. Alternatively, ask for any known genetic disease that is already known to be running in the family. There is power in knowing. You will be surprised what could turn up in your findings.

b) Metabolic disorders: diabetic mellitus, high blood pressure and liver cirrhosis.

c) Infections: HIV, syphilis, gonorrhoea, chlamydia, herpes virus, papiloma pirus are all common ones you may consider.

d) Test for good functions of the kidneys, thyroid, heart and liver. Also, while it may sound extreme, one of the issues that cause most intense unhappiness in couples is childlessness. Will it be out of place if you test the fertility potency of both of you? Remember, you are embarking on a life-long journey with a partner who may be with you forever.

e) Good family history to trace as much *backward* as practically possible for previous mental health problems in the family. This should include misuse of drugs and alcohol. It may help if you enquire about depression, mania, schizophrenia, personality disorder, suicides, eating disorder and obsessive-compulsive disorders in the family. At least you can make up your mind up, if you want to continue the relationship or not.

Endnote: The key to success in life, as in any relationship, is having good desire, good intention and purpose. Be strategic, know what you are doing. Know where you are going and have good plans before starting. Know the implications of your actions from the very start. If you plan well, all things being equal, as the economists would say, it will end well. Here is my advice: enter into a relationship with someone who values whatever you value and who would continue to do so. If you get into a relationship with someone who does not value what you value, you may end up with your productive efforts, and everything that you have, as a waste. Good luck to you.

***

CHAPTER SIXTEEN
Conflict Resolutions In Relationships

"For me to have the opportunity to get advice, good counsel and fellowship with these individuals is extraordinary."
President Barack Obama
On meeting his four predecessors on
7 January 2009

Let us face it and let me say it from the very start. In relationships, in marriage and its variants, conflicts are inevitable. It's part of the package. I hate to fluffy you with flowery words. This is not the place for it. You need to grasp the reality now before it's too late. Conflict will come. When two people come together in any form of relationship, conflict is inevitable. It may be a platonic relationship between daughter and mother. It may be a relationship between friends or business partners. It may well be a conflict in a relationship between spouses. Ideas and desires will clash and intentions will collide. Conflict will result.

Yet, for the sake of all the advantages and for the interest of your mental health and for the benefits of your children if you have any, you are required to endure all the heat in the kitchen of the relationship. You are caught between ditching the marriage so that you can have solace or carrying on with likely consequences of angina to your heart and the sleepless nights you spend brooding over what your spouse has said. There will be times you may be in a dilemma, asking yourself if you should bail out now, in keeping with the principles of self- preservation, or stay in order to preserve your wealth and also protect your social status as well as your children. Perhaps, you are selfishly eyeing the pension that is about to mature and you think, "I will lose all if I go my way now so I will stay. Things may become better". You are caught between the deep sea and the immovable object. Your personal affairs are now affecting your job and your boss is asking if all is well with you. You pretend and respond that you are OK, while anxiety about the future of your home is eating into your very fabric. Alternatively, your concentration is faltering.

As a business person, your client may be asking you questions, but you are in a dream land, carried away and consumed by your domestic affair. You are falling asleep in board meetings. Your board members and employees are asking if you need help. In your office, alone, you reach for the wine with 10% alcohol concentration to suppress your unhappiness, anxiety and depression.

In the extreme, you may think that life is no longer worth living, for the burden of the crisis is now too much to bear. The problem and conflict refuse to go away. Your life is now gradually falling apart and your home is no longer what it used to be. Friends are either supporting or deserting you in your most vulnerable period. Somehow, life turned out to be contrary to your expectations. You simply can't explain why you have faced so much opposition and failings.

Should that be the end of the relationship? Of course, "no" is the answer. If otherwise, no relationship will stand. Therefore, be prepared for it. Again, conflict is unavoidable in human relationships. The core causes of conflict and crisis are to be found in defeated desires and intentions that ultimately give rise to anger and unhappiness. Anything that threatens the enjoyment of life, the fulfilment of desire and anything which may tend to jeopardise an individual's survival or self-interest, will undoubtedly lead to anger and conflict with people and things around him or her.

***

Crisis, unlike conflict, conveys a condition of urgency. Crisis is an emergency that requires immediate attention and action to resolve it. Let me cite some examples. There are many conflicts that go on in the world everyday between competing power blocs, within nations in civil wars, in communities, in our homes and indeed in our individual lives. These conflicts are not crises yet. In crisis, there is alarming or devastating and ongoing risks to life and property. There is a dramatic turn of events from simmering conflicts which have now transformed into actute crises. There may be some form of permanent damage which may occur if the crisis is not checked. There is a sense of urgency to stop further and damaging deterioration in events. Conflict on the other hand, may be subdued, flaring up in argument, or it may be a confrontational quarrel or disagreement between those involved. It may crawl along for a very long time. Compared to crisis, conflict can be a long drawn battle.

***

Conflict, if not contained or properly managed, may develop into crisis. So, it is better to contain a conflict before it develops into crisis. Should crisis emerge from conflict, which is either between individuals or between communities, it may by then involve the police, social services, medical interventions and other emergency services. In much larger crisis, but at an extreme, the military may be involved. This is because life and property are always at greater risk of damage in crisis. Crisis, if possible, should be avoided at all costs for it is extremely damaging and often the devastation is not only irredeemable, but also irreparable.

The problem for individuals in a relationship is that they very often overlook or do not realise the gravity and damaging effects of a simmering potential crisis which has stayed below boiling point for some reason. Further problems could arise as a complication of the crisis. This can be in both long and short term. The actions of single or combined individuals can lead to forensic records against you. This means, the government may begin to apply scientific methods to probe your mind to determine what is really wrong with you and why you committed, what may now be considered, a crime. This is in spite of the fact that you consider your action as a mere domestic affair!

It can lead to detention and curtailment of the liberty and economic freedoms of such individuals as they may now be subject to control by the respective state apparatus. Bad records of having being involved in domestic or public crises can have serious economic implications too. You may no longer be able to apply for certain jobs and positions. Your movement could be subject to monitoring by the authorities. From here, you may be interested in knowing, your life may begin entering a downward spiral. Why? You were in a *relationship,* you remember, that was not suitable for you.

Now the next question is, where do crises come from? Let us see.

***

Origin of conflict in a relationship
The foundation of any conflict is when the desire and intention of, say, person "A" is *opposed* by the desire and intention or acts of person "B".
Meanwhile, as in any other partnership or relationship, ironic as this may seem, two *opposite* genders go into a relationship on the basis that their desires and intentions would *merge* as one in the form of a *union.* This is far from what happens in marriage in real life. Often, the opposites truly oppose each other, with each person attempting to enforce her or his desire on the other, all to the disadvantage of the union.

As we shall see in business relationships, two persons or companies form a relationship on the basis that their intentions and desires will come together as one. This is also true for people who are working together in organisations. They do so especially when the expected result is greater than the sum of their individual capabilities. This is otherwise called *synergy,* which we saw earlier.

Practical experience has shown that in relationships of all sorts, this beautiful scenario is far from what happens in reality. Desires and intentions and acts do conflict. This can still occur even when their combined desires appear undivided from the start. As they go along, there may be an error or mistake which may give the impression of division in the desire. This is what the military refers to as *"friendly fire".* This means even in a united front, conflict of acts can still occur.

Nevertheless, the major causes of conflict anywhere are, as I mentioned above, are fundamentally anything that will threaten the survival of the person. Such threats can be against what the person holds morally, legally, financially, health-wise and materially high. It may also be a threat that tends to impair the enjoyment of life. Nations go to war when their way of life is threatened, you remember. Families, too, will defend their positions and belongings against the intentions of violent intruders or burglars.

The question is, how do we apply this great insight into relationships, or put in another way, how does this come into relationships?

To get an understanding of how this affects relationships, first let us look at the major causes of conflict in intimate relationships, of which marriage plays a central role.

The clear causes of conflict in relationships/marriages are:

***

Financial issues including properties:
I have mentioned elsewhere that money supports marriage and relationships. This is without regard to the fact that some individuals form a union with another person with the singular aim of getting rich or with the aim to get out of poverty. Such relationships survive by a thin thread. What happens when money is not forthcoming or the source of money dries up? Argument upon argument will therefore ensue. The relationship will now be on the brink of collapse. This is because the bridge that links the two and the bond that binds the two are no longer there. The money is no longer as it used to be.

Therefore, basically, money and what it can buy is a major cause of conflict in a relationship. It may be that one person is not making enough of it or the other person is spending too much to the disadvantage of the other. It may also be about reckless spending on frivolous things by either of the individuals in the relationship. When there is no agreement, verbal or written, on how and when to spend money that belongs to a team in any relationship, and not least in an intimate relationship, then arguments about money will not only be as hot as burning sulphur, they may never end. That may be the start of the end of the relationship. As I have said in other chapters, money can be shield and it can also be a sword. I will not repeat those discussions here.

***

Sexual matters.
Ever heard of sexual frustration? Driven by the aggressive testosterone hormone, men love sex; that truth has to be admitted, with some exceptions though. It gives them a sense of dominance and satisfaction. Men, when they have a desire for sex, want it right away in a manner that suggests that it's the oxygen that keeps them alive (see the chapter on: Is sex necessary?).

Women, less so, with some exceptions, are more placidly laid back, though some women are more sexually active than a lot of men (see chapter on Gender and Individual Differences). These are perfect examples of oppositions. You want something and the other person does not, yet you have to stick together without causing offence. However, the important thing to note is that, conflict is inevitable when a person in a relationship desires sex, but such desire conflicts with the other person's desire. There has to be a negotiation between the two. It could be by signs or by spoken expressions. It could be by good motivating words and legitimate physical acts. It may also be an enabling physical, as well as mental health, environment that promotes sexual intercourse. Good and legitimate sexual acts can not take place in the midst of hostility.

***

Except when these conducive conditions are created, quarrelling is a certainty. Sexual matters relating to style, frequency, intensity, places of doing *it* as well as the enthusiasm during the acts are all areas of differences in relationship intercourse that may lead in one way or the other to serious conflicts. Even in some lower mammalian animals, these conditions must be created before sex can take place. If not so, you can bet that the male may *suffer bruises* as the female repels him. I am not saying by any stretch of imagination that we as humans should behave like lower animals. I do not want to be misinterpreted on this matter so I need to make that clarification. The issue here is that sexual frustration against either of the individuals in a relationship can lead to conflict which may in some way be expressed in other ways as crisis. The trouble is, if you ask any individual, they are likely to talk about something else leading to the crisis, thus putting a cover-up to the main issue of sex.

***

Matters that affect children
Children are a third party to any relationship. Note that a relationship must have been formed between two people before children, either biologically belonging to the couple or adopted, ever join them.

The views of the individuals in a relationship on how to raise the children, the number of children to bear, the morality or discipline to impose on them, the school to attend, the friends to keep and so many other issues that surround children are major causes of conflict and crisis in a relationship.

Children themselves can constitute a challenge to the spouses. These kinds of problems may be seen, for example, in problems relating to birth, such as birth defects, in which one parent may blame the other as the cause. Others are diseases, as well as when life-death decisions have to be made. For example, if you have conjoined twins and one of them has to die for the other to live, except when the parents agree on the way forward, conflict is inevitable. What if the child is on life support machine and the spouses must make a joint decision about the fate of the child? Except if the couple make a joint decision, there will be serious family conflict. The cause of conflict may also be the behaviour of the children, such as issues of illegal drugs, where one parent may agree on their use and the other parent may disagree.

I have seen situations where one parent sees nothing wrong in a child smoking cannabis or going out with a particular boyfriend who does. The other parent sees something wrong with the arrangement. To an independent observer, this is a perfect recipe for crisis now and in the future. Such situations can become major sore points of conflict to the individuals in a relationship. It may split the marriage or relationship. Whatever way this goes, either it splits the relationship or the child continues on the said path, where the end can not be said to be bright.

***

In-laws and friends
Sadly, in-laws (mother, father, brother, sister etc) and friends are notoriously noted to be a factor in ending some otherwise stable marriages, due to the conflicts that they may cause through bad and divisive advice and acts. I will not belabour this here as it is common knowledge among married and unmarried couples. Besides, I have discussed it before now.

Other causes of conflicts are religion
Few people can boast that they share major religious differences with their spouse and yet the relationship ends well (that is until death separates the couple). In those that are played out in the public domain, such relationships almost always end poorly.

Imagine if you call on different gods in the same home! It is like someone putting one foot in a boat and the other on shore. When there is a wave, he may certainly not remain standing. Let us even consider religious differences on minor grounds. Even in homes or marriages where the *mode* of worship of the same God is different, e.g. Catholic and Baptist, conflict may even flare up here. Do you remember the fact that 80% of Americans attend churches every Sunday? Yet there is about 50% divorce rate in the USA in total! Computed, this means that the majority of divorce occurs amongst those church attendees of various denominations!

It is clear that human beings just don't like opposition to their intentions! Therefore, another common source of conflict in marriages or relationships is religion. My advice; only enter into a relationship with someone who reflects your views, shares what you share or values what you value.

Career/work
If there is competition for time, prestige and money in the sense that one person in the relationship develops his career or her career more quickly than the other, especially if one individual humiliates the other, then conflict is a certainty. Conflict is also certain if one spouse fails to support the business or the career of the other spouse, yet he or she wants some of the profit of the business. It simply doesn't add up.

Health (mental and physical)
I know for sure for I have seen it so many times, even in case law, where the development of mental health illness is a defeat of intentions and desire of the partners in the relationship. What I am saying here is that reasonable partners do desire that their spouses should remain in health. This desire may fail which is a clear conflict with one's wish and aspirations. This sometimes leads to divorce or separation. The cause of this may be exhaustion from caring for the other person who is ill or general unhappiness about association with someone with mental heatlh problems.
This statement is also true for physical illness. That said, health issues being the cause of conflict is more of a problem as in HIV and other sexually transmitted diseases, whereby the cause can be attributed to an individual in the relationship.

Culture, social up-bringing and influences
No two human beings are the same. Even twins behave differently though they may have been raised in similar ways. Now consider individuals in a union who are raised in different homes, different communities, and even different nations and from different beliefs. Individuals who are married are often raised in different *social* backgrounds and have different rules of enforcing self discipline and the discipline of others. Unless they *agree*, their *ways of doing things* may be poles apart from each other. Conflict and crisis may rule the relationship until, perhaps, it comes to an end.

***

Manifestation of conflict
Conflicts and crisis do manifest themselves in different ways. There is likely to be more attempts at violence in a crisis than a conflict, which may in some occasions remain as verbal attacks, especially between couples. Verbal attacks, nonetheless, can cause psychological injuries which may lead to physical injuries and economic retardation. You might ask me how? There was a woman, who told her daughter, "You are good for nothing. You will never amount to anything substantial".

In truth, the daughter could not get the words out of her mind. She became depressed and indeed, as if it was a curse, she failed in so many ways. She became engaged in self mutilation, not because she did not have the required skill or capability to succeed in life, but she failed because of the words that continued to trail her. If this can happen between a daughter and her mother, imagine for a moment, what spouses can say to each other in the heat of crisis.

Other examples are words said which may be abusive, discouraging, antagonising or words not said, such as omissions, silence, prejudice and malice. But the intentions are otherwise clear. Words are a powerful tool and can cause considerable good or damage, depending on how you use them.

Unresolved conflict, now transformed into anger and unhappiness, is manifested by such acts as hostility and violence. Sometimes it may be the deliberate omission to do certain things. For example, an angry ex-spouse may be so angry at the behaviour of their other "ex" that they could refuse to pay child support. If you need an answer, it is a gently building-up anger that arises from a conflict, whatever its nature.

Conflict may also manifest itself as the rejection of offers and approaches by the person who feels offended. It may also, in general, be a refusal to perform expected duties. Examples of such refusals are the refusal to have sex, refusal to do the cooking, rejection of requests to look after the children, withholding finances such as child support, physical and virtual avoidance of the person, making ironic and painful reference statements, or outright and direct or physical opposition. All of these could arise as sources of arguments at the initial stage.

If they are not resolved or if no common ground is found, the argument may transform to direct enforcement or *"direct action"* in which one person attempts to ensure he or she physically *enforces* his/her desire, whatever the cost, over the other. The law calls this kind of act *violent behaviour.* From here, anything could happen, from personal injuries to criminal damage.

***

Manifestation of crisis (the absence of peace)
These "enforcements" which I mentioned above may take the form of physical attack (violence), damage to property or attack against a person verbally and physically. It can be behaviour which is described as "out of character" and a rejection of any existing arrangements.

Other manifestations and "enforcement" which may be employed are subtle or open involvement of the police and other emergency services. This particular move may sometimes bring the crisis to an end or it may worsen it. It may worsen it as the bitter experience of involvement of a third party, such as the police, in domestic affairs often lingers on. It may also bring the original intention that was opposed into fruition as one of the opposing persons may have to give way!

The *original intention* that resulted in conflict may now also be realised in the light of the involvement of the police who may now have taken one opposing individual away.

For example: Imagine the following scenario. You are the father of say your 16-year old daughter. You advised her that at this stage of her life, for her benefit, she should not have an intimate sexual relationship. Her mother, your spouse, opposed you. Now the issue results in argument (conflict) and suddenly in a crisis (as anything could result in crisis in a marriage), and the police are called for incident of "DV" or domestic violence. Believe me; the door will now be opened for the girl to have her desire and for the mother to support her daughter. Why? This is because by now, the man, who opposed the daughter and mother, may have been removed from the scene and home. Here, the man has been "disarmed" and "kept away" or as one of my patients put it "emasculated". As we shall see later, legally, men have a greater chance to being at the receiving end of DVs. That is, they are more likely to be accused of causing domestic violence regardless of the preceeding verbal exchanges that precipitated it in the first instance. Of course, men are by nature a more aggressive of the human specie while, based on currently socially accepted data, women are more likely to be the victims of DVs.

Clearly, at this stage the mere conflict has become a crisis that now needs to be contained in order to avoid further damage. Curiously, one of the partners, the "enforcer" (not the police) may be so determined to have his or her way that the enforcement may take the form of conspiracy to murder the other person or unseat/remove the opposition from his/her home and work. Have you not heard a lot about some spouses murdering the other for very flimsy reasons, such as insurance claims, or fear of the spouse discovering extra-marital affairs? Remember, as I said before, human beings like to hide their deeds.

Returning to our discussion in the above example, at this stage of crisis now involving third parties (police and other emergency services), all manners of decency, confidentiality between the two in the union and those around them (in-laws, friends and neighbours), has virtually disappeared. If not at this stage, it is only a matter of time before you see it in the tabloid newspapers. At this point, the "battle" has become winner takes all, whatever it takes. The stakes have been raised, even in monetary terms.

The *lives* of the children in the middle of it all, and the lives of the parties, now matter very little. It is a fight to the finish. This is "war!" By now, the newspapers, may have taken over as spokespersons for either parties if no lesser persons have done so. Hostilities are likely to be intense and sustained because the stakes are high and may involve wider participants, such as in-laws and neighbours. How it will be resolved, if it will be resolved at all, depends on the principal participants, the spouses or couple in the relationship (see the Chapters on Broken Marriages and Broken Relationships).

All said, most if not all relationships/businesses and personal friendships/marriages will go through conflicts in their life time, but few will transform to crisis.

***

Management or controlling your anger
Conflict/Crisis. There is a common saying amongst the sages, that in all forms of disagreements, words will be the tool to end and settle conflicts. Remember that all conflicts started with words too! Amazing, isn't it?

Prior to application of words, there are some key ideas that need to be recognised:

1) In any relationship, not least in marriage, there is a presumed *mission* to be accomplished, otherwise, the relationship will fall apart as there is nothing to do or there will be nothing to defend in time of crisis. The parties to the union will simply give up in time of crisis if there is nothing to either defend or look forward to. All those who are involved should share the same vision and mission and speak with one voice.
2) In any given relationship, even if everyone in it is legally or naturally equal, there has to be a *designated person* to lead the union. Clearly, if everyone leads, then there will be a major leaderless problem. In time of challenges, fingers will be pointed at one another, in accusation.
3) Conflicts arise and are sustained and crises arise when there is a failure of leadership.
4) Whenever there is a leadership and followers, it is a fundamental principle of any union and a sign of unity that the

follower or the led as well as the leaders should be (a) loyal and (b) be defensive of the leadership and the union.

5) Similarly, it is a cardinal principle of leadership and union, that leaders should not cause harm to the led/followers and leaders should protect, defend and secure the led. This is otherwise called "love".

6) It is crucial to the survival of any union that the leader(s) should be tolerant but firm, attentive, strategic, foresighted, pragmatic, obey the law, be fair to all, trustworthy, maintain the trust of the led, pursue justice, lead by example, be a good listener and *sometimes* flexible. The same principle applies to the followers too.

7) The followers should not undermine, betray, conspire to harm the leaders, save in cases where the law compels the person, and only if life and properties are in danger. It should be remembered that in any union, conflict arises because someone at least is breaking the rules (man-made law or God's law). The other people feel threatened and largely "*do not know what else to do*". In some ways, lack of knowledge about legitimate unharmful things to do to resolve conflict can lead to more conflict, crisis and violence. This is often stated as "*I do not know what else to do...Doctor.*"

With these in mind, one can go on to providing an outline of what can be done to resolve a given conflict.

***

"Cooling Off Periods"

a) The first thing is to appreciate the power of words, which, paradoxically, are the tool in all conflicts. One would advise that at least one party should leave the scene of conflict immediately, especially if the verbal/physical aggression of the other can not be contained. The idea that one should leave for a neutral place is valid to avoid escalation into crisis.

b) Also, leaving the scene of confrontation is vital if at least one of the parties can not maintain a state of silence or if the silence will feed into the aggressor, who might be using it as an excuse of weakness to launch a violent attack against the other.

Leaving for a neutral position will also allow the parties to reflect, take respite and provide some necessary leadership, if this had been lacking. This is not legal separation as there no intention to pursue this path. The duration of "leaving for the neutral postion" or place can be as long as possible provided that there is no intention to separate or divorce. This is crucial as intention is necessary before divorce can proceed.

Here is a teaser for you to consider: to underscore the value of your spouse and how you should probably support them in crisis, here is a true clinical story. Amongst many such clients whom I have seen in similar circumstances, this peculiar but pathetic story comes into my mind. It concerns a woman in her early forties. She had a partner of many years. But they were cat and mouse, according to her own account of events. Mostly, she loathed the man. They would fight without end; a fights that could be physical or verbal with severe physical and psychological injuries to match. Suddenly, the man developed a rapidly deteriorating illness and died. The woman, having lost a long term companion, got depressed for two reasons. One, she lost a human being she was close to. Two, she lost someone she could at least shout at, or transfer her problems to.

When I saw her, she was extremely miserable. I really pitied her. It was her words that caught my attention. Granted that she was still in grief, but the genuineness of her touched me. She said while sobbing, "If only I could have him back, I will never fight him again…Now I have nobody….I will look after him…It was my fault…I used to fight him…" Then, it dawned on me what the sage of the English language had said for a long time, the true saying that "a bird in the hand is worth two in the bush".

**

Short Term Strategy
Someone will have to pay the price for this leadership failure. Thus, someone in the union must assume the position of a leader in keeping with the qualities spelt out above. The union will fall apart if this is absent. Someone will have to take the "insults" for the sake of saving the union, provided there is something worthy of defence (an objective and mission of the union). The

person assuming the leadership will need to steer the marriage or relationship towards its destination without it falling apart.

Long Term
For the long term, a more sustainable strategy will have to be put in place which should in fact incorporate the short term strategy as well. I shall divide this long term strategy into parts.

a) Genuine talk and negotiations should begin after the cooling-off period, when tempers should have waned and serious dangers have been averted.

b) Negotiation to reach an *agreement, including possibly written marital agreement,* a new start in a trusting environment with a mindset of flexibility, giving and taking, should be set up with a truly *wise* person (counsellor) e.g. a family member who is acceptable to the parties in the marriage or union. It could also be with an attorney. The negotiation would fail if one or both parties maintain a rigid position for their demands. Real issues should be discussed without pretensions. Alternatively and in order to avoid further disputes about the agreement, it could be committed to a "marital contract".

c) It would be very damaging to the union if either of the parties resort to litigation or legal means, since the law may empower and successfully enforce an intention but it may lead to unhappiness in the end. It may be the end of the relationship with all the impact that comes with it. (See the chapter on consequences of divorce)

d) Finally, the relationship should have a focus, an aim or something that must *always bind* them together, for example children, maintaining of social status, belief in God etc. The clearest example of this is the principle of *companionship* that underlines or should underline all successful marriages and relationships.

It is in this respect that, for the sake of the common good, forgiveness of each other should be considered. This is given added weight considering the human frailty, to which each one of us is so much a subject.

e) Maintenance: communication (words) and trust are vital to sustaining a relationship. The words should be open, gentle, non-hostile, constructive, supportive, inspirational and encouraging to each other, and all who are involved, in addition to the necessary joint pursuit of life's essentials, such as money and property.

f) Counselling: Counselling, which I mentioned above, is one of the methods to deal with conflict and crisis. It may be sought and may be given in times of urgency or it may be sought and given when things have calmed down. Human beings react to situations when they have tried all they could and have reached a point when they *"don't know what else to do"*. This is where counselling reaches its most important value to the individual, by providing strategic and tactical insights to the person in crisis or conflict.

What is counselling? Counselling is a form of intervention in an on-going event. It is an ongoing event as it may not have been resolved. Such events (or multiple events) often act as a disadvantage to the sufferer or the person who is seeking counselling. It is something that needs to be dealt with. Otherwise it remains and it troubles the person. It torments the individual and may affect the quality of his or her life. An on-going event is one which is unresolved and which continues to impact on the overall health/happiness (well-being) or decision-making process of the individual. Such decision-making processes may be related to work, relationships, marriage, finances, or issues that surround children.

***

Legally, counselling implies that a counsellor encourages or aids another person who is seeking counselling to achieve a certain set objective or desire. For example, it may be counselling to help deal with alcoholic abuse that often causes conflict in the relationship. It may also be advice about how to deal with drug misuse in children or school truancy.

Primarily, the need for counselling arises because there is a conflict between one and another entity (spouse, employer, children etc). This is the conflict that needs to be resolved. Without you knowing, this conflict is a threat to your happiness.

***

How is counselling delivered?
There are various methods to provide people with counselling. It could be by phone. It could be by video link. It could be face-to-face or via email or the internet. Advice could be provided by text messaging. The significant thing is that words have been creditably exchanged between you and the counsellor.

Regardless of the methods used (face-to-face, internet, email, books, TV, DVD, demonstration, telephone etc), one undeniable element common to all is that words are the tools that are employed. To most scientific minds, even clinicians, they may not realize that words are the most powerful creative tool that exists. With them, aims and objectives can be achieved or can be defeated. Words are the tool of communication. Words are the tool of counsellors in the ancient and in today's world. Counselling in short is delivered through words.

Such delivery may employ technologies such as the internet, telephone, emails, and letters, to reach the intended recipient, who is you. In its earliest and traditional form, words are delivered through face-to-face interaction. Some people have said that this is the best method. Granted, but this method may not be very efficient nor be available to everyone who needs counselling.

***

Common names and substitutes for counselling
Some common names for counselling are used among mental health professions: counselling can take the form of Cognitive Behaviour Therapy (CBT), psychotherapy and "talking therapy". In geek speaking terms, counselling is also called, e-therapy, email therapy and online therapy, online help, online advice and so on.

I have listed these names since readers may not necessarily be aware that counselling is somewhat synonymous with these names. In younger age groups, they may prefer the technology-learning names rather than the traditional name of *counselling*. In specialist industries, they may have their own "counsellors" who are unique to that industry. An example is the financial industry, where the counsellor is called a financial advisor.

In some cultures and local government politics, the public administrators, otherwise called politicians, are called "counsellors" by virtue of the fact that they "advise" the public. Also, in some professions including business and Law, terms for counselling exist. In legal profession, for example, there are variants of counselling. The British Monarch for example has lawyers as Queen or King's "Counsel", as the President of the USA has "Advisors". They both offer advice on key issues on which these office holders must make a decision.

Others names for counselling are: "to support", "to instruct", "to direct", and "to help".

All these terms imply that someone is giving the other person tactical information, advanced and strategic knowledge about how the "on-going issue" will or should proceed towards its, hopefully, happy ending for the one seeking, shall we say, advice.

Why do people seek counselling?
You might be forgiven for asking this question. You might also be pardoned for thinking that people should "get a grip" with their problems. Well, we all need help. No one can have it all. Also, we will at some time in our own lives need some help or advice on one thing or the other. No one is an island of knowledge. As I mentioned above, in spite of their powerful positions, monarchs, Presidents, Prime Ministers, Kings, Queens, politicians and businessmen all, at some point, ask for counselling. So there is nothing strange about it. Women (especially) and men, the low and the high, search for and conduct counselling in one way or another. No one can

completely function without it, though it may not be obtained in a formal way. After all, we do call our friends to ask: "What do you think of *this* matter?" or, "Can you *help* me here?" If you have ever done this, and I am sure you have, you sought and possibly obtained, counselling. Also, women do call their mothers and friends for advice on matters concerning their husbands. Similarly, men seek counselling from their fathers and friends too, all in the name of *help,* even if it is only encouraging words.

***

How does counselling work?
Counselling works by modifying our thinking/word formation process. The counsellor will listen and then analyse the problem. By offering "solutions" the counsellor if effectively working by modifying the way we "see" or perceive things. It works by replacement of the information memory store in our brain. This process will subsequently modify our actions, the way we see things, and therefore the way we behave and do things. Words do matter. Take an example: your husband is on holiday in a foreign land, say, Paris, France. You then hear from a friend that he has started to go out with another woman in spite of the "love" between the two of you. You become flustered and anxious. Then you threaten the worst consequences for this betrayal. You decide to take practical actions, but first you decide to seek counselling on "what to do". You approach a counsellor. He *advises* you first and foremost to call you husband and find out more about it. Also, he *suggests* that you should find further information from your friend. You do as suggested. Ultimately, you discover it was all a lie as your friend had malice against your husband. The outcome of this is that you have saved yourself the trouble that may have ensued if you had acted unwisely.

***

Who is a counsellor and what qualification is required?
In brief, a counsellor is ideally someone who is an *expert* in the matter in which he or she is providing counselling. An example would be a relationship counsellor.

Who is an expert? By law, an expert is someone who is skilled in the art or profession under which he is claiming to be skilled. It has nothing to do with education. In some, education is a recognized criterion, as in some professions, such as law. It may be necessary to have qualifications before becoming an expert, though not always so. *Experience* has everything to do with it.

Take for example a poorly educated plumber of 30 years experience. He has little education but he can teach a hypothetical academic professor of say "plumbing", everything that is practical about plumbing. If you ask me whom I would rather call for my plumbing advice when my kitchen pipe is leaking, I know which of these two people I would turn to.

Similarly, nobody goes to marriage school. We learn from experience and pass it down the line. Even though there are relationship and marriage counsellors who have never been married, they have gathered experiences over the years from resolving many difficult family problems and so can guide and advise the married and unmarried. This is also the basis why some pastors, priests, prophets and friends or family members are good counsellors.

***

Who can benefit from counselling?
Just about anyone can. "You," "me," "him," "her," "they", "us," and "those," "them," the rich, the poor, the bereaved and so on. Children need counselling *always* as they grow up, in the form of *guidance* from parents, teachers and guardians. Adults and children who may have suffered mental/psychological and physical injuries need advice. Women and men in marriage/relationships need appropriate counselling to resolve conflicts in the family with spouses and children or neighbours. Strangers who are hurt and injured by others on the street need legal *help*. Workers come into conflict with employers. They both need strategic *advice*.

What do you require to use a counsellor?
You need determination and confidence to deal with the matters that are affecting you. You need some boldness that you will not be defeated and to face up to the issues. You require the honest intention that you want to resolve the matter with the aim of getting over it and moving on with your life.

You need to trust your counsellor and he/she need to trust you, that all matters will be kept confidential and that there will be no abuse of the process.

You will need to seek an appropriate counsellor who matches your needs. You need to determine which media is good for you: e.g. internet/email, face-to-face or telephone etc. Each has its advantages and disadvantages

What matters will you bring to a counsellor?
Just about anything that bothers your mind. Anything that is interfering with the enjoyment of your life; anything at all. Remember, words change things. Examples are: Marital/family conflicts, relationship issues, children matters, work matters, sexual issues, financial matters, legal conflicts, health and mental health issues etc.

***

Relevance of counselling in relationship matters
Although a number of individuals and couples would be able to deal with their personal challenges by themselves, there are millions out there who are too in-ward looking and bound by their problems. They have no personal solutions. It is couples like these who may benefit from counselling, especially if they do not have the motivation or confidence to sit down face-to-face to discuss their issues without deteriorating into confrontation.

Also, a fresh view and perspective from a non-interfering third party, who may bring in fresh impartial ideas as an independent mind, may provide vital solutions to the challenges.

That said, the downside is that couples may be too intimidated and shy, to the extent that they do not have enough confidence to discuss extremely painful and intimate issues.

On the other hand, if couples have taken a firm, unyielding, pre-determined position prior to seeing a counsellor, then it may be difficult to change their minds. This is even more so if they have not opened up in real terms to the counsellor.

Also, I have seen conflicts and crises continuing in spite of prolonged and expensive counselling, simply on account of non-yielding and non-forgiving parties who refuse to "let go" of the past.

In all, counselling may be worth trying in time of crisis and conflict, though it is not a panacea for strategic foresight before entering into a relationship. In saying that, I must advise potential partners to seek counselling on issues they are not clear about before a serious relationship is formed in the first place. That is the essence of this book.

***

Other methods of coping:
The two individuals in a relationship can certainly not maintain the same unyielding positions permanently. Along the line, after the "cooling-off" period, one of the couples may have a softer heart and reflect more deeply. This application of *words* may achieve a considerable effect. Ever heard of poems and relationship quotes? Words can achieve a lot. Poems can soften a heart of stone. Wise encouraging words in the form of romantic quotes can make all the difference. That may be all you need to resolve your conflicts. Either of these can be sent preferably by text/SMS. It could also be by email or letter.

Imagine, if your spouse had offended you, how you would feel if he sends you this line, from Bayard Taylor: "*I love you, I love but you. With a love that shall not die. Till the sun grows cold, and the stars grow old...*" (Note I have modified this quote: I have replaced "thee" with "you"). The choice of your words is yours. Words, we know, have the ability to change minds. Use them to your greatest advantage.

***

CHAPTER SEVENTEEN

Sex in Relationships: Snare or Serenity? Is Sex Necessary?

"One half of the world cannot understand the pleasures of the other." Jane Austen

Sex is central to intimate sexual relationships. Sex is the critical difference that separates intimate relationships from all others, or from all other forms of relationships. Every other relationship is platonic. Although in business relationships, the aim, strictly speaking, is directed at making profit, and any other activities that may accompany this in the course of the profit making are certainly not the main reason as to why the business was established in the first instance.

I have often wondered why human beings are so curious about sex and why they can spend so much energy in pursuit of intercourse. The reader would appreciate that sex and its images are used in practically all human endeavours. Its effect spreads through and is present throughout human activities. If it's not tittle-tattle in a big business, it will be a scandal in a presidency, royal houses, schools, monasteries and churches. Sex is everywhere: on the internet, TV, mobile phones and newspapers. It is used in marketing great products, some authors rely on it to sell books and some television channels depend on it to make profit. It is a multi-billion industry in the USA and in many more countries across the world. Big individual names have tripped over because of it. There is perhaps no other inter-human engagement that catches our attention or could arouse our embarrassment as much as sex. In spite of its pervasive nature, human beings pretentiously do not like to talk about *it*.

Yet the questions remain, Is sex really necessary in human existence? Is sex necessary for reproduction? Is sex necessary in human intimate relationships? Do you really have to have sex?

Sex, for the avoidance of doubt, is discussed here as pertaining to intercourse between a genetic man and a genetic woman. This is the surest measure to know who a male and female really are.

***

What is sex?
By the account of authorities on this subject, sexual intercourse is defined as the act of sexual reproduction between a man and a woman, whereby the man's penis is inserted into the woman's vagina and excited until orgasm and ejaculation occur. I suppose most individuals in marriage and relationships will agree with this view. Another name for this act is "coitus" or "copulation".

It appears, human beings (and indeed animals) do not have to *learn* this act in a formal way. I suppose this should be otherwise. Human beings could and should have formal educational introductions to the act. The reason is that there are too many misunderstandings of what sex means and therefore it has been subject to too many tangential interpretations in both theory and practice. The reader may recall how the world was "entertained" at the close of the 1990s by the shrewd attempt by the former President of the USA, Clinton, to define what sex actually means. It was a serious but entertaining issue. For the sake of decency, I will not go over the argument of what constitutes sex. This is a book that I want all ages who are capable of forming relationships to read and I should therefore spare the young minds in our midst any trouble in that area.

Primary Purpose of sex

From a biological and religious standpoint, sex is directed, primarily, at reproduction. The Catholic Church, in particular, has been outspoken about the relevance of sex in marriages and has indicated on many occasions that sex is primarily meant as a reproductive tool. That is its purpose, the advice goes. Let me stretch this argument to some extent. Let us take a couple who want *three children,* for example. Let us assume, they both married each other when they were 22 years of age. These assumptions are actually real and not fished out from some vacuum.

Does it mean then that the couple would and should have sex just three times in all their marital lifetime? Now, assuming on each occasion the woman did not get pregnant immediately but did so after three sexual attempts for each of the children.

That means, the couple would in total have had sex nine times in their entire marital life.

On the other hand, if she got pregnant on each occasion of trying for each of the children, it means that the couple will only have sex just three times in their entire marital life.

You can do the maths if the couple want 10 children or 20 children. Now assuming they didn't want children at all, which is perfectly within their legal and biological right to decide, it means they will not have sex at all!

I am not certain if this is realistic, although I have heard of marriages in which one partner of the couple refused to have sex with the other, to consummate the relationship. Perhaps the ruling in the Catholic Church is meant to be that sex is meant to be within marriage and not necessarily for reproduction. If one may take the religious argument a little further, there are certainly many married, but initially childless, couples in the Bible who, as it were, tried for babies at some point. How can we describe their sexual intercourse when they were trying for children? Needless? Perhaps, we could call it fruitless.

***

Conduct of sex
The definition which we saw above has given us some indication as to how sex is conducted. However, the manners, the preparation and the actual conduct are a matter for the individual relationship---perhaps within this definition. Years ago, a male colleague of mine asked another male friend of mine, in a light-hearted way and in my presence, a very interesting question. No sexism was implied neither should it be factored into this discussion. My male friend began, "I know you have been married for a while." Every one of us present lifted up our heads in anticipation of the curious interjection into the existing discussion. "How do you do sex?" he asked, to the puzzlement of everyone present. The room fell into silence for a

while and my friend, who the question was directed at, paused in total surprise and his mouth dropped. He summoned his courage and responded:

"When you get there, she will teach you what to do!" I think that wraps up the answer to the question on the conduct of sex. Couples will have to teach each other.

The answer was concise and nearly accurate except for the fact that there are many reports in which, after the marital ceremony, one partner in a relationship may simply refuse to have sex---for whatever reason. Often, that is the beginning of the end for the relationship. Having said this, I wish to share another interesting experience. Years ago, I was consulting in an infertility clinic which, as the name implies, is a clinic for childless couples/people. There was a couple who were unfortunate in many ways. They had been looking to have their own children for a while. In my role, I had to ask them about the conduct of their intercourse. To my greatest surprise, the couple who were actively looking to have a child were having "sex" through a different entry point! Of course, without a doubt, their childlessness and its cause was not so mysterious, in the end.

Meanwhile, it is not the objective of this book to explore human sexuality, save that it is important to all intimate sexual relationships, as the name appropriately implies. As a result, it is very important that I should explore a related theme that may seriously affect the stability of a relationship, as we know that sexual frustration is an important cause of divorce.

***

Is sex required for reproduction?
This might appear as an unnecessary question until we look deeper into what is happening around us in the world, as well as the advances in science and technology of human reproduction. Until the birth of the first test tube baby, Brown, in England, this question would have been answered in the clear affirmative that sex is required for reproduction. With the development of test tube babies, surrogacy and possibly cloning, the question as to

whether sex is necessary or required for reproduction has been thrown into confusion.

The reader might be forgiven if he or she says that this statement is not applicable to stable marriages. Actually, it is. A lot of marriages go through test tube baby processes each year. Surrogacy is also increasing in use, especially in the Western world. Therefore, all these could potentially affect the role of sex in a relationship. This is poignantly important if all that the couple required or that joined them in the first instance was the common need for children. Alternatively, as we see in the case of some rich pop stars, they could "marry" but actually "buy" the service of a woman for insemination or surrogacy without a single act of sex! The question then arises: What is the purpose of sex? Also, what is the key link between the individuals in a marriage relationship? That question brings us to the functions of sex in a relationship.

***

Functions of sex in relationship
To a certain extent, the function of sex in marriage is basically for reproduction. That is the biological and natural function, as I stated earlier. At least that is what it appears to be, looking at it from a keen and casual observer's point of view. However, it is clear that there appears to be more to it than meets the eye. Before I continue, let me state that there is no documentary evidence in recorded human history that child-bearing or procreation has ever been made compulsory. In fact, the opposite is usually the case, whereby governments, even in our modern days, could restrict child-bearing because of overpopulation. On the other hand, there are instances where governments do persuade their own people to have more children (France). They even sweeten this policy, especially when the population is dwindling.

Now imagine you are married but do not intend to have children. What would you be doing otherwise to strengthen the link between the two of you in the relationship? Would you be holding hands, looking at each other face-to-face? Will you be watching TV and chit-chatting as friends do? If sex is important or not important in an intimate relationship, let us see it under closer examination of some functions of sex in marital relationships.

The starting point is that few, if any, would doubt that sex is an act resulting from a *union* of two people, no matter how short the relationship may be. Marriage, as we saw at the beginning of this book, is defined as a union of two adult opposite genders. Sex, it would appear, is the point where the union itself comes into reality: in union. Two individuals who are supposedly "married" but who abstain from sex are not doing the marriage great justice, it would seem. Alternatively, it may be that one denies the other the benefit of sex. That denial may be the clearest sign yet that all is not well with the *union.*

Sex, it would appear, functions to calm anxieties in the participants. This is even more important in relationships that are troubled by frequent wrangling. This internal strife can and is usually suppressed on the few occasions when they can "see eye to eye," (if there was light during the act) away from their bickering times. If we put it more medically, sex tends to act as a "relaxant". Sex, at least during the act and for some time after the act, promotes intimacy between the couple. After all, that is the principal purpose: intimacy. And sex makes that intimacy possible: skin to skin and heart to heart.

We should remember that all the *natural assets* that are given to us are meant to be used. "If you don't use it you lose it" is a common saying amongst the wise. Therefore, if the organs of sex are not used, they gradually fall into what is called disuse.

This is also true for the brain. If you fail to use your brain, dementia may not be far away. If you fail to use your arms, they may begin to waste and wither away. The same is true for organs that we all use in sexual intercourse. If you don't use it legitimately, it may just fade away. Of course, you don't have to use it, if that is your choice. If you use it illegally, you could be in trouble for a long time.

***

Does that mean that sex is necessary or compulsory in a relationship?

The short and long answer is "no". Sex is not compulsory in a relationship but it *helps*. This is because the couple can rise above a relationship that depends on sex to survive. The euphoric needs of sex may not be necessary for the relationship to blossom. For example, I doubt what the impact of sex or its absence may be in a truly bonded couple in which one is severely disabled, physically. Yet, in another scenario, the absence of sex, especially in very old age, may not diminish their fondness for each other. If this were not so, then the divorce rate might be higher than it currently is especially among the senior adults or Old Age Pensioners as it's commonly called. Another example: in relationships where one of the couple suffers from sexual dysfunction, as in failure of erection in men, does that mean the relationship should end, considering the spirit of "for better for worse" vows that were taken by both on day of the union?

In fact, a relationship whose primary objective is set at the outset as sex is likely to fail. The reason for this is that, like everything else that is being, "tried and tested," and, "once the novelty wears off," as is commonly said, the relationship will lose its magnetic attraction. The couples will fall apart. At least, one of them will simply *"move on"* to the next sexual project in another relationship.

Therefore, the question with regard to whether sex is a necessary condition in relationships does not always hold.

***

Advantages of sex
If you do think that sex is unimportant and unnecessary in a relationship, what have you got to gain in the relationship?

Apart from the likeliness that sexual intercourse may result in pregnancy and therefore children, what are the other benefits that may be derived from sexual intercourse? I must say that some of the claims to support advantages of sexual intercourse that I have seen in the course of writing this book are very dubious. Nonetheless let us look at some of them.

1) You use up considerable amounts of energy during sex. Some people have estimated this energy to be about 200 calories in 30 minutes of sexual activity. This amount of energy represents, approximately, a whopping 10% of your entire daily energy needs! On this account, it may actually look as if you have done some rigorous exercise. The benefits of this, one can claim, is that it even helps lower cholesterol, because you burn some reserves, reduce the risk of heart attack and high blood pressure and improve your digestion. The list of beneficial projection could go on! Remember you have just lost a whole lot of calories in less than half an hour!

You may become hungrier and eat more. Now imagine if you have sex five times in a day or in a go. Believe me, you will be as we say in medical circles, "a vegetable," almost lifeless and barely active. Now consider if you do so everyday! You can bet that you are by your own actions shortening your life. The trouble is, except with care, people who suffer heart problems and high blood pressure may actually die during sex, due to the high energy usage that follows, or due to the stress of the occasion and the strain on the fragile heart.

In all, the above stated advantages are good for those of you who want to lose weight. But remember, it can not be a substitute for reasonable exercise.

2) The muscles of the pelvis, buttocks, abdomen, hands and back are at work during sex. So it may help "tone" these muscles. On that account, the argument goes; it may help your vigour. Remember the danger, if you overuse the muscles, you will also lose them too.

3) Anxiety. Due to the relaxation that follows successful sexual intercourse (with *orgasm*), the individual feels relaxed and problem-free for a while. To benefit, intercourse must come with orgasm. Note that when you come back to reality, your

personal problems may not have disappeared after all. It can give you a temporary sense of well-being. Despite the physical and mental health problems you may be suffering from, sex can temporarily give you a euphoric and transient sense of well-being.

4) It reduces bad temper, for the time being; due to the effect of relaxation on muscles and mood, sex reduces irritability. This is logical in my opinion. Time spent on preparation for sex is probably the time you are least likely to argue with your spouse. That is where the calming effect begins and continues throughout the act of intercourse. The calming effect may help explain why individuals may feel psychologically younger, more self-assured and with a better point of view on life.

5) It helps with depression if the person's depression stems from anxiety, lack of previous intimacy, lack of confidence and lack of self-esteem. Now that the person can confidently have sex, all these failings may be relieved although it may not remove the fundamental impairments. If not having sex is driving a person into despair, it is obvious that once this objective is accomplished, the despair may lift. If the hopelessness is due to something else other than sex, it is difficult to see how intercourse can help the person. In any case, sex must be conducted in a legitimate manner; otherwise it may land the person in further trouble, irrespective of the existing depression.

6) Sleep. Again, due to high muscular activities that accompany sex and the high energy usage and the relaxation that follows, the person becomes tired after the "exercise" and may fall asleep thereafter. This is probably why sex is mostly done at night, which is when biological couples meet after work, and it also helps them to gently fall asleep in each others' arms. This, though, helps to raise doubts in my mind in the claim that sex does not reduce one's sharpness, post-sex. People testify that if you have sex early in the morning prior to setting out for the day, your energy and alertness may not be the same as when you do not. This makes sense in light of what I have outlined above.

7) Meanwhile, anyone with experience will tell you that sex *connects the individuals emotionally. It also increases the individuals' level of supposed devotion to each other. This will happen either if they have any children or not.* This point of "devotion" should not be taken lightly as sex may act as a *snare*, which I will discuss later.

8) Religious Advantage: Christians are urged to marry (if that is their desire) and hence have sex instead of "burning". Burning should be interpreted to mean, lusting and having unfulfilled thoughts.

9) Having a regular sexual partner could prevent moral, religious and legal crimes, such as rape, indecent exposure, solicitation for sex, sexual abuse of children and vulnerable adults, pornography and lusting.

But then, sex is really not compulsory, neither is it necessary for the survival of an individual. Abstinence, as we shall see, in the absence of "lusting", does not cause mental or physical harm.

***

Disadvantages of sex (These are the dangers you could avoid if you practise abstinence).
1) The first one is that if you do not want children, the most effective preventive measure is abstinence. Why do you want to have children children, if you don't need them? Why do you want to have children if you don't know their value? Avoiding sex is a form of absolute contraception. Abstinence can help prevent unnecessary child abuse as you will not have the children that you don't need.

2) The second point is that sex is always a risk, like any human enterprise. You may die in the course of doing it from heart attack, because of the intensity of the exercise, especially if you are already vulnerable. Many people have died like this before.

Even if you are not fatally wounded, you may contact sexually transmitted diseases, such as HIV (human immunodeficiency virus) or chlamydia, especially if you have sex with multiple individuals on different occasions, or if you do not have a regular sexual partner.

3) There are some people who feel a sense of guilt after sexual intercourse. The reason for their guilt is not clear but it could be because of long held religious views on the matter. It may also have something to do with the way the individual was brought up. On the other hand, if sex has been done immorally and illegitimately, such as sex with a minor, it may bring guilt feelings. You could avoid this sense of guilt by avoiding sex.

4) On the other hand, as I mentioned earlier, in the absence of sexual intercourse, your relationship may blossom in other areas. For example, if you as a spouse are also a carer for your partner in illness, the pleasure and reward for such caring may transcend sexual intercourse. For example, someone who is caring for an ill spouse will likely devote his or her time and love towards the caring, rather than seek the pleasure of sex.

5) Getting involved with somebody sexually may act as a very dangerous snare for you. There are individuals who have met their untimely death through unguarded sexual activities. Also, in some cases, sex has been used as a weapon to kill in the Cold War, as well as in relationship disputes, and as a snare to "catch" real criminals. Some innocents individuals have fallen into the police trap as if they committed the offences being investigated by the police. These innocent individuals have been caught when they have been offered cheap sex by alluring entrapment police officers and the unwary individuals have sought to to take advantage of cheap opportunities.

6) Overuse and unguarded sex may become the object and act of abuse. You may lose so much energy that you could no longer function well. What I am saying here is that, for example, if sex has become your focus, like misuse of alcohol, you could lose much of your vitality. It may also become a disease that you will need to seek help to cure.

7) Sex can result in deep psychological hurt or result in over-possessiveness of the other partner. If you are over-attached to

your spouse, you are likely to suspect every move he or she makes. You may begin to suspect that he or she is sleeping with someone else when he or she is not with you.

8) Sex, especially with partners carrying an STD/STI (sexually transmitted diseases/infection), such as herpes, may increase cervical cancer risk in women. In men, papiloma virus may increase your risk of getting cancer of the penis if you happen to catch this very ugly virus. Other STDs which you may get include gonorrhoea, chlamydia and many others.

***

Can sex be a snare?

Caution: Before the reader continues, please understand that this book is about openness, truth and facts. Some of the issues which I have mentioned here may make your skin develop goose pimples if you don't like detective stories. You may pause or skip the rest of this chapter now.

Sexual intercourse is an extremely powerful tool in the hands of those who are shrewd enough to know its inherent power. It ranks alongside money in its ability to entrap individuals. It ranks along and also complimentary to drugs and alcohol in causing you to lose your sense of mission and focus. To make this power more effective, there is a complementary side to it. Men love sex. They think about it. They seek it, sometimes to their own peril. Some adore it. They can give all that they have, including their life, for it. Money can buy you sex. Men have the money and wealth in this world. Women *apparently* love money, so the claim goes. They also have what it takes to demand money and make the man pay the full price—in kind and riches--- whatever it takes.

Sex makes men feel that they have "conquered" *that* woman. After he has conquered one woman---apparently---the unwary man moves to the next conquest.

Prima facie, as they say in the legal profession, women are not stupid at all. They are smart, wise and they take their time. Women understand the stony hearts of men. They know that sex is one of the weaknesses that men have to endure and which women have to exploit to the fullest. The stage has been set from the "crucible" which I mentioned in the opening chapter of the book. As it was then, so it has been ever since, even up till this day. The meal is set for the eater. The poor lamp is now ready to be led to the slaughter.

The question is how can sex be a snare? The answer is that sex can be used in detective works. For the shrewd person who has a certain *intention in mind,* sex can be used to achieve the intention, especially if the person who is being lured into intercourse is reckless about sex. It may also be exploited against those who are engaging in unguarded indulgence. If you are doing right and legal things, keep doing them, for this may not affect you. If you are on the wrong side of the law, the snare may be wide upon for you. Let us see.

To answer the question above, I shall undertake some case studies: please follow me into the labyrinth of treachery. Please note that except if the principal characters and their cases are well established in public knowledge, I shall use the abbreviations or mere letters to represent them.

***

Case study 1
Criminal investigations
In the early 1990s a young beautiful woman, R, in the South of London, UK, met her untimely death in an open park. She had been brutally murdered. The death touched the national conscience for two reasons: one was that the son of R, who was about 3 years old then, was beside her. He was shouting at the side of the dead body—his mother's--- "to wake up". Second, this death was apparently senseless. It was imperative for the police to catch the killer. Police were determined to do the job effectively and at least to earn the praise and confidence of the wary public. In the course of the investigation that followed, the police set a scene such that a policewoman was empowered to

search out the perpetrator. She was empowered to have sex with the potential criminal who killed R. She did so with one CS. The CS "confessed" to have "killed" R during the ensuing sexual encounters between the policewoman and the CS. The case went to a court of law, but the case later collapsed like a pack of cards. Why?

Reason: the CS did not actually kill R. The CS had been led to "slaughter." The CS wanted sex. He got his heart's desire in a trap with a "chain" around his neck at the end of his sexual encounter. CS was lucky. While he was ultimately exonerated and the real culprit caught in 2008, there are many men who have not been so lucky. Many men in their little ways and in their own private lives in different lands, races, politics, businesses and religion, have fallen to this Achilles' heel of men having been ensnared by the claws of sex. Talking of religion, are we not living witnesses to the crushing and trapping power of sex in the lives of prominent pastors and preachers the world over, who have fallen from grace to grass? And of politicians, need we be reminded of many White House hopefuls in the US, and prominent politicians in Europe and elsewhere, whose careers were slaughtered on the platform of sexual intercourse?

On the positive side, "the snare" has been used in many ways to lure real and potential rapists and child sex abusers into the noose. At least, this method has reduced the numbers of those who will cause misery on others and/or be a nuisance to the safety of the public and innocent children.

Case Study 2
Here is one. During the Cold War, sex was a powerful tool--- a landmine for the easy prey---with the predator's true intention cocooned in the unsearchable heart of human beings. The hunter could ideally be a foot away, shadowing the innocent but unwary "gazelle". The lioness in human skin was ready for the kill. The time was set. The trap was perfect. It may have been a cold winter's night, but in the warmth of a walled and well entrapped apartment in Prague. It may have been on a sweating summer's day in Moscow, or in the freezing temperature of St Petersburg. Many secret service agents are said to have lost their

lives to sexual entrapments. If they are lucky to be alive, by the end of the encounter, the secret agents may have let the cat of their nation out of the sexual bag.

Case study 3
Many people will be familiar with two prominent characters in the Bible. One was Samson. He was a great warrior and trusted defender of his dear country. Like the case of the agents during the Cold War, a secret "hunter" with deadly poison in her mouth and kiss had befriended him. Her sweet talk and pretensions wer a hot knife that sank into Samson's defenceless "butter" --- or, shall we say, he befriended a killer. He loved sex beyond his soul. His sexual partner/girlfriend was going to deny him sex unless he told her the secret of his might. The bargain was perfect. As soon as he told the secret behind his might, from that moment, his days on earth were numbered. A larger number of enemies, who were lurking in the corridor, swooped on Samson and gorged his eyes out. Though he revenged his poor treatment, he died in the midst of his enemies. He sold his life for sex.

***

Indulgence
Case Study 4
Similarly, the hearts of warriors, sages, kings and presidents can easily be changed and ensnared by sex. I hope the reader is familiar with the story of Bill Clinton, the former president of the US, and King Solomon of ancient Israel. "Sex" made the former "ridicule" his office, and of the latter, his office was brought into laughable disrepute.

Case study 4
Interestingly, and for the sake of balance, the snare of sex is not for men as the victim only. Women, too are often victims, notwithstanding in different circumstances. Women, as I have said, and as many people believe, "love" money. That is at least the popular view. They could "chase" money even into rat hole in the rate race of this world. Why? Just to make ends meet, but sometimes in the belief that they can hold their own even in the most dangerous places. Also, because of their conviction, they entrust their lives into the hands of even dangerous men. Money,

after all, is no respecter of persons. Without money one is doomed into poverty. With it, you may be doomed into indulgence!

Many unsuspecting women have been killed or maimed by men with twisted intents. This is even true in the case of prostitutes. It is equally true for someone looking to obtain security or money, and maybe material gain and money, by offering sex in return. They often do not know that the trap has been set in the mind of men to take revenge for the cheap offer of sex in exchange for hard-earned money.

Sex may not be enough to satisfy any previous disappointment the man may have had. He may be bent on fulfilling his desire to kill in revenge for previous pains and disappointments he may have suffered in the hands of other women.

The perfect snare is often therefore set for anyone who has not done her homework properly and then falls as a prey falls into the hand of a waiting but watchful tiger. Many women have met their early death this way: sex for money, materials and security.

In sum, actual sex act could well be a snare for the unsuspecting, for it may make you so weak, mentally, physically and emotionally during and after sex, that it may make you vulnerable to physical attack. Besides, sex causes intimacy. You may be ensnared even for something that you did not know about. You may wittingly or unwittingly be emotionally involved with someone who is undesirable. Sex can tie you into a relationship that you never wanted. Enough said for the wise.

***

Can sex be an escape into serenity?
I will not be doing you my reader any good if I did not tell you the greater value of sex. Provided that sex is done in an atmosphere of moral, social, legal and biological legitimacy, the short and long answer to this question is that sex can be an escape into enjoyable euphoria and serenity, though briefly. On the other hand, as you can see from the foregoing discussion, it

can be a terrible snare for the naive and gullible person. I hope that helps.

***

CHAPTER EIGHTEEN
Gender Differences: What You Should Know

"When you struggle with your partner, you are struggling with yourself. Every fault you see in them touches a denied weakness in yourself." Deepak Chopra

I do attach great importance to this chapter, not least because it is a core area in human relations that is easily overlooked at the outset when we all form one type of relationship or another. Depending on the culture in which we grew up, each of us has pre-formed ideas about how the opposite gender should behave and conduct themselves. We also have, at the back of our minds, questions in respect of what drives the behaviour of a female or a male. Well, in a lot of ways, a significant amount of work has been done to unravel this question. So as to avoid plunging myself into academic works and controversy, I will not be entering that debate, for I will stick with proven and observable behaviour and conduct.

I know some readers may be expecting me to write about the anatomy of the genders here, as a means of highlighting gender differences. In truth, that is not the aim of this chapter. If the reader is interested in some anatomy of the sexes, he or she can consult my book: *Your Health in Your Hands: Comprehensive Guide to Healthy Living,* or any good book dealing with the anatomy of human beings.

As a general observation though, let me say that a woman is a man's Achilles' heel: his weak point. She carefully, sometimes trustingly, observes anything and everything that the man does rightly or wrongly. She acts as a reality checker. These weaknesses, the male reader may wish to know, could be his downfall when conflict emerges. But if the man is upright and does things right and legitimately, he will stand firm in days of potential peril. Let me cite an example: the British Broadcasting Corporation once broadcast news that a businessman was reported sixty times to the tax authorities for alleged tax irregularities, by his wife, apparently his closest ally! On each occasion nothing was found to be illegal by the taxman. Imagine if this man had done something wrong! History tells us that most great men who have fallen from grace have had a connection to one kind of sexual relationship or another, as anyone can tell.

What about the weak point of the woman? The man, her nemesis---the formidable opposition who she can not beat or overcome---is the object she loves to hate, or shall we say hates to love. The man is the one she can not do without. Yet, aggressive as the man is, she finds herself unable to disentangle from being in a relationship with him. However, despite the man's physical power and domination, he has a vulnerable point. Therefore, she can sting him on or through his Achilles' heel: his weak point.

A lot of harms that occurs in an intimate relationship are played out on the platform of these two points that I mentioned in the last two paragraphs. A passing look at these types of harm shows the tendency for men to be more (allegedly) physically aggressive against women (some research is now doubting this claim), while women are more likely to be subtle, innocently or maliciously lurking and verbally ferocious regardless of whether they are showing support, as well as "love," for the husband, while doing so or not. Evidence, we know, points to some facts. Women can still *"love"* their husband while conspiring with others as to how to ensnare the man the spouse, while ironically, she remains in the same bed and under the same roof as him! (See case studies). Shall we call this ambivalence or mental conflict?

To these ends, let us look at further differences between men and women.

Male Characteristics

A brief biological chemistry (biochemistry) background might help us here. Men are men because of the chemicals, called hormones, which control their behaviour and appearance. In men, the principal hormone that controls their sex drive, behaviour and appearance is called testosterone. In men, all roads lead to this powerful chemical. If this chemical is taken from men, then they will become placid and gentle and possibly like a dove. This is called chemical emasculation. Their sexual spirit is gone by this removal or suppression of the hormone. Please note that the hormones that control both genders are present in men and women but at different quantities. Testosterone is greater in men and estrogens/progesterone is higher in women.

Aggressive behaviour
Men are mostly controlled by testosterone (and to a lesser extent some hormones that are found in women) which by nature gives them aggressive behaviour (along with other hormones common to both men and women called adrenaline) and puts them in an attacking mode. Men, it has been shown, speak fewer words in comparison to women. It would seem that men tend to compensate for this lack of word power by reacting to events physically. This may possibly explain, amongst others, why men are prone to accusations and allegations of assault and domestic violence in relationships. Even then, this statement on domestic violence (DV) should be taken with a pinch of salt, since there are some reports that in the USA, the rate of DV against men by women actually equals, if not surpasses, that of men against women.Certianly women make more report of DV to the authorities than men.

All said, men's aggressive nature, surely, makes them more likely to react physically than the placid woman who is more enamelled by the words of her lips. It may also be the reason why men are more likely to go to war and declare war on other nations. Remember though that most nations on earth are ruled by men.

Behaviour of men in looking for a relationship:
Taking a cue from observations that one can see in public and in research, men are usually the "aggressor" and the ones who are more likely to approach the opposite gender for sexual friendship. In the last 40 years, this supposed approach by men is being taken over by women in some countries. We should remember that the primary thing in a man's mind is his plan to "possess" the woman he fancies, no matter how many of such

women that caught his attention, and so to satisfy his primitive desire for mating. Man, except if he's well-disciplined, could use all means, even to his peril, to achieve this sexual objective. Having children is not a major or main priority to a *typical* man. If anything, children may be seen as a problem or an obstacle to his "free spirited" sexual nature. But social norms, maturity, aging process and laws constrain this masculine behaviour. In the main, we all know that man is the one who seeks out sexual friends/relationships, or converts ordinary friends to sexual friends, most often.

Behaviour in domination
Men loathe to be controlled by the opposite gender. A look around the world leadership will easily confirm this observation. This may be due to the aggressive posture and defensive consciousness of men. Men are very conscious of security matters. Therefore, anything that will alter this position is looked on with dim eyes by most men. This behaviour is also carried into relationships and intercourse. Men are known to lead and want to lead in the home; ensuring things are put in a certain proper order or "done my way." Put it this way: "Everything in its place and a place for everything," is an unspoken driven principle of conduct in most reasonable men. Man does not like to be dictated to but human-made laws and the advent of emancipation of women have tended to change this balance of power.

Sexual behaviour
Men, controlled by testosterone ---a hard-line hormone--- tend to overlook dangers and to seek pleasures wherever they can find them. In doing so, as well as being urged on by man's uncompromising attitude, he will almost always want to have his way sexually. The need for gratification is enormous. The pleasure centre in the brain can not wait for too long; it must happen soon or it must be now. Feed me with pleasure, it tends to say.

That said, the behaviour of men is under their conscious control and testosterone can not be blamed for all masculine acts that destroy social and legal boundaries. Nonetheless, men tend to or want to explore *"varieties"* or innovations of sexual processes and with *several numbers of* the opposite gender albeit at different times. This is what accounts, in my opinion, for the lack of sexual satisfaction that is seen in men. Also, this observation explains the difficulties in staying with one woman which is seen in a lot of men. Perhaps inclination for domination and sexual adventure forms the basis of adultery. As I mentioned above, the sexual adventure tends to give men satisfaction, secured in the sense of domination.

Sadly, this behaviour by men, often characterised by undue risk taking and irrationality has at times made men prone to accusations and allegations of rape and other inappropriate sexual behaviour against women. Men should therefore be aware of these important issues. In many ways, along with money and power, sex forms the Achilles' heel of a typical man.

Men and money
The majority of human beings love money as it helps us to satisfy our needs. Money for its own sake is barely useful; rather, it becomes so when it can be directed at achieving a certain purpose.

Considering the forceful nature of men and the risks that they can undertake, as well as the need for domination and the tendency to "control," there is therefore little wonder that the substantial wealth of the world is in the hands of men. Money makes men feel confident and able to put their homes and lives in order with the added security that comes with having a lot of money. They loathe anything that would put them in a position of vulnerability whereby they can not have their *say or have their way*. Intimate relationships could easily dissolve if men encounter issues that would diminish their motivation for work, sex and money-making: The triad that ultimately leads to a sense of incredible power.

Men and work
A reasonable man who is jobless but willing to work is a man who is in the position of a *wounded lion*. This is so since he may

be losing his confidence, motivation and ability to "control" things. The society is even more at risk with such a person. If a man who is able and willing to work could not find a job, he could become angry, unhappy, acting out his anger in violence, engaging in petty behaviour that is out of character, and may even become depressed. The important thing is that if the man has no work, he will feel "out of control of his domain"---home, spouse and family. He will feel very vulnerable and may view his life as being dictated to by the woman, his spouse or partner. Some may even want to commit suicide and/or be involved in criminal acts. His desire to dominate has vanished and his power of sexual prowess and to impress his spouse has been cut short. The man may thus feel worthless. At this stage he needs understanding and sympathetic help from his friends and partner. I have seen many men, in my career, in depression clinics who suffer from nothing other than joblessness and a sense of worthlessness leading up to depression.

Men and Cars and Tools for Work
I want to caution the female reader not to toy with a man's tools for his work. It may be the plumber's tool box, farmer's harvester, it may be a computer, or it may be the pen of a writer! It may also be his car. Considering the man's priority for defence, security for his family, financial domination at home and in the community, therefore, the man would certainly remove anything on his way that would stop him from achieving these objectives. A man who is losing money because of adverse weather against him would fume and be upset at his helplessness at the ferocious weather. I have seen men in agony because their farm produce is going to be damaged by torrential rain. Well, you might say, he agonises because of the likely wasted efforts that he has put into the farm. However, the extended truth is that he would have calculated the amount of money he will lose because of the disturbance.

Men: Emotion and betrayal
This varies from culture to culture. It also varies due to differences in up-bringing. Some men are emotional and some are not. Some are shy and some are not. However, one thing a

man can not stand is being embarrassed in public by his partner or spouse. On occasions such as this, emotions may be and are often subdued by the man, but his delayed anger may be palpable. The man does feel belittled and may feel that the relationship is not worth saving.

As in any reasonable human being, men are very sensitive to betrayal by spouses whom they may have trusted. I was told a story in law school by one of my teachers. A couple had been undergoing divorce; the man had negotiated to keep his marriage but the woman pressed on. The marriage was due for divorce and the lawyer or attorney had by now issued threats against the man to cooperate. In anger at the betrayal by his spouse, the man simply packed all that the attorney had asked for and emotionally "dumped" them at the attorney's office. He could no longer care less even if the marriage was to end immediately. The betrayal was disgusting to him and emotions wer running high.

Men and words
In numerical terms, men speak fewer words per day than women. Evidence has supported this. Some other works have also indicated that men and women speak nearly equally. The evidence for who is winning this "war of words" is in practice. Try living with a typical man if you are a woman and if you are a man, try living with a woman. Forget about the research for the time being. I leave that to you good people out there to judge for yourselves what the outcomes would be.

Nevertheless, the concern of this writer is in the *content and context* of these words. Men are in general more subdued in the *type or kind* of words that they say. More or less, men are more refrained in what they say. This is, women's use of words in "nagging" men takes a superior hand over men as women tend to say the words that will send the man really *mad*. Nagging, in reality, is a refined way of saying that the woman is repetitive on a subject that may (or not) have been dealt with. Women tend to say words that belittle and embarrass the man in private and in public places. This, in my view, is compensation for the laid-back nature of women (no offence please). "Nagging," as any married man can tell, may end a relationship.

A couple of years ago, I was called to dissolve a crisis which a couple had gotten themselves into. The man was suffering from bipolar disorder: a kind of mental illness. This condition could make him talk literally without end. The woman was in her early 50s and undergoing *change (menopause)*. This condition could make her irritable and hence talk and complain, even over minute things, endlessly. Their two adult children were no longer living with them.

They were having, as they had been for a while, a heated argument and none of them were ready to give in. Firestorms of words were being exchanged. "Thunder and brimstone" were being sent to each other. The atmosphere was charged. The man, now oversensitive to the woman's words, would scrutinise and take personally every word that the woman uttered. "Good morning" greetings were now being seen as a very bad omen by the man—the start of, potentially, something awful. So often, the couple would, by choice, keep each other in selective silence so as not to cause, as a friend would put it, a "Third World War!" As we all know, even in silence, actions speak louder than voices!

The man was in fear of engaging in conversation. When he did, it was really bad. The man, emboldened by mania, would shoot back with considerable and powerful words. The woman would burst into tears at the most innocent comment by the man.
In the end, I had to explain to them the various reasons (illness in the man and *"change"* in the woman) why the atmosphere was so charged. The bottom line here is that words matter and can make a man decide and act in a manner that was never associated with him. On the other hand, motivation and encouraging words from the woman can propel the man to the greatest heights ever known. Words can break or make a relationship. Words can make and unmake a home.

***

Female Characteristics

Women are in the main, controlled by *estrogens* and *progesterone*. These are two hormones or chemicals that make women look smooth, desirable and beautiful. They are also the chemicals that make them look mild-mannered and inviting. These chemicals, as I have said, are responsible for women being (in the majority), less aggressive *compared to men*. Of course, there are exceptions to these rules. Some women are the aggressors in a lot of homes. The hormones also control their "monthly period" as well as supporting pregnancy and childbirth.
Readers should note that I am not comparing men and women in this chapter. What I am pointing out here are the main features that characterise the gender, or what he or she is. Therefore, I will not be comparing what I said for men in women: like for like.

Let us look at the principal desires and acts of women

Money
Every one of us needs money, including women. Now, money is a form of power and liberation from a grip---be it that of a man or husband or of something else. There is a general perception that women "love" money. This is really a meaningless statement. What women love, is to acquire power from the man. The reasoning is possibly to liberate themselves from the man who, in their perception, is oppressing them. Therefore, women would go to any length to get the money, even if it means exchanging some biological services (sex) for it. Money, in many ways, is power and the road to liberation.

Emotion
Females are more emotional. They cry easily, shout easily, complain more often and feel cheated all the more often. Both sexes express and suppress various feelings. Men typically hold back emotions like sympathy, sadness and distress, while women suppress their feelings relating to anger and sexuality. Men and women do not differ dramatically in their immediate

reports of emotional experiences, even in contexts that are of relevant differences for men and women, some reports have suggested.

Estrogen is closely linked with women's emotional well-being. Depression and anxiety affect women in their estrogen-producing years (child-bearing age) more often than men or post-*change* women. Estrogen is also linked to mood disruptions that occur only in women – pre-menstrual syndrome for example.
What these effects mean is that an *individual woman* is *impossible to predict,* according to the online Web MD.

Law and third party intervention in a relationship
Women are more likely to use the law, the agents of the law or enforcers of the law to execute or ensure that their intentions are carried out against the man. They are more likely to call the police to intervene in domestic disputes. Sometimes this is a protective mechanism from what they might perceive as threats from the spouse or the male partner. Casual observation also shows that women, unlike men, are more likely to involve extended families, law officers and friends in their domestic affairs.

Decision making at home
"To explore decision-making in the typical American home, a Pew Research Center survey asked men and women living in couples which one generally makes the decisions in four familiar areas of domestic life. Who decides what you do together on the weekend? Who manages the household finances? Who makes the decisions on big purchases for the home? And who most often decides what to watch on television?

The survey finds that in 43% of all couples it's the woman who makes decisions in more areas than the man. By contrast, men make more of the decisions in only about a quarter (26%) of all couples. And about three-in-ten couples (31%) split decision-making responsibilities equally". This is according to Pew

Social and Demographic Trends. As we can see, it's not a man's world, in spite of everything.

Note that while this may be true in the USA, it does not hold true in the rest of the world, especially where traditional roles of gender are strictly maintained. Further, in most places on earth, religion and culture intermix. This blend of religion and culture helps to put the genders in their specific roles without blurring the biological and social responsibilities of each gender or being oppressive to women.

Caution, fear and risk-taking
Considering the laid-back effect of the hormones on women and the emotional state they may be in, women are generally lesser risk takers than men. Women are more likely to express reservations on a matter that they are not overwhelmingly certain about the outcome. These fears of uncertainty make women more cautious than men. Under the same umbrella, this caution appears to allow women to scrutinize matters more closely by weighing up, often, the adverse effects. The man, on the other hand, may actually have perceived the benefits better than the woman. Try doing some shopping with your female spouse if you are a man in order to establish the truth of this matter. The importance of this is that often this difference in perception may lead to argument and conflict in the relationship.

Women, in general, need more convincing on matters that will take money away from the family/relationship, especially if they are not certain of a return. It's all part of the risk-shy process. On the other hand, in a typical relationship, women tend to be more vulnerable to the sales gimmicks of a salesman. Do you know why? Women are quick to trust a man and to be taken in by "sweet" words.

Issues with children
Either in a traditional role or not, regardless of the geographical location on earth, women are biologically in charge and socially responsible for looking after children. This duty, it seems, can not be taken away from them as they tend to do it with enthusiasm, protecting (in most cases) the children, even to the

detriment of their spouse. In saying this, I have not considered that there are some men and women who are also dangers to the children and the family. That is not the aim of this book but there are some men and women who are threats to their children.

If these crucial differences are borne in mind in atypical relationships, there is likely to be less tension and conflict. When the individuals in a relationship are not fully aware of these issues, crisis may later ensue, which may in itself transform into the dissolution of the relationship. Once again, the objective of this book is to allow you to make up your mind on these matters.

Yearn for freedom
I have mentioned earlier that men love domination and power. I don't need to prove that. Take a look around the Presidents and Heads of States around the world. Count the numbers who are men. Take a look at the governors in the 50 states of the USA. Count the numbers who are women. Do the same for the Senate and the House of Representatives. Do the same thing for county and local governments. Finally come home and take a look at the data from *Pew*. The figures speak loud and clear about who is in charge in this world. Since the "crucible" which I mentioned at the start of this book was formed, women have been in a struggle to free themselves from the authority of men.

Women (like men) cherish their freedom and the ability to take a decision free from interference from men---albeit within the union of a marriage or even other forms of relationship. That said, this agitation for freedom is true everywhere in every culture, but is more subdued in areas outside western societies. Even in far-flung, or if you like, "primitive" societies, women take measures to free themselves from the sometimes masculine "yoke". Some women do see men as the stumbling block that needs to be removed in order for this freedom to be enjoyed to its optimum.

Thus, conflict will arise and does arise when this freedom is not forthcoming or when it's thwarted by other forces. As we shall see later in the case studies, some women will do anything, even conspiracy and murder, to ensure that their desire for free will is not obstructed by men.

The conclusion here is that women want to do what they wish, just as men are doing. The caution here is that a union will be fractured when there is no unity of decisions or if the individuals in the relationship have divergent visions as to where the relationship should be heading. This division in vision is borne out by the 50% divorce rate in the USA and 33% in the UK. Everyone is, it appears, to his or her *"tent"*----their separate ways, so to speak.

As matter of reflection, men don't like competition for power, career, profession, prestige, finance etc. in their domain. Women loathe competition for attention or any thing and person that may divert the love of their husband or partner away from them. This competitiveness and the dislike for it have led to a lot of murders and harm in the world (see the Chapter on Case Studies). There was a story of late about a prominent member of the elite group in NASA who went to a great embarrassing extent to dislodge someone who was competing with her for the love of her partner. She drove several miles and took desperate steps in the course of doing so.

On the other hand, women don't like repression, or "oppression," as some has called it. Nobody likes it, hence the "yearn for freedom" which I wrote about above. Meanwhile, men have found themselves in a difficult position, "ruling" their home without appearing to be "oppressive".

The bottom line therefore, is that as a woman; do not marry someone whom you perceive, in the short and long term, might *oppress* you. For men, you may have to distance yourself from someone who will compete with you for power in all its facets. This simple advice, which is provided on the grounds of compatibility, is frequently ignored by individuals intending on forming an intimate alliance. Remember that the aim of this book is that you can see afar from your current stand point. That is why I have made that piece of advice.

Some researchers have wondered aloud why relationships tend to flounder after the first 10 years, when each individual seems to seek their freedom with keenness. Whilst this is not an academic book, I am tempted to provide some explanations here. The reason may be that once the mission of a partnership is satisfied, it tends to be dissolved. After all, there is nothing else that is left to be achieved. Also, couples seem to be fed up of seeing each other routinely. However, this being "fed up" with each other is unlikely to be the case if the original objective had been set as a life companionship. I just mentioned these points for completion. Please forgive my lurching into academic thoughts.

"Little things" that cause irritation to partners but which can develop into serious conflict when added up

In general, when people get into relationships, especially intimate relationships, they are put to the test everyday by tiny little things wish may badly annoy them. Such little things (except when they are discussed or get resolved, almost immediately, in an honest and open non-confrontational way) may gradually aggregate into bigger and bigger issues that could threaten the survival of the relationship. Alternatively, you may just overlook them without any grudge. You may also count it as a weakness in your spouse that you may need to turn into his or her strength.

***

In both women and men

In general, life is about continuous learning until you die. Continuing a relationship, even when there is a written contract to guide you, serves as a form of permanent schooling from which no one ever graduates.

One of the things that upset couples more than any other is apparent wrong-headedness or inflexibility. For example, you may have identified a minor wrong and irritation in your partner. An example of such an irritation may be that your spouse forgets to put down the toilet seat. You have noticed this previously, and you have advised your partner or spouse against doing this, but the advice has not sunk in. This "wrong" or as someone who wrote to me called it, "silly things", soon gets repeated five times on the same day and 100 times in a month! If you do not talk about it amicably or overlook it outright or count it as a "weakness" in your spouse, it will soon merge with other irritants, such as exasperating habits, like unrelenting knuckle cracking or flatulence. This deadly blend of wrongs, if not properly managed, will soon gravitate into a crisis.

I heard of a story which I found very interesting. A married man noticed that his wife came to bed at about midnight, even though there were no problems between them, and that she remains in the home all these times of the night. The man went to bed early. However, the property had stairs. While the man would be sleeping, the woman would go up and down the stairs, stamping her feet on the floor. She was not doing this intentionally. The noise from her stamping would wake the man up. He initially, at the onset of the marriage, thought it was a chance occurrence. He called his wife and told her about his concerns. The next day and many days after, the same irritation, waking up and discussion took place. It continued until the man realised it was never going to stop, and not only did he just get used to it, he stopped going to bed before his wife so that she could fall asleep first.

Here is another example. A man likes cooking as much as his wife does. Now there are two garbage bags in the house. One bag was for kitchen waste and the other for other household waste. If the specific items were not put in the right bag, the collector will not collect them. The wife advised the husband of this and he appeared to take notice. He actually did not. He simply mixed up the garbage and household bags until the collector refused to collect them. In spite of this, the husband continued the mix-up until the wife decided that she would personally collect all garbage from the man and put them in the right bag!

What do you say to a snoring by one spouse? --- A biological habit that refuses to go away, yet you have little control over it, if any, although this irritation disturbs your sleep so much. What if he always likes to leave the window open in winter against your wishes? What would you do?

Human beings, you may have noticed, are very complex. Even if you happen to overcome a given habit, there is not a single assurance that a new one may not develop. You learn and teach everyday! That's the odd beauty of matrimony: it's full of tough times that no one can ever prepare you for. All said, those are the things that collectively give wealth to your life.

***

CHAPTER NINETEEN
Sample of Marriage/Partnership Agreement

"Love is blind, but marriage restores its sight."
Georg C. Lichtenberg

I need not reiterate that the marriage rate is falling and the divorce rate is going up. Romance and love are, in most cases, not worth the effort that one puts in, to verbally express it. "Till death do us part," no longer means anything substantial. At the same time, in the wider society, crime rates are going up as divorce rates also go up, though not at the same quantity. But there is a link. Human beings in general hate to be caged by rules and regulations. We don't like boundaries, as we like to do what we want at any given time. But, without these boundaries, there would be chaos in society. As individuals, if we fail to put our behaviour in check, we risk running into troubles. Law therefore exists in order to instil discipline, orderliness and peace in society and between human interactions.

This fundamental reason is the foundation why marriage or prenuptial agreements make a lot of sense. For your information, whether you agree or not, your marriage is based on an invisible contract. What you are doing by constructing a marriage contract is to make this "invisible" contract clearly visible. All our conduct as human beings with each other is based on one rule or another, so a marital agreement is no different.

For the interest of readers who may be apprehensive about any form of agreement, and in particular a pre-marital agreement, please relax as I attempt to put your mind at rest.

First I need to deal with an urgent issue of terminology. The terms "pre-nup", "prenuptial agreement", "pre-marriage" or "marriage contract" all mean *essentially* the same thing. They refer to the agreement that you enter into with your fiancé/fiancée before (pre-nup/pre-marriage) you become spouses or before you get married. The agreement serves the purpose of defining and stating what you have agreed about, in terms of management of the marriage or relationship.

On thing or difference to note though, is that a "pre-nup" is before marriage and takes effect on the date of marriage. If you sign it after your marriage, whereby it's called a marriage agreement, it takes effect immediately. Also, it is a legal document. This is very important to note. Therefore the reader should draw strength from that fact these terms refer to the *same* kind of documents. It is true that there has been a lot of public discussion about pre-nups, especially in recent times in divorces that involve high- profile individuals. Despite this, the value and importance of this crucial document still eludes wider individual consideration.

***

What is the importance of a "pre-nup" agreement?
First, a prenuptial agreement is a sure way to open up crucial communication with your potential spouse or partner. The significance of this is that it's a foundation in which your future desires, intentions and expectations are laid. It is important to commit these desires and expectations to a written document so as to avoid the defeat of these intentions. Besides, it is a mutually agreed "mission statement" which commits the couple to what will shape their future behaviour.

What does a pre-nup do?
A pre-nup goes as far as or to the extent you may want it to go. Often, it covers the protection of your interests in as diverse areas as your monetary and non-monetary contributions to the union. The assets that are covered include, for example, your pension, savings, and landed property which you may have had before the union was formed. The pre-nup helps to protect inheritances and other assets which you may have owned before your marriage. It also helps to provide for any children who are in the relationship, either whom you have had before the marriage or will have eventually during this marriage.

Looking into the future, a pre-nup will help protect your non-monetary contribution to the marriage. An example of this includes when you give up your career to stay at home to care for the home front or looking after the children. This is not a retirement but a choice by the spouses especially if they want to save cost on child rearing. In that case, you are actually contributing to the marriage. This kind of "service" had come before the British Courts and has now been settled as a contribution to the matrimonial income.

Further, in death, you are certain (while still alive) of what you will get and to whom you will give it, if you have a will. This may help your estate to avoid difficult and expensive litigation. A pre-nup also protects you from inheriting the debts of your spouse which may have been acquired before marriage. These and many more, are some of the benefits to derive from, and are also the function of, a pre-nup agreement.

***

How do you go about it?
Ideally, a marriage contract should be discussed well before the marriage takes place in a relaxing atmosphere devoid of argument and acrimony. Be prepared to go into details and specifics as the relationship gets more serious. You should be free to express your concerns and expectations. You should also be free to discuss your goals and life ambitions, family, children and the role of each person. Be free to initiate the discussion openly and directly. Once again, the principles of cordiality and agreement come into the discussion.

All in all, it will be a serious mistake to put off a pre-nup agreement until a later period when things may have gone too far in the relationship. Note though that a marriage contract or pre-nup as the case may be, may help the two of you respect each other's rights so that you can avoid disputes that lead to trouble.

Territorial recognition and differences: Legal power of the agreement

In Britain, in the main, the courts may look upon it under the principles of a contract, especially if the individuals have taken independent legal advice. In other countries such as Canada and the USA, provided both spouses have obtained independent legal advice and the agreement is reasonably "fair," it would be enforced by a court if one spouse has tried to pay no heed to the agreement. However, contracts that are manifestly unreasonable to either person may be set aside or varied by the court, particularly if no independent legal advice was obtained prior to its execution.

Some things will not be enforced by the courts: Limitations
With or without an agreement on paper, the law already makes certain obligations compulsory for the individuals in the wedlock, which cannot be excluded in a contract. Also, a contract to be childless, or to end the marriage after a certain period of time, may not be imposed in any court. In addition to that, one major advantage of this agreement is that it offers some degree of certainty to the parties. And the agreement is often used by people who have experienced a first marriage, as they are more realistic considering their experience.

In effect, needless to say, this kind of agreement represents a failure of the larger society, as represented by the various governments to stop the tide of human disappointments in marriage. It reflects the apprehension in people about being let down by partners or spouses. To avoid this disappointment, a private contract such as this is called for between intending parties.

Agreement can be reviewed
Certain issues can always be reviewed by the court. An example of this is the care of children, where children should live and the support to give the children. Also, if you and your partner agree, you can alter or change the agreement, but it must be signed by the two of you and be witnessed by a third party.

A sample of an agreement, below, is proposed for illustration only. You may use this sample as a guide to what you intend to achieve, taking into consideration the laws of your territory or state. Similarly, you may modify it to reflect your religious and moral views. Remember that human beings will, generally, not obey a law or rule unless there is a severe enforceable penalty for disobedience. Therefore, do not forget to incorporate this idea into your marriage agreement.

If you are attempting to create a cohabitation agreement, ensure that it covers ownership of property and, specifically, the care of children.

In the agreement below, you can strike out and replace or redraft any part that is repetitive or does not apply to you. It is crucial that you both must have obtained legal advice.

***

<u>Sample Marriage Contract</u>
(Note: This is for guidance only. You should obtain independent legal advice so as to formulate a contract that suits your particular situation).

SECTION A

Whereas the parties/spouses/persons to this agreement/contract desire to marry under the laws of the State/Country of _____, and now wish to set forth in advance of their marriage the rights and privileges that each person will have in the property of the other in the event of death, separation, divorce, or other circumstance which results in the dissolution of their marriage: Now therefore...

Or

I. I as the BRIDE

Full Name:
Father's Name:
Mother's Name:
Date and Place of Birth:
Marital Status: (never married / divorced / widowed)
Address:

and

II. I as the BRIDEGROOM

Full Name:
Father's Name:
Mother's Name:
Date and Place of Birth:
Marital Status: (never married / divorced / widowed / married)
Address:

...stated here as Future Wife and Future Husband, hereby agree, as follows:

> Future Husband and Future Wife consider marriage in the foreseeable future and desire to create their individual and collective rights and responsibilities as regards each other's earnings and property and the income and property that may be obtained, either individually or jointly, in the course of the marriage.

B.

Future Husband and Future Wife have made a total and whole disclosure to each other of all of their financial possessions and burdens which are further outlined in the attached and accompanying Financial Statements, attached herewith as Appendix I and II.

C.   Unless as otherwise stated beneath, Future Husband and Future Wife relinquish the following rights or privileges:

i) Acquisition of parts or whole in the other party's estates upon their death.

ii) The maintenance of spouse, both provisional and enduring.

iii) The division of the individual's property and estates of the individuals and signatories to this contract whether at presently held or acquired in the future.

iv) Acquisition of part or in whole of the pension, profit division or other retirement accounts of the other party.

v). Acquisition of part or in whole of an increase in value during the matrimony of the separate property or estates of the parties.

vi). Any claims relating to the period when the parties cohabited.

D. (Please see the relevant exceptions which are set out below)

E. {Further terms of this contract are set out here. These can be in respect of children raised from other cultures, households and previous relationships, morality, religion, dissolution, the benefits to be derived from the relationship

Other things to consider but not in the order in which its written here.

Shared sexual congress
How do you want to conduct your sex encounters? Don't shy away from very important though sensitive issues such as this.

Shared rearing of children
What do you consider as discipline? What constitute abuse? What kind of education, religion and culture should they have? These and many more should be well discussed to avoid future conflict.

Financial obligations
etc. By all means, talk about this now, thrashing your responsibilities and also who cares for the other in times of trouble?

F.   Both Future Husband and Future Wife are being represented by different and independent legal advisers who they have chosen of their own volition.

G.   Both Future Husband and Future Wife have individual and sufficient income to support and provide for their own needs. The parties (husband and wife) agree that each shall be responsible for any tax liabilities associated with their separate properties
.

J.   In the event of separation or divorce, the parties shall have no right against each other for division of property existing of this date.

K.   This contract represents the entire contract of the parties. It may only be modified in writing validly executed by both Future Husband and Future Wife and witnessed accordingly.

L.   Should it be determined that any section or clause of this contract is in conflict with applicable laws and therefore unenforceable, such section shall not invalidate the rest of the contract so that the rest shall remain valid.

M.   This contract is made in keeping with the laws of/ England and Wales/the State of_____. Any dispute as regards its execution will be determined by reference to the laws of England and Wales/that State.

N.   This contract will take immediate effect upon the formalization of the parties' marriage.

I hereby confirm that I have read and understood the terms of this contract and I give my signature below in execution of the contract.

----------------------   ----------------
Future Husband   Future Wife

Sign name/date----------------
Witness

End of the Contact

_____

***

Moral standards which may be considered and included in the agreement:
Prohibitions such as for adultery, dangerous behaviour, abortion, assault against a party, criminal behaviour, ejection from matrimonial home, habitual alcohol misuse or drug abuses, should all be provided for in the agreement.

In addition, most agreements will spell out the remedies for breaches and severe penalties for the breaches.

Also, the agreement should provide for possible resolution and reconciliation. If it all fails, the agreement should provide a route for decent separation and divorce in keeping with the religious or secular terms that you have agreed upon.

In situations that relate to co-habiting parties, the agreement is tailored to be more individualistic. It reflects the recognition to each other that the cohabitants have a non-binding lifestyle in the absence of a written and enforceable agreement. The agreement should spell out who pays for what. For example: should there be a specific contribution per month or per week for telephones, food, electricity and so forth? But such petty things as who washes the dishes or cleans the property should not form part of the agreement.

The basic sample agreement that I have provided here can be modified to reflect the wishes of the cohabitantss. In any case, I would expect that intending parties will talk to their attorneys or solicitors before signing an agreement such as this.

It might be worth remembering the caution of Stephen Covey, that, *"All broken relationships can be traced back to broken agreements,"* regardless of whether it was a written, implied agreement or not.

***

SECTION II

Platonic Relationships
(Non-Sexual Relationships)

"You cannot be lonely if you like the person you're alone with." Wayne W. Dyer

CHAPTER TWENTY
Friendships
"There is no greater form of relationship than a friend."
Dr. Joel Akande

Friendships are different from intimate relationships that involve intercourse. For a start, there is no "contract" to be respected as in marriage. Friendship is a loose association with another person, presumably of like mind. Secondly, there are, strictly speaking, no children to look after. This is not withstanding married couples who divorce and later become "friends," albeit without intercourse. Therefore, a friend is someone who *shares your values*. A friend should ideally be someone who shares your pain and, sometimes, your gains, worries, tasks, failings and successes. It is very difficult to find a true friend.

Therefore, it is crystal clear that to have a friend who will be there always, with you in thick and thin, you must choose your friend carefully. On some occasions, it takes time for friendship to mature. At other times, you can find a quick friend and the relationship may last for a short while. It's still friendship nonetheless.

There is something that a friend does like no other relationship: friends can influence you to do extremely good acts or "friends" can induce you to do terrible, as well as morally repugnant and legally revolting, deeds. There is no middle way in friendship, for the relationship is about exerting influence on you. You can either tilt to the right or bend to the left. There is no middle ground. If you do not agree with a friend, he will reject you and shrewdly or violently call off the friendship. Meanwhile, the agreement might be for good or for bad. In truth, a friend is someone who adds positive value to you, rather than devaluing you and taking your credibility away.

There is only one option in friendship: you *agree* and flow together or you do not agree and then part ways.

Unlike, marriage, there may not be a need to go to court to untie what was tied under "oath." There is no oath to take in law in public places, such as the marriage registry or in churches. Friends, unlike co-habitation or marriage, are sometimes made casually, by accident and by chance. In intimate relationships, such as marriage, there is a gradual and steady understanding of each other. Unlike marriage, friendship can be called off at any time, even without notice!

***

Now, the question that arises is, *Why do you need a friend?*

I have mentioned previously that not every one of us can stand intimate relationships. The truth is we are not all made for intimate associations. Some of us are, by nature, going to be decently single, either by choice or by our personal circumstances such as religion, illness, deformity or for other reasons. Whatever may be the reason, one thing is also certain: not every one of us as men and women will have our own children and form a family.

Yet, I said at the outset of this book that none of us can survive in this world in isolation. You will need someone to lean on at some point. Even if you have your own family, they can still fail you and your children can desert you. A wife can desert the husband and a husband does sometimes desert his wife.

In scenarios such as these, who do you bend over to? Whose shoulder can you cry on at your time of most need? Who can you call in the dead of the night to help you in the midst of winter or in the rainy season when all hope is nearly lost. Who can you call when families can not reach you or when you feel let down by those whom you look up to as siblings or as husband or wife?

When money is running out of your hands and your children and wife (or husband) is asking you to do something in the midst of nothing, who do you run to?

When you have been retrenched from your job in the middle of "re-organization" of your company and your life is on the edge, who do you call for advice?

Think about it, when all you had worked for disappeared or a big money lender had seized your property and your family had been taken hostage by an economic downturn, who do you call for support?

Imagine you were incarcerated due to one unwise act or another. Acquaintances have deserted you, trusted associates have dissociated themselves from you, and then you remember there is another who would not. The person would even go through the tunnel of the thickest of darkness with you. What do you call such a person? Alternatively, perhaps, the most embarrassing situation has befallen you. Help from other sources has disappeared. But there is a stranger who listens to you and helps you out. How can such an individual be explained?

***

Who is a friend?
The English proverb describes such an individual as "a friend in need is a friend indeed".

Therefore, a friend is someone who, in spite of risks to his personal life, be it financial, job, family, physical security or any other form of risk, stands by you in the days of your misfortune. A friend is someone who shares in your pain and values. A friend is not someone who deserts you in time of your greatest need, be it physical or emotional. Your friend is not someone who knows your inner secrets, but chooses to conspire, to your chagrin, with others to embarrass and ridicule you. Your friend is not someone who laughs at you in public, with others when you are there or not, but sympathises with you in your privacy. A friend, I mean your friend, is not someone who supposedly works with you but secretly plots to unseat you when you turn your back. The English people describe such individuals as, "a green snake in the green grass."

Therefore a friend is someone who is openly honest and always tells you the truth even if you don't like to hear it. He tells it anyway: the truth. He tells you that you are falling when you are falling, and does not tell you that you are firmly on your feet, when you are indeed lying flat on your face.

A friend is therefore someone who adds constructive value to the life of his friend. A friend is someone who enhances the quality of life of his friend and shares in his vision.

A friend is no longer your friend when you both enter a joint enterprise to cause harm. Such association is best described as a bunch of *criminals* with a joint vision to obtain their hearts' desire. Such a person is not making you a better person but gradually *destroying* your future and leading you into trouble. That is not a friend. Such a person is *hostile* to your future and your very existence. In such a case, you *have taken an enemy as a friend.*

Here is why. I have seen teenagers and other age groups who came to my clinic, or whom I have met in the course of my work in prison and other secure centres. The vast majority of them came to that position because of failed family relationships leading up to a lack of proper guidance for them. Alternatively, they came because they had been affected by the use or misuse of illegal substances. As a matter of curiosity, I have often asked how they got into drugs in the first instance. The response can be staggering: "my mate gave it to me," or, "my father was an alcoholic," or, "my mother was a drug user." From these, one can deduce one thing: bad association can get you into real trouble. Bad friendship can lead you into a big problem. Bad communication, they say, corrupts good manners.

***

How do you know you have a friend?
You have a friend when the person does not *pretend* to be what he is not. Neither does he or she try to pull a fast one on you. A friend will be truthful and sympathetic even to his own discomfort. A friend will almost always find ways to

compromise and meet you midway when his desire and yours clash. The same can be said for time sharing. A friend would want to spend time with you. A friend will almost always defend you until you prove him wrong! A good friend will confide in you and would expect you to keep a secret.

A "friendship" whereby the bond is tilted in one direction and in dependency may not really be friendship in the true sense.
Such friendship will nearly always bring some burden on one individual.

How do you choose a friend?
A friend can be anyone: white, brown, black, pale, blond, ginger, tall, short etc. He or she could be a male, a female, a child or an adult: a friend. That person should be someone to whom you will not cause any harm. An individual who will not cause you harm either. A friend can be from anywhere. Frankly, your friend may, at first, not appear as angelic, to your disappointment. He or she may be the most smelly or dirtiest person around, when you first meet. But the person is a human being: a friend in the making.

Most friends are chosen or most individuals become friends when *help* is exchanged. This is a crucial yardstick to measure whether a friendship is about to be established. I have never seen nor heard of two individuals who became friends without a preceding act of help being exchanged between the two individuals.

Let me re-state that in a short form: *the foundation of a friendship is that a help, care, attention or something that adds value to one has been offered by one of the parties to the other, prior to the friendship developing.*

This is especially so and such help is often valued when the person who receives help is going through a time of distress.

On the other hand, a *gratuitous gifting* which is not asked for may also cause friendship to develop. Again, this is a kind of help being exchanged. Has is not been said that, "your gifts will make way for you." It may be friendship or a favour that you will need to render in return. The basic truth remains that offers of *help* always precede friendship.

Still, even if help is offered from one person to another, that alone does not make them friends. The key thing is that the individuals must share an enhancement of *values and providing help* towards anything that binds or will them together for the common good.

The other important factor to consider is that you have found a friend when you have someone who can *share time and dialogue* with you in an atmosphere of warmth, jokes and seriousness. The individual must be free to discuss issues of concern in confidentiality with you, knowing that your heart is a fortress for keeping private matters and a stronghold for holding secrets.

You have found friend, a pearl, when you call at odd times and he rises to your call. You may choose such individuals as friends.

***

What should you do when your friend leads you into trouble? How do your get rid of bad friends?

Pretenders as friends may get you in deep water to your great dislike. But you need not always get rid of such friends. This may be one of the human weaknesses that have shown up in such a person. However, if you continue to get into trouble with such friends, it may be prudent to consider the option of getting rid of the friendship.

The answer to this question may appear to be as obvious as, "just get rid of him or her." It is not that simple. There are friends who would not go away even if you no longer need nor want them. There are some "friends" who would also plot to harm you if you dare attempt to get rid of them. They are prepared to spill the beans of your secrets in the open after merely a slight disagreement with them. The important thing is that these kinds of people were, in truth, never your friends to start with. They were snakes lurking in the green grass ready to strike at you. To avoid people like this is to choose friends carefully and to separate the trees from the woods.

Yet, there are genuine individuals who would understand your needs, and apologise for the offence, and then gradually disappear into the mist of this world---never to be seen again.

Now, to get rid of an unhelpful friend: gently say so, clearly and without acrimony or bitterness. Alternatively, gradually show a lack of interest in his/her affairs. Also, you could change location, although this is likely to be an expensive option. It may be worth it in the end. My principle toward such people is: "If you don't move away from me, I will move away from you, before you cause me further damage".

On the other hand, if life and property are at risk, you may need to take serious security measures to ensure your safety. Consider the option of reporting illegitimate activities to the police and distancing yourself from breaking the law. Remember that friends can mislead you into big troubles.

***

How many friends can I have?
Frankly, it is better to have no friends at all than to have one thousand friends who cause you to stumble. On the other hand, you may have a friend who would mean more than a thousand troublesome "friends." There is no limit to the number of friends. However, it is not the number that counts; it is the quality of true and honest friends that matter. Remember, you will be defined by the friends that you keep. Again, the British have a description for it. They say, "Show me your friend, and I will tell who you are." This is important, as you will necessarily be a reflection of your friends. Why would you be a friend to someone who could drag you through the mud? A friend is, in the end, someone who is your reflection after all. Remember, no other relationship is greater than friendship. In all, here is the counsel of a clever man, Leo F. Buscaglia, on this matter:

"Never idealize others. They will never live up to your expectations. Don't over-analyse your relationships. Stop playing games. A growing relationship can only be nurtured by genuineness". End of the matter.

CHAPTER TWENTY ONE
Children, Siblings and Extended Family Relationships

"You don't choose your family. They are God's gift to you, as you are to them." Desmond Tutu

Earlier, I mentioned that, no matter where we turn as individuals, you are in one form of relationship or another. At home, at work, on the street and in many other places, you are in relationships that are sometimes governed by invisible rules. One such relationship that you never made yourself are the family relationships. You just found yourself in it as a member of the family. Now, let us look at some family relationships.

Parent/Guardian and Children Relationships

The parent or guardian and children relationship is uniquely different from any other type of relationship. There are three reasons why this is so. First, the *child never made a decision* to belong to the parent in the first instance, as far as human knowledge can discern. The child was chosen instead. Even if the child did choose his/her family, as in cases where social services might place a child in care and the child might, just might, express some preferences, there is no guarantee that the view and choice of the child will prevail in such a placement.

This means that it is the parent or guardian and in some cases, representatives of the government, via the social services, who, in the final analysis, choose to have the child. The vulnerable child finds himself or herself in an environment in which she or he is put. He has had no choice in the matter. He or she does what he/she is told and possibly acts in the manner that she or he may be directed. This is what gives rise to the second point. The relationship is based on *trust*. It is overwhelmingly a trusting relationship on the part of the child, who believes and trusts all information and acts that the parent/guardian may bring or direct.

The third point follows from the earlier two reasons. That is to say, the relationship between parent or guardian and children is one of dependency, in which the young person not only trusts but also depends on the adult guardian and parent for safety, security, defence, instruction, guidance and provisions of life essentials.

Sadly, it's on the foundation of this trust and reliance that the abuse of a child can arise.

However, abuse will only take place the moment the parent or guardian, in some strange circumstances, may have lost sight of the *value of the child*. Once a person loses sight of the value of a thing, or is not aware of its inherent value, the thing may become an object to be abused. Someone once said, when human beings do not understand the value of something, they will abuse it. It's no less true in the case of children.

Strictly speaking, often, the child has no choice in many of his circumstances and therefore can not be held responsible for the errors and outcomes in a relationship in which he or she had no say at its formation.

There is another important point which is noteworthy of discussion here. Thus, all I have said under relationships involving intimacy is not applicable to parent-child relationships. Under the law, even under moral codes in many cultures, a child can not form binding sexual relations with an adult. We all know that such a relationship is repugnant to any reasonable person, apart from it also being illegal. Such a relationship will amount to sexual exploitation and it adds up to abuse.

As a result, the responsibility is on the adult to protect the growing and innocently vulnerably person.

***

Why would you want to have a relationship with a child?
Parents, naturally, have a relationship with their children. It is a natural bond that comes with parenthood. The parenthood can be one that comes with natural biological birth as parents. It does not matter if the birth occurred in marriage, cohabitation or from a "one night stand". So long as at least one of the parents made up his or her mind to have intercourse, then such person should be held responsible for producing the child. Alternatively, in modern times, sex is no longer required, one hundred percent, before you have a child. It can be by means of a test tube baby. Well, hold it, cloning is also a possible route for having a child, but this is currently an illegal means.

Parenthood can also come from adoption of a child. It may also come via fostering a child, no matter how long or how short such a relationship may be. Those people who decide to bring a child into this world have a duty and responsibility towards the child in what is termed legally as parental responsibility.

Therefore, for parents, without them realising it, they are forming a relationship with a potential child the moment they make their minds up to bring a child into this world.

***

Why do you want to have children?
Only individuals can tell for what reason, on earth, they want to bring children into this world. I have often wondered why anyone on earth would want children. Most parents, whom I have spoken to, have not had a reason or purpose for having children. They say it's a biological duty. A call by instinct, they state. No need to reason, they tell me. It means, we are embarking on a mission without a purpose. Are we therefore surprised that the world is full of children who have no purpose or direction and therefore become targets of abuse?

Even at that, one can only make some guesses as to why people have children if one takes a scientific look at the actions of parents and human beings in general. Here are some:

Such reasons might include what most people have cited as their reasons, the need to continue their lineage in this world. That means they want their name, blood, genes etc. to continue in this world. Sadly, this may be cut short in future generations if the child decides not to continue the perpetuation of such lineage.

The second reason why some people would form a relationship with a child is that they might want company, someone to talk to and to share time with. This also means such children may, when they grow, help on the farm or in trades that the parent or guardian may currently or in the future be engaged in. Unfortunately, most children will leave their homes as soon as they reach adulthood, or when they go away for schooling.

In some cultures, bizarre as it may seem, parents have children for the main purpose of making money out of them later, either when they are in childhood or when they are able to be "traded" as a commodity in marriage. Such use can be in forced labour or as sex objects. Are we not living witnesses to a world that sells or "traffics" children for money and prostitution? The issue here is that millions of parents have no plan, not least a credible purpose, for having children!

Yet, some parents are looking for children who will take care of them when they (parents) become infirm in old age or earlier. Still, some have a point to prove that they are biologically sound and do not want to be seen as failing in their biological reproductive function. This is pathetic, as this aim may conflict with the true intentions of the individual. I have seen parents before who set out to have children without a shred of intention to keep the children. They simply wanted to prove a point. On delivery, such children are taken into care. What is the point of having children who are likely to be abused or discarded and who may end up in a mental health institution or prison on account of childhood instability?

There are some, for religious reasons, who are just compelled to have children. They can not stop until they are, either by overuse, death or old age, compelled to stop.

Also, some individuals, out of indulgence or negligence during intercourse, have a product of their actions without the intention to do so. I have seen depressed individuals who fall into this "unwanted, one night stand" child category. No trace of their parents. No siblings. They are unwanted. They describe themselves as a "waste product", or "a mistake": they say that is what they are.

Most of the children in the last three categories will either be abused, depressed or abuse others, and they achieve little in their lives. It may be a combination of all of these.

If I could therefore sum this up, it means the majority of parents want children for reasons of money or care. Some have no clue. Either way, it amounts to self-preservation and selfish reasons for having children.

What is the purpose of a child or children?
A child, like every other human being, on earth, has only one material, as opposed to spiritual, purpose: *Productivity*. This is a combination of *reproduction* and *economic* productivity. But, there are times for each of these. There are also set times for the combination of these in order to achieve the optimal effect. If the child is rushed to be productive too soon, it may become exploitative and illegal, and the child may break down mentally or physically. Too late, children who are now adults become less productive. For the sake of certainty, a person is at their peak of productivity (reproduction and economic) from 22-35 for the former an 18-65 years of age for the latter.

While children remain, they give reassurance to the parents as the future of the parents. Also, children are good company if they are well brought up and if they are well behaved.

***

The joy of relationships with children
Children can give joy to their parents and guardians in many ways. Not only as good company, they are also smart at perceiving what parents may not consider as important, or what

parents may not perceive. In so doing they may save the lives of the family. Children, when they are much younger, to some may form a crowd in the home, if they are many, and so give the home liveliness with their noise and vigorous exercises. They are good at encouraging parents and adults to reach into their greater depths, such as asking parents to tell stories and to do incredible things that parents and guardians would otherwise not do. Children can make parents laugh and be comical by virtue of their words and acts. They do ask funny, sometimes bizarre, questions. In that regard, they create happiness and help drive moodiness and loneliness away. All these advantages come at a high price: the price of caring for them!

***

The danger of forming relationships with children
Children are extremely vulnerable. They trust and obey the carers, parents and guardians. They are therefore at the risk of being exploited by cruel adults. There are recorded stories, all over the world, of parents and guardians who exploit their children sexually and physically. There are also credible stories of adults exploiting the children of other people. This can take the form of sexual abuse, but it can also be physical abuse.

If you form too close a relationship with a child who is not yours, you are at risk of being accused of many crimes, not least sexual and physical abuse, regardless of the truth of the accusation. Some readers will remember that prominent pop stars have fallen into disrepute on account of this. Therefore, caution is required in forming relationships with children, needless to say.

That is not to say that all close relationships end in abuse. No, not so. There are good carers, teachers, guardians and professionals who are in impeccable relationships with children.

I have already directed my attention to the issue of child abuse which unfortunately is a global issue (under the Chapter on Abuse of Relationships). I do this because this is a relationship issue. Also, children in-between two adults in a relationship (as in cohabitation or marriage) may become an innocent "stumbling block" to the relationship and may therefore be subjected to abuse by either of the adults in the relationship. As a matter of rule, most abused children are in relationships with someone whom they know.

Sadly, there are also child-to-child abuses. All said, the burden of responsibility still lies with adults and guardians to prevent such devious occurrences.

Relationships between siblings
Apart from the relationship that exists between the children and parents, to the majority of us, the relationship that may appear as eternal and seemingly so close is the one that exists between one sibling and another: that is to say, for example, the relationship between brother-sister or sister-sister or brother-brother. In some sense, it may even be closer than the relationship that exists between one parent and a child. In others, a sibling relationship is a direct competitor to a relationship that involves sexual intimacy.

In fact, in some families and cultures, because of this competition, matrimony may be divided if one parent prefers to show greater preference in the relationship with one child as against his/her partner/spouse/cohabitant. I have seen in practice cases where the wife/mother in a family became upset because the man/husband/father had devoted more time to the offspring than to the wife. On such occasions, the wife may say, while seething with subdued anger: "He doesn't touch me any more... His attention is now on his children." Similarly, the man may also become unhappy if the wife shows more care and attention to the children at the expense of the husband/father. The family dynamics, as we call it, may become fractured as a result of the imbalance.

***

Why is sibling relationship important?
The reason for this is not, by any stretch of imagination, far-fetched. First, the children may have been brought up at about the same time so that they have similar beliefs and morality as well as views about life. This is a plus in comparison to their own parents who were certainly raised differently; siblings have somebody to relate to who shares similar views as theirs. For example, identical twins and non-identical twins are most likely to be raised in the same household.

Secondly, true biological siblings come from similar genetic (at least from one parent) pools and thus have a common heritage and identity.

The importance of all these is that, sibling relationships, from practical experience, continue even when their parents have aged and died. Siblings often realise this much later (than much younger years) in early adulthood or when one of the parents has died suddenly. This is even truer, and may come as a shock, if the parents have not emphasized earlier on the need for closeness amongst the siblings.

With this come the greatest benefits of sibling relationships: *trust and loyalty*, which are perhaps the strongest benefits, especially if the siblings see each other in the light of *friendships*. That is, if the siblings have seen each other as friends (see chapter on friendships), then they can trust and be loyal to each other.

Thus, siblings, just as in any relationship, do influence each other for good or for bad. Siblings do have different genetic make-up, except in identical twins. They also have different personalities, ambitions and desires. These differences are what may help one sibling influence other ones. One sibling might encourage others in good deeds, such as schooling, to behave well and to be obedient.

Also, siblings do "plot" to get things done. This "plotting" or cooperation, if it happens in early childhood, might be to get some toys or material things from the parent. If it works well into their adulthood, they can be very successful as trusting partners or friends in business.

Perhaps it is obvious to say that siblings do learn skills from one another. In fact, there are some claims that, children are very good at teaching their siblings skills.
Personally, I have put this principle into use with great effect. I would, for example, teach the senior child something and then ask him to teach the junior while I observe. It is a method of entrenching learning and cooperation in both junior and senior children.

***

Problems with sibling relationships
In spite of the fact that siblings come from the same or similar genetic pool, they are still human beings with different identities. They may have similar or different desires and intensions, even amongst identical twins. These desires and intentions may come into conflict at some point. It may be so in early childhood as one sibling makes innocent efforts to ensure self-preservation in a benign way. The love and care which one sibling has for another may, for a temporary period, be set aside. This kind of behaviour may lead to some "fights". Any parents who have had children (even when they are not all theirs) could attest to this observation. The reassurance is that it does not last long. They soon make up and continue where they left off, before the fight. This "fight" may sometimes be verbal or it could be physical too. The truth is that siblings at ages before 11-15 years know that they have nowhere to go and therefore no choice but to play with anyone who is close to them. They have to make up as soon as possible after fighting.

Also, siblings in this age, rarely bear malice and grudges against each other. Therefore, pain and disappointments are forgiven and forgotten with ease. In my career, I have seen only very few instances where childhood disagreements carried on into adulthood. Another major cause of sibling tension is when one or both parents show unbalanced love and affection for one child over and above the other. A child may thus feel alienated and unloved.

Psychologically, these feelings may be carried on into adulthood and it is a worrisome thing if this happens amongst siblings. I have seen this occur in my clinics, whereby a depressed person may ruminate over the fact that he/she was not as loved as the others in the family. Some have called themselves, "the black sheep of the family," referring to their isolation as well as the lack of love they have suffered in their family.

Siblings may also actively seek the favour and love of the parents. The other siblings may not be as active. On such occasions, the parents will need to manage this carefully. Take, for example,, a disabled child among four children. Obviously, more attention will be directed at the disabled child. But, the other children may be innocently jealous for not receiving equal attention.
Therefore, the advice to parents is that they should consider, carefully, the need to balance and share "love" fairly in the family, so as to avoid future damage to the emotions of one particular child or another.

How the family way of life shapes a child's and siblings' behaviour
Children learn by observation and by direct instruction. We all do the same, even as adults. Therefore, both good, bad and criminal behaviour of parents, and the behaviour of other siblings, will influence the children and the siblings too.

***

Effect of siblings on their parents' relationship
Siblings may strengthen or weaken the parents' relationship. If, for example, you listen and act on rumours, feedback and other half-truths from one sibling, which are directed against the other parent or other sibling, it may cause severe disharmony in the family. The advice would be that information such as this should be confirmed, be dealt with and managed properly.

The downsides of sibling relationships
One major characteristic of the relationship between siblings is that there is no legal contract between them. If there is a "tie in" at all, it is cultural and social. While it may be socially and culturally odd to sever a tie with siblings, there is no reason why it can not be so, legally. Severance, though, of such ties may also be frowned at, on religious grounds. At least, it is a relationship that is also based on trust, mutual benefits, dependency on each other as well as the "cause no harm" principle. In reality, as the readers may have noticed in the news, brothers and sisters can do strange things.

I have mentioned good things that siblings can do to each other, such as teaching and empowering skills. They can also do bad things to each other and in cooperation against outsiders. First, siblings can be so jealous of each other to the extent of inflicting injuries on the other. In early childhood this is easy to manage, as the parents can impose rules and boundaries on the siblings without taking sides in the matter. Matters become more difficult in adolescence by which stage outsiders have influence on their lives.

Have we not heard of one sibling sexually and physically abusing the other? It is there in the news if you search and listen.

What about *joint enterprise* of bad behaviour by siblings? In case you have missed some, there are lots of studies which have shown that having a criminal father or brother may influence the other siblings into criminal behaviour. This is not an academic book, but was it to be so, I could have cited one hundred examples to convince you, the reader, that siblings can join hands to commit crimes, or a sibling can induce, aid and abet the other to commit crimes. This kind of behaviour may be an attempt at self-preservation or an attempt at preserving the life of the other sibling.

***

Why then are sibling relationships relevant to the reader?
First, as I have mentioned earlier in this book, you are not an island or beacon of loneliness, even though you may decide to live a lonely life. You will still come across people who may influence your life. Such influences begin in childhood with your siblings (if you have any), at home. But you can also be managed by your sibling if he or she is responsible and older than you. This can happen, for example, if the parents are dead or disabled, or not available for whatever reason.

If you are in this category, then as you grow older and you have come to some awareness, you will need to decide if these influences are right or wrong for you. You will need to ask if these influences are doing you good or bad. Then you can make a decision if you want to continue your life under such influences, even though they are from your siblings.

In making such decisions, you will need to bear in mind that brothers (and sisters) are made for days when misfortunes occur to you, and friends are for all seasons. This means that if your brother or sister is also your friend, then you will be likely to feel more secure. If not, then your brother will only come to your rescue when you run into trouble, but your friend will always be there for you, in good or bad seasons---only you can decide, but the words of Kurt Vonnegut, Jr. might just help you in your decision making: *"Don't be reckless with other people's hearts, and don't put up with people that are reckless with yours"*. Enough said.

***

Extended family relationships
The starting point is to decide what constitutes your extended family. This is important if you are to gain the best possible benefit from extended family relations. If we are able to identify what is an extended family, it will help you to avoid dangerous relationships in the name of extended family. Remember, once again, that there is no escaping the fact that you will be influenced by other human beings around you, distant or close, friendly or not so friendly.

An extended family is a group or type of family in which relatives, in addition to parents and children (such as grandparents, aunts, uncles, and cousins) live in a single household. It may also be that they may live apart in far-flung corners of the world. That is an extended family. Some readers may not necessarily agree with this definition. Let it be adequate to say that, it will help us to explain the issues around our extended families.

I have in my career seen individuals who are so miserable and so depressed, for the simple reason that they can not trace their immediate and extended family members. They think, they belong to nowhere and no help may come from any relatives.

Why do we need the relationship of extended family?
You might be forgiven for asking this question, considering that our world in modern times has gravitated towards individuality. You want to be on your own without the burdens of others on you, you might reason. Also, given that, daily, we face personal economic struggles and the social fragmentation of families whose emphasis is on "self" over collective living, why on earth should anyone need an extended family? Are we not stressed enough?

The truth is that you are "lost" on earth without being able to trace your ancestors. Your extended family might be the next governor or great scientist without you knowing about it. Thanks to the internet, family trees have come more into vogue in modern times.

The short answer to the above questions is that you can hardly claim to have any roots or be related to anyone without the recognition that they are part of you. Similarly, these individuals, as well, can collectively influence your life for the good or for the bad. You need only be careful and possibly be selective, just as in any dealings in life that you may encounter.

How do you form relationships with members of your extended family?

The first thing is that the relationship is a natural bond by virtue of your biological "blood lineage," which was due to both parents of yours. You can not deny its existence. Even if you do, it can be proven by genetic testing that you are related to a particular person. He or she may be a good person, or a bad person. That does not mean you are necessarily good or bad either.

Now, in spite of this biological and blood lineage which you can not do anything about, you may decide to maintain the link or sever it. The reason you may want to maintain it might be for financial support, jobs, housing, social support or help in any other areas that the relative might be in a position to provide, either now or in the future. You may be surprised at the impact of the extended family in some cultures, especially when there is something to celebrate or when there is a loss to "share," as in bereavement. You may need someone, in those days, to lean on.

How do you get to know who your relatives are?
The answer to this question might appear simple on the surface of it. Looking closer, it is not that straightforward. Nonetheless, the use of technology and simple enquiries may be all that you require.

Let us start from the simple ones. Ask your parents. If they don't know or "don't want to know," ask an uncle or cousin for clues. Start to chart the family tree. With the clues that you may have, try some family tree database on the internet. If this is unsuccessful, then you are now facing the "leg work," as they say. Then, there lies the hard part. Some governments, local and state offices (in developed countries) do keep long-standing paper work of family trees. This may be where you will find help.

If this fails and you are still lost in the woods, try interviewing relatives who are still alive and then gather as much information as possible and as far back as possible.

If you really want to get to the bottom of it all, you will need science to help you. This option is expensive but nearly foolproof: genetic testing of individuals, if they agree, whom you think may be related to you is the surest thing.

When you are sure, you may then begin to socially interact and develop your bonds further and not allow for future generational breaks in the association of the relatives.

***

What are the benefits of an extended family?
The answer to this question depends on your culture. In some culture such as in Asia, Southern Europe and Africa, the extended family holds sway in maintaining social and family cohesion. It goes beyond the official social security support that is offered in some of these countries and also in North America or Western Europe. In reality, the social security services' support, unlike the extended family, is provided by strangers who come to your home to help you. This kind of "help," while it is welcomed, has its limitations, as it may not offer the heartfelt psychological empathy that extended family members who are able to go "through the thick of it" with you, can offer.

There are other huge benefits that one can derive from one's extended family. Let us see some of them.

An extended family relationship is a way of preserving biological and social bonds. Biological bonds are preserved anyway unless you choose not to be socially associated with them. These bonds can stretch back into thousands of generations. Have you ever wondered why a tiny Irish town would, on the election of a new USA president, suddenly start to celebrate? Do you know why? They always trace such presidents, many of them, to Ireland, no matter how long ago the great and great-grandparents immigrated to the USA! Remember though that nothing succeeds like success. Who, if you think about it, would want to be associated with criminals?

So, relating to one's extended family is one sure way to know where you belong, especially in the modern, selfish, and fragmented world that we live in. In addition, it helps to preserve one's heritage. On clinical use, you may also discover certain ailments that your relatives have suffered from which you may now want to take step to avoid. It is common sense that human beings do bond. We bond with people we know. No reasonable individual bonds with total strangers. That is true. Therefore, people are more likely to be comfortable with individuals who can provide real reassurance and affirming positive experiences, which extended family relatives of diverse experience can and do provide. With some cautionary note, whom will you trust more---a stranger or your direct relative---even if he or she is leading you in the wrong direction? It takes courage to trust strangers over one's relatives. You must be operating with certainty on such occasions before one can trust a stranger, especially in today's dangerous world.

Furthermore, your extended relatives can support you in many areas, such as in education and in the exchange of information which you may not have had, until then, an opportunity to know.

Therefore, with all this positive support, one is not at all taken by surprise when researchers say that knowing your relatives does improve lifespan and physical health, and that extended family relationships provide some stability.

***

What are the downsides?
The first thing is that you may distance yourself legally and socially from your relationship with siblings or families but you can not deny or biologically sever it. It is permanent, biologically speaking. You can not flush it out. You can not erase it.

What if your extended relation is a criminal of the highest order? Does that make you criminal? No, but you may be guilty by association even though you are innocent!

What if your connection is bringing you problems, medically? That is to say, for example, you may have inherited some illness by virtue of your extended relationship. Well, remember that you did not choose to belong in the family either. You just have to accept or take steps to minimise your disadvantage. Also, you may take steps to ensure you do not pass on the disease to future generations.

Similarly, if you know the problems in your extended family, you can try to improve them socially or distance yourself from the problems. Perhaps the time has come for you to re-consider the words of the sage, George Washington: *"Associate yourself with men of good quality if you esteem your own reputation; for 'tis better to be alone than in bad company"*. All said, the choice is yours to make.

CHAPTER TWENTY TWO
Business Relationships

"Before we can have a successful relationship with anyone, we first need a perfect personal relationship." Russ Von Hoelscher

In this chapter, I will deal with relationships whose sole objective is nothing else other than creating wealth. For clarity, some people go into a personal relationship with a view to making money. The primary objective of personal relationships should be a benefit in kind and not money making. That may explain why a lot of personal relationships do fail. With or without money, a relationship such as friendship, or one of intimacy, should still flourish since the primary purpose is not money making. In reality, it is clear to anyone who can see that money is also important to make personal relationships work. Money is required in marriage, for example, but anyone whose primary objective in such intimate relationships is based on financial reward, will fail.

It would be better if people in a marriage or cohabitation, whose objective is money making, abandon, such primary reasons and simply enter into a business partnership. That said, a marriage is fundamentally a "business" in the way that I see it, for it is sealed under a visible or invisible contract or covenant that you signed at the marriage ceremony.

So, it is possible that people in wedlock may also enter a secondary business relationship to make money.

In the meantime, there is no business relationship without personal relationship. It is the people who make business, for business does not make people.

Therefore, the first foundation of a successful business relationship is the personal relationship of the people who are in it. Can you successfully and reasonably work to make money with someone who opposes you all day and night? If you attempt it, you may spend all your days, time, and energy dealing with conflicts. You may end up making no money for all your efforts.

As a matter of further emphasis, a business relationship in one way or the other will involve the exchange of money. Let us take one example, which are not strictly in business to make money, but behave like a business. If that is accepted, then we can also say that if your government, for example, is not doing the business of the government properly, you may hold them to account. But you can only do so if you pay your dues in taxes for the government to run properly.

Therefore, a business relationship could also be seen in the duties that the government owes you and the duty that you owe the government. If you like, you may call this one a legal duty or relationship between you and the government. You will also recall that if there is a strain between the citizens and the government, then someone in the relationship is certainly breaking the "contract" that establishes the relationship.

In the light of these examples, the aim of this chapter is directed at the relationship between an entity which is set up with the sole purpose of creating wealth, and an individual who transacts business with it. This is called the business and consumer relationship. It is also meant to focus on an entity aiming to make profits and another business whose objective is still money making. This is called a business to business relationship.

We need this simple clarity so that we can best direct our attention toward how best to make use of our relationship with either of these entities. It will also help you the reader to decide if your relationship with a business is serving your interests or if you are being made to work for nothing.

***

One fundamental thing to note is that there are striking similarities between personal relationships and business relationships, not least because at the heart of the two forms of relationships are human beings who initiate and operate businesses, and who make the relationship work.

In both relationships, as in any relationship for that matter, there is always implied (unwritten but assumed) and/or written agreement not to cause harm to the other party or to the relationship. This is in addition to any agreement to defend and protect the relationship. There will be problems if these contracts break down.

In personal relationship, it's rare until lately perhaps, to have a "contract", as in a marriage contract, though in truth, an "unseen contract" is always part of the relationship. And this unseen contract operates behind the scenes without the couple knowing. In business association though, there is almost always a contract, written or implied.

One essential similarity between a business relationship and a personal relationship is that trust is a most important element. Would you want to do business with someone who can not keep his word, not to mention keeping the terms of a contract? Certainly not. Meanwhile in a personal relationship, if your husband is not keeping his word, you might just tolerate him. If your wife is untrustworthy, for other reasons such as for the sake of the children, you might just accept that as part of her weakness as a person. In a business relationship, on which considerable efforts, money, and the livelihood of others may depend, the security and safety of society may be at stake. Who would want to work with someone with a lousy trust history? If your son or daughter betrays your trust, you may just adjust. This is because, after all, blood is thicker than water and a blood relationship is not so easy to sever. In business relationships, failings in trust may cost lives and "cost the earth"! Literally.

***

Also, if a friend lets you down personally, you may rise above it. In a business relationship, it may not be so easy. You may be down for a time that seems eternal.

I need to emphasise that this book is about you having foreknowledge of where you are going, even before you start the journey. It is also about helping you to assess your status if you have already started the journey. It is not about teaching you the day-to-day activities that you need to undertake, but it's about helping you to avoid pitfalls. Some of them are clear and some of them are not so clear. Let us take a closer look.

Who do you have business relationships with?
Your customers, your workers, including consumers, employees, investors, regulators, and communities are your likely partners in relationships.

Just as in personal relationships, it is the human beings who run, the business including the workers in the business. It is human being who will have to manage everyone who in one way or another associates with the business, be it customers or your suppliers. These people constitute the driving force behind the business.

Therefore, in order to be successful, you will need to be well equipped. You will also need to equip those who are associated with the business with appropriate tools in order to make the right decisions. Making the right decisions will help everyone who is involved to focus on expanding and making the business profitable, as well as developing business relationships.

There is no successful business without concrete and excellent personal relationships that come in the form of the business relationship. This applies to the managers who have to turn the resources into profits. Compare this with a personal relationship where husband and wife must work together to make their marriage function, or friendships whereby the friends must focus on a target objective in order to achieve their stated aims together.

***

How do you build a business relationship?
In order to build a lasting and profitable relationship, we need to go back to the very basic principle which this book is all about.

You will need to put all that you have learnt in this book about personal relationships to maximum use. That is to say: You should endeavour to know all that needs to be known about your business partners. "To know," means you are aware of a thing beyond a shadow of doubt and beyond any contradictions. Just as in personal relationships, you should find out about their personality, likes, and dislikes, their values and what is important to them.

Let us deal with the crucial issue of trust. Readers may recall how I placed emphasis on trust in personal relationships. It is equally important even in business relationships. Remember that a friend is someone whom you can rely on in the most difficult of circumstances. Business is about operating in difficult circumstances and doing impossible things. There will be no business if we can do all things by ourselves. Since we can not do all things by ourselves, we call upon those can do what we can not do, to help us out. In such an environment, you will need a friend or someone to lean on, and trust that he or she will do the job without failing you. Therefore, in establishing business relationships, the mistake people make is to treat human beings in an aloof way.

To build trust, you will need to share ideas and the mental picture that you both would like to achieve. Not just any ideas, but something in exchange or that blends together and which will be mutually beneficial. Money, for example, changes hands for a helpful service in customer/consumer relationships. A friendship, you may recall, will only be established if help of some sort has been exchanged. Therefore, the starting point for a business relationship is to exchange information that is helpful to your partners. This is the starting point of connecting with people. After all, why would I want to be associated with you if what you are going to give me is damaging to me?

With this consideration in mind, you can build as many friends and business relationships as possible. No business can exist without the product or service providing help for the user. Why should I buy something or engage someone to provide me a service that will cause me harm? Or why should I work with someone who opposes me and who will cost me highly?

The reason why the principle of friendship is valid here is that, under these circumstances, you are more likely to be forgiving and less likely to want to cause harm to your friend. If there is a mistake, you are not likely to institute legal proceedings, but to resolve it amicably.

This is where the same element of companionship, which we saw under personal relationships, can be harnessed in building business relationships: What do you have in common? Is it interests and life experiences? This will allow the partners to be opened up and less defensive about talking with you. You should have something in common that binds you.

The truth of the matter is a business relationship is the practical application of the principles of personal relationships
Let us assume that you are meeting someone for the first time, compared to hanging out with some of your personal friends in the same place. Do you treat the meeting differently?

In fact, you may need to consider, without being unduly over-familiar, "recruiting" the new person into your fold of friends. There and then you can offer help, share experiences, provide information and introduce your great ideas. That may be the only opportunity and chance you will ever have with the new person before you strike the next deal!

Another issue that we should consider is respect. Apart from trust, respect is another principle which we discussed under personal relationships, and which should be applicable in business relationships. Would you want to do business with someone who is rude and disrespectful? Who in his reasonable senses would want to have an intimate relationship with someone who is abusive and rude? Remember that rudeness and abuse are sometimes at the bottom of separation and divorce in personal intimate relationships.

Respect is like the glue that holds partnerships, cohabitation, marriages, and indeed business partnerships together. Like friendships and marriages that last, in business there should be admiration for one another's differences and the need to negotiate on certain points. It should not be that only "my way" or "your way" is right.

Respect helps to accept a person for what their values are. Such acceptance leads to trust. Trust may lead to opportunities, yet unseen greater relationships and new ideas.

***

The tools you need in business relationship
Just as in any human relationship, you need the power of words to do things for you. You need to communicate effectively.

Without words, nothing can be achieved in personal and business relationships. You need good words to motivate and encourage your partners in the relationship. A relationship in which a wife speaks badly to her husband is on shaky ground. In business, you need words that give directions to the managers and workers, as well as the customers. You need words that convey motivation in your communication.

In communication, what you say and the way you say things matters. The communication can be verbal or non-verbal, as long as the intention or message is conveyed appropriately. The tone that you use and your body language do indeed matter. If communicating with employees or customers, for example, they may have come from different backgrounds. It is therefore important that the style of communication should take due recognition of the individual culture, if possible. Even if you are rejecting an idea or product, you will still need to be friendly and use less hostile words.

What makes for a good business relationship?

Business flourishes on relationships. What appears as a small relationship may in the future become a gigantic success which may last for years to come, providing mutual benefits (help) for the parties in the relationship. What to bear in mind though is that all along a service, something helpful and something special is being provided for the other party. If this good service can no longer be provided, then the relationship may indeed come to an end. Why should anyone be associated with another except when there is something to give or receive? In personal relationships, if desire and intention is defeated, you may recall, there will be frustration, anger, and unhappiness.

In business terms, this is called dissatisfaction. It means that needs and desires are not satisfied. The relationship may simply end, though anger may be subdued so as not to damage the party's social and economic standing.

As in personal relationships, whereby you deal with individuals, the same applies in business relationships. You deal with individuals. Provide good service and the individual will lead you on. Provide bad service and the relationship may fail.

How is a business relationship sustained? It is sustained in the same way as a personal relationship. Be kind with your words. Show appreciation with gifts and enhance the value of the partners. Little gifts and promotional materials may go a long way to enhance the relationship. It is up to you now, the giants of the universe.

SECTION IIII

Value

"The bond that links your true family is not one of blood, but of respect and joy in each other's life...."

Richard Bach

CHAPTER TWENTY THREE
Maintenance of Relationships
"...When the foundations are destroyed, what can the righteous do...?"
The Psalmist

Maintenance of a relationship is as vital as the formation of a relationship, if not more important. In some relationships, personal, or business, once formed, there is no going back, especially if they are based on a contract. In some instances, in legal circles, dissolution is even more problematic. In any case, there will often be serious financial, psychological, and social penalties for breaches of the contract. As I mentioned in the preceding chapter, marriages and human relationships are based on some invisible contract which can in some cases be made visible, e.g. by written marital agreement.

In a business relationship which is guided by a contract, it is almost impossible to go back on the relationship without some penalty being incurred by the person who want to breach the contract. In some personal relationships, such as those that are based on some religious obligations or on a marital contract, there are almost always some repercussions for the possible breach of the relationship.

It is to avoid these risky and costly outcomes that some relationships have to be maintained regardless of the huge inconvenience of doing so. In some intimate relationships that have children, the relationship may be maintained for this reason. A relationship may also be maintained for political reasons as well for social reasons, for example to ensure the social status of the couple is not affected by separation and divorce. In political terms, there are positions of which a certain relationship status is expected of the office holder.

Nevertheless, a relationship can only be maintained if there is a reason to keep it going. If there is no identifiable reason to sustain it, it would amount to a waste of resources and time to expend energy to maintain the association.

Meanwhile, in business relationships, there is only one reason why such a relationship should be kept alive. There is only one reason for the existence of a business relationship and that is money. When money is out of the equation of a business relationship, it transforms to a personal relationship which is maintained on a different platform, such as moral support.

Therefore, in short, a relationship---business or personal---can only be kept alive if there is a reason or a bond that needs to be protected. Short of this, a relationship is dead. The most important thing, however, is that if the foundation on which the relationship was built is weak or is destroyed, what work can any reasonable person build upon? Therefore, for the sake of emphasis, a relationship can only survive if it is laid on a solid foundation which can not be shaken, even though storms may beat against it.

How is a personal relationship maintained?
Let us, as usual, begin with intimate relationships such as marriage and cohabitation. There are many people who would offer one thousand and one ways to sustain a relationship. Apart from trust and loyalty, which I have discussed previously, maintenance begins with good words and is followed by good deeds. Some people, especially women, respond to poems and intelligent, romantic, or loving quotes. For example: *"I would fly you to the moon and back if you'll be . . . if you'll be my baby,"*---from a song by Savage Garden. Any woman would certainly be moved by this kind of persuasive words. Word matters.

For some, all they want to hear now and then is *reassurance,* encouragement, and motivational words---that all is going well and that all will be well.

To some, if an offence has been spotted, the best option might be *"to come clean"* with a promise that it will not be repeated. This is very relevant is cases of adultery and unfaithfulness. Defensive and evasive action may cause more damage than repair.

Yet for others, the gesture towards repair and maintenance must be *practical deeds*. Some have advocated *exotic holidays* with or without the children. The couple alone may travel to the "other side of the world". This is even more important in time of an impending anniversary or landmarks such as wedding and birthday anniversaries. For all those men out there, take note that women are more sensitive to these events than men, it would appear.

While for some, this deed toward the spouse and relationship is only acceptable if it comes in the form of *token gifts* of high or moderate value. The attitude and presentation must be genuine. Could it be diamond, gold or silver? You decide.

The maintenance could be a combination of all of these. It could simply be that the spouse should be available and willing to spend time together. That is, to fall in the loving arms of the partner/spouse at any time in public and in private places, without any hindrance --- complete with wholesome attention and care. In some relationships, all that is required is the ability of one half couple to have the *listening ears of the other* ---just someone who can *share* in the other person's thoughts, worries, tasks, successes and failures. All these should be continuous and not just in knee-jerk reactions.

***

Let us look at the maintenance of friendship relationships. The only sustaining bond in friendship is *trust* and the *reliance* that the friend will be available in times of crisis or in times of urgent need to *provide help*. A friend who fails in time of crisis is a most undependable person. Who can rely on or who would want to maintain a relationship with such a person? Of course it goes without saying that *good words and deeds* are part and parcel of a friendship. Good counsel when a friend is at a crossroads, when he or she is wondering where to turn, would prolong the life of such a friendship for a long time to come.

Showing appreciation in words and deeds is fundamental to all relationships and not just friendships. But since friendship is the ultimate hierarchy in relationships, appreciation should be part and parcel of the means to sustain all forms of relationships for the duration of a couple's lives.

How is a business relationship maintained?
I have said earlier that a good and ultimate business relationship could potentially be transformed into one of friendship. In no other form of relationship is trust to perform and not to be negligent as strong, and indeed required, as in a business relationship. Therefore, to maintain a business relationship, it requires a *continuous attention to the contract* so that there is no breach. It is important to keep the service to be provided in focus and to *meet the expectations of everyone* in the relationship. Do not take things for granted even if the business relationship is with your dad, mother, or siblings!

Key events, such as New Year and Christmas periods, are times of opportunities to *show appreciation.* The appreciation may be made by gift items or by any means that is appropriate. Associates may simply show more *admiration* for relationships that identify with the business ups and downs, or those relationships that show great understanding in difficult times. This is the kind of relationship that can transform into friendships, despite the fact that it was originally a business relationship.

Who would want to maintain a relationship with a business partner who runs from you in times of trouble but shows up in fair weather?

In sum, and in the same way that human beings are affected under personal relationships, human beings in business relationships have emotions, desires, and intentions quite apart from the corporate entity that constitutes the business. Thus, the maintenance of personal relationships is and should be similar to the business environment. If you fail to care for business partners in times of their trouble, who then would want to bother about you when you run into difficulty? Friendship, in the final analysis, is not just about mere relationship; it's about offering help in times of need, and support and understanding in periods of shortfall.

***

CHAPTER TWENTY FOUR
Instances of One-Sided Relationships: Abuse of Relationships

"Great ideas often receive violent opposition from mediocre minds." Albert Einstein

I mentioned earlier in the book that none of us can live in absolute isolation; even if you live as a single person, you will in some ways come across other human beings in shops, work places, on the street and in a host of other places. If you do decide to relate to others, these bonds could be with children or in intimacy with adults. It could also take the form of deeper bonds, as in friendship. On the other hand, it may just be an aloof but important relationship such as a business association. In all of these connections, value is added to us and to the individuals or organisations we associate with. They are often priceless relationships. On some not infrequent occasions, an individual, or some individuals, can conspire to devalue, oppose, damage, and destroy these invaluable associations that, in a real sense, are meant to help the individuals in the relationship.

Opposition and damage will often arise to these relationships out of selfishness, a lack of appreciation of the value of the association itself, as well as from an absence of insight into the gifts and people we associate with. It's on this account that I take on the instances of abuses in relationships. Let me begin with that innocent and vulnerable individual called a *child*.

***

Child abuse:
Child abuse is any resultant ill-treatment or, as commonly said, maltreatment of a child. This definition should not be confused with discipline or any treatment that will in the short or long term bring benefits to the child. The key words, as will be explained below, are benefits and value. Let us expand on each of the component words in this definition.

"Treatment" is a process of modifying or altering something. It is the action or behaviour towards a person. Also, to be "ill" is to be poorly and or be unsound mentally or physically.

***

Who is a "child"?

To avoid complicated legal arguments, let us take the definition of the World Health Organization into consideration: A child is defined by the Convention on the Rights of the Child (CRC) as "every human being below the age of 18 years unless under the law applicable to the child, majority is attained earlier."

From this, we can begin to see that child abuse is any form of behaviour towards someone who is under 18 years such that the behaviour alters or modifies the child detrimentally or makes the child become unsound mentally or physically. This may be sexual or verbal abuse, as well.

To answer this question, we will use a car as an example: your car. I suppose you have one. It could as well be a house or any acquisition of any material thing. Similarly, anyone who intends to make a car would first desire it (in the case of a child, this would be the desire to have children).

From this desire, he would consider how to bring the desire to pass (in the case of a child, this would be to have sex with an appropriate adult, or in modern times, by assisted reproductive technology, also called test tube baby). He would have a plan about the care of the child. This is called intention. After this, he would act to design and fashion the car (the birth of the baby in the case of a child). When the car is made, he would care for it (in the case of the child, look after him or her), "love" it and ensure it does not rust nor be involved in an accident. This same process applies to any reasonable person who intends to purchase a car or build/purchase a house. More significantly, the people acquiring the car or house have a *set purpose* for the acquisition. This is to drive the car so that the car can move people and the owner from point A to point B. If, say, the car or the house is left neglected, then anyone passing by could easily conclude that the owner is wasting the car or house. This comparison is significant to understanding children and human beings. As illustrated above in brackets, these processes are similar to how we have our children. Accidents of birth abound in the world.

Value of a Thing

Anyone who is familiar with gold or diamond or land (or even petroleum!) as a treasure, would value it, keep it, care for it, protect it, even, as we know, fight to defend it from being stolen or destroyed. This simple process is called "love". This means that the owner of the gold, land, diamond etc. would do anything to ensure *no harm* comes upon the treasure.

***

The Problem with "Acquisition" of Children

Sadly, it would appear that unlike the issue with cars or houses as illustrated above, human beings tend to "acquire" other human beings, in this case, a child, without a reason or purpose for their "acquisition". Thus, in general, the beginning of abuse of anything, and not least human beings, is whether the "thing" lacks a constructive and legal purpose. If it does lack a purpose, it would be devalued and mistreated. The word "legal" here is applicable to both the laws made by man (governments) and, like it or not, God's laws, for there are reasons why human beings exist on earth. In sum, if you do not know the true purpose and value of human beings, you will abuse him or her, regardless if the person is a child or not. That is a foundational principle.

What is the Value of a Child?

The question, then, is what purpose and use do children have in the world? Basically, a child, for want of most appropriate word, is an "asset" or entity to the parents, extended families and the society at large. Like all other assets that arise from or within the earth, they must be well looked after---that is, be loved. This is because such assets, and, in particular, the biological assets that children are, can be subject to infection, decay and impairment. Therefore, the value that a child brings, or the use of a child, depends on the input from parents, the community, and Godly design. This value that a child brings is enhanced or diminished by the mental (through words and images) and physical influences the child receives. Nonetheless, unlike any other "asset", the child must be useful and have a purpose in life. Short of this, the child is a wasted entity. This abuse happens almost always through abuse!

The Reason for Child (And All Forms of Human) Abuse

There are many reasons that had been put forward. These include the fact that:

1) Current abusers may have, in the past been subject of abuse. While this may be a factor, it does not completely explain the rampant issue of abuse of harmless children who are clearly at the mercy of their abusers.

2) The abusers lack the *social skills* to engage with adults or they feel intimidated (or afraid) to seek relationship with adults. It is therefore reasonable to conclude that adult and in some cases, children themselves abuse children because of their vulnerability.

3) The victims are easy prey or easy touch and are vulnerable.

4) D*rugs and alcohol* is clearly an issue that one can trace to impairment of their early development. Thus, if the issue of abuse as a result of lack of social skill is to be addressed, one should consider proper family rearing and almost faultless childhood education and orientation.

Individuals in this category may sexually abuse anything that is vulnerable so long as their sexual desire is satisfied. It is also important to start advising young children who may be subject of abuse (or all children as part of parenting/education), very early on sounding early warning of what an abuse is, and emphasizing the value or sanctity of all human parts and their respective functions. Example, it may be imperative to teach what the private parts (genitals) are for and when they should be used. The purpose of mouth, hands etc and when they should be used etc.

5) The other important reason why children get abused is to be seen from view point of *anger with or without existing mental health problem. Frustration in general is a cause of abuse.* This is true for sexual, verbal, and physical exploitation of children. Anger is directed, as it always is, at indefensible or vulnerable object. Any object--animate or inanimate. In this case, children are easy targets. Unexpressed anger and pathological anger, *lack of insight* (see below) are the main culprits here. The anger could be about anything but may be about failure in life, failure in relationship, health, disappointment with adult relationships, desire to sexually destroy/exploit the children in a failing or troubled relationship including domestic violence, and so on.

Reader should note that children are easy victims in *domestic violence*.

6) Another reason is that children are *easily led* and they easily establish trusts in relationships. They will almost always do what they are asked to do believing that what they are being told is the right thing because they do not know otherwise. In such occasion, the adult abuser may lure children with sweets, money, chocolate or any promises. This is true for sexual, physical, religious, cultural, financial, and labour abuses.

7) In some occasions, the *financial condition* of the family or adults may be in such a *miserable state* that the children may be compelled voluntarily or involuntarily to do something about the

family situation. This is true when children put themselves up for labour, financial, and sexual exploitation.

It should be noted, that all of these causes and reasons for abuse will have serious psychological impact on the children in the immediate and in long terms, often leading, as stated below to a host of psychiatry / mental health problems (see more below).

8) Yet, closely tied to the most important reason for child abuse are the fact that, unwanted children (children from unplanned pregancy ---one night stand--- etc,) physically or mentally disabled children and unloved children are clearly and clinically at risk of being abused.

9) Still, the foundation for child abuse lies in what I have listed below as the most vital reason for child abuse. Closely aligned to this reason is lack of *parental skills* and in almost all cases, *Godlessness* (lack of true fear of God). Being Godly is not the same thing as being seen in some religious attire or designated buildings or being called a certain religious names and positions. There are afterall, many wolves among the sheep. As public evidence have shown, many abusers use their respected trust, authority and position to commit terrible child abuses as well as execute their dark heart desires in the name of God.

10) The critical or perhaps the most important reason why child and indeed human abuse occurs is very simple. If the *value of a thing* is not known and if the value of a child is not known, such child or children are subject or vulnerable to terrible abuse. Regardless of the social and psychological excuses that experts may give for anyone abusing the other, the abuser would most certainly stop abusing when he or she acquires the *insight* and comes to the *realisation* of the abuse or understands the value of human beings and children. No one who knows the value of his gold or house would damage it. Therefore, *insight* is crucial to understand the priceless *value* of children.

***

The Great Conspiracy between Governments and Parents

Instances of abuse or misuse of children are rampant in the world, crimes against children are on the increase, and death and infection devour children because various governments across the world pretend that parents who acquire children do know what they are doing. The sad truth is that most parents neither plan for nor have good purpose in mind, nor know the value of humans beings who are represented by children as the most valuable and incomparable creature in the world. If they, governments, and parents do, they would guard against the enormous waste that goes on in the world's children.

Manifestation and Forms of Abuse: Effects of Abuse

An abuse by definition is a devaluation of the individual or thing. Let us concentrate on human abuse by other human beings.

Psychological Effects

a)   While the person who is being abused may not realise it at the time of the abuse, or he or she may be defenceless, the psychological effects will start to emerge as soon as the person who was abused comes to the knowledge and realisation of the violation. Ignorance conceals wickedness. When the abused comes into awareness, he or she will react to the abuse. This is why an abuser will always try to hide the offence and prevent the abuser from coming into the knowledge of the abuse.

That said, the following are some of the psychological effects of abuse. A sense of violation and infringement on one's dignity, as well as one's value, are perhaps the first and immediate effects. It has the same effect as if someone had stolen from you something that is irreplaceable and of greatest value. These feelings and impacts have rippling consequences. Thus:

Unhappiness will ensue from this knowledge. This unhappiness will lead to anger (see the chapter on anger). Anger will lead to belligerence. The belligerence will lead to further unhappiness, depression, and possible violent conduct.

If these ripple effects are not recognised there would be further problems. If there is no sympathy from the family or from professionals, and if this behaviour is not properly managed with restitution by the offender, there will be further complications. The restitution should ideally include justice for the offended/abused, counselling for the abused and true forgiveness of the offender. If these steps fail, the victim may be diagnosed as suffering from mental health disorders which may actually manifest as depression or psychosis. The behaviour may become unpredictable and complex.

Sadly, the person could be labelled as suffering from personality disorder ---PD--- pejorative term for maladjustment to one's social and biological circumstances--- no matter how painful or traumatic that may be. The world and the professionals expect traumatised individuals to adjust to the trauma! Child abuse can lead to personality disorders, anxiety disorders and major affective disorders, research work has confirmed.

***

Still, bitterness may linger on and may continue to haunt the abused, except perhaps if he/she forgives and "moves on" in life. If the memory of the traumatic experience continues, it could be very hard for the abused to make substantial progress in life and regular admission to psychiatry hospital or frequent visits to a therapist may impair the victims' prosperity or mental, social, and biological stability in life.

It should be remembered that if medication is prescribed at all, the side effects may contribute to weighing the person down, mentally and physically.

In verbal abuse, the effects can be even harder to shake off. Physical abuse follows an intention to harm. Intentions are unexpressed words. Now, words are the most powerful tool that exists. I have seen a young lady who was told by her boyfriend that she was ugly. She became depressed because of this and could hardly shake off these words. The effect of verbal abuse is that it can be demoralising, discouraging, demotivating, and ultimately destructive and may cause real fear in the person.

b) *Biological effects and impacts on the next generation*
Depending on the nature of the abuse, the victim may attempt to or actually avoid the kind of circumstances of the abuse. That is to say, if sex was the biological function that was abused, the victim may avoid sex completely. Thus, sexual performance in marriage or child bearing may become a major difficulty in someone who was sexually abused. Someone who had suffered financial abuse, for example, may also decide to take revenge on others. It should be noted that such revenge abuse could stop if the original victim came to the realization of the value of human beings and or he had forgiven the abuser. So it's not true that an abuse always begets abuse.

I have also seen hatred for and poor bonding towards the gender that caused the abuse. For example, women tend to project to practically all men and to loathe men or avoid men in the belief that "all men" are most likely to behave in the same way. There is no doubt that a lot of sexual abuse is committed by men. On the other hand, further encounters with men tend to remind the abused woman of the sad experience of the original abuse. This is called projection. The same can be said of children who were abused and women who abuse men. Such men may avoid women because encountering women might remind them of the abuse they may have suffered at the hands of their mothers.

Some people lose their sense of worth so much that they may actually give up protecting what was abused. For example, if the reproductive organ was abused, the victim may see no reason in protecting the sex organs. That is, the victim may become promiscuous in the extreme; after all, there is no longer a value or need to protect the thing that was abused.

It has been said (there is much debate on this) that when there is a physical abuse or sexual abuse, the victim may tend to vent his or her anger against other vulnerable individuals, such as children (even their own children), women and men. In some instances, the anger is directed against the larger society that so wantonly failed to protect the abused person. This manifestation may be in the form of criminal damage to properties (see below). The grey area in this is the element of discipline in the case of physical abuse. The question is where does discipline stop and abuse begin? The denominator, however, is that with discipline, it benefits the child and "causes no harm", while abuse does otherwise.

The abused person may suffer a lack of confidence, intimidation, fear, social phobia and lack of motivation.

***

c) *Economic Impact of abuse*

Abuse is a misuse of a thing or person. Therefore, improper use of a person, leading up to devaluation, is a clear indication that, except when the abused person forgives, forgets and moves on, he or she carries a risk of not reaching his or her economic optimum in life. The reason could be due to the impact of likely mental health problem, bitterness, and lingering physical trauma.

***

d) *Impact on Society*

Every loss of productivity, devaluation, and diagnosis of mental health illness incurs costs of care for the abused. Lack of, or poor, productivity is one effect and individuals who are unhappy in our midst are others. PDs are seen as threats to the existence of society as they can pose a threat as sexual predators, violent offenders and sport hooligans, as well as the fact that PDs constitute security risks in general, not to mention the issue of persistent offenders, regardless of the nature of the offence.

e) *Physical Effects*

In physical abuse (including sexual abuse), there could be physical injuries which may be permanent. In forced sexual entry (vagina), the victim may be so scared that it may give rise to difficult sex in normal relationship. It may also lead to difficult labour during childbirth.

In boys who are abused anally, they may lose the control of their bowel and this may become permanent. It may also cause friction with medical teams who may want to examine them in future. Transmission of infections such as HIV, syphilis, etc. from the abuser to the abused (and vice versa) may occur. Bleeding from wounds, scars, fractures, bruises, brain injuries and death may occur as a result of physical abuse. Non- sexual infection may come into the wounds as time progresses, if not treated.

In some individuals, they reject the organs, or related organs, that were abused and may attempt to remove them from their bodies in the belief that such organs are agents of attraction that caused them trouble in the first instance. Examples are more pronounced in women, as they may attempt to remove their reproductive organs, skin, and breasts so as to disfigure and make themselves less attractive to potential abusers. In all, the attempts can lead to all sorts of self-mutilation.

f) *Abuse and the law: Legal Ramifications.*

Whilst this is not exhaustive, there have been suggestions in Britain that PD individuals should be locked up in mental health hospitals before they cause havoc in wider society. The opinion of the medical profession is that some PDs are untreatable (remember forgiveness though). As a result, the option being considered is to send them to prison anyway, especially if they commit heinous crimes. In the alternative, the PD may be sent to a high security "prison-hospital". Note, however, that not all PDs are as a result of abuse and not all abused persons end up as PDs. Also, there is a debate, regarding whether discipline, including physical discipline, is a type of abuse. The jury is out on this. However, except in moderation, and which is also beneficial to the child, extreme discipline, both verbal and physical can easily become abuse. Many innocent children have died on account of anger and abuse which is camouflaged as a form of discipline.

***

g) *Religious Effects:*

Clearly, abuse of human beings is a violation of the divine Christian laws to "love" and to "cause no harm" to others. The implication of abuse in this respect is to effectively prevent the recognition of God's authority, and to prevent others from enjoying the liberty, love, kindness, grace, and resources that are made available by God to the inhabitants of earth. Further, abuse prevents the victim (who may now be ill), and in fact the abuser, from reaching or experiencing the manifest glory of God in the individual and on earth.

***

Child abuse may lead to substance abuse, self-injury, suicide, depression, rage, and strained relationships with women or men, depending on who caused the abuse. Self-concept and identity issues (sexual orientation), and a discomfort with sex, are other possible outcomes.

In sum, what am I trying to prove by going into this length? Why did I say this much? The idea of this book is to allow readers to come to their own conclusion before they take certain crucial action, such as having children. If you make children without thinking ahead of why you make them, and if you do not have plans for them and your relationship is not well thought out, then they may suffer these effects. Relationships matter. Relationships matters even more in one that involve children.

Relationship affects children, influences their way of life and impacts on their future. Relationships with children can be very rewarding if done so under the ambit of great morals and convictions to protect their interests. In so doing, the adult can always be assured of trusting and rewarding relationships.

Domestic Violence (DV)

I have touched on this subject earlier. The bottom line is that both verbal and physical attacks by either or both members of the couple against each other are an abuse of the relationship. The sad truth is that physical attacks are given more prominence by the police and legal authorities in DV than verbal attacks--- a weapon which can cause enormous damage equal to or greater than physical attack. In dealing with DV, the law and the law enforcers do not consider what led to DV such as embrassment, hurtful name callings, devaluation of the partner, taunting of the spouse and so on. Thus, the often claim by men that "she was abusing me or calling me names" is at best tenuous in defence against DV. It is the physical attack in evidence or attempt at physical attack that now matters. So take caution. Words and intentions, however, are the forerunner of physical attack in most cases. Both, however, is an abuse of the relationship. Period.

Exploitation of Vulnerable and Unaware Adults
Let me first remind the reader that human beings have the propensity to exploit other human beings that are either ignorant or who may be in vulnerable positions. Such "vulnerable position" may be mental illness, physical illness or any condition that makes the individual not function to his or fullest capacity. It may be one disability or another. This is also why children are so vulnerable. There are adults, therefore, who are in vulnerable positions which I have mentioned above.
Exploitation of vulnerable individuals is usually by a person with whom they have a relationship. It may be spouses or carers or family members. It may be a stranger who is actually a member of the community and who has a relationship duty to protect other members of the same community.

I have said all these, so that the reader, who may be in a vulnerable position, or their family members, should take measures to protect the unaware or vulnerable person. But of, course; you have the option of not doing so---to your peril.

***

Stalking

Stalking is an irritation, or nuisance, in an unwanted relationship. It's a pestering of one person by the other in a supposed relationship, which is actually one-sided. The person who is being pestered does not want the relationship. But the person, who is doing the stalking thinks, believes and acts as if the person who rejected the relationship wants the bond between them. This in fact, is a relationship that is *causing harm* to one person and therefore is an abuse. The person who wants the relationship may lurk in places at times that the other person does not desire. In effect, it can cause a lot of distress.

You may ask, why have I mentioned this here? Well, it's a "relationship" that is known to cause great harm, distress and even death to the person who rejects the stalker. So the reader should know when a relationship is truly over and should take caution appropriately. Again, you have the choice.

CHAPTER TWENTY FIVE
Stories of Successful and Dreadfully Failed Relationships

"The fundamental glue that holds any relationship together is trust." Brian Tracy

I have written here about what Hollywood might call, "the good, the bad and the ugly," of relationships. The idea is that readers should learn lessons from these issues in planning their relationships. These cases will hopefully also allow readers to assess their existing relationships.

Prevention, the doctors have said for millennia, is better than cure. A good beginning may just have a good ending. A bad start may also end badly except when participants are alert to what dangers a bad beginning may bring.

Human beings in general are very lively, sneaky, witty, fast-talking, lurking, conspiring--- all into one piece --- and likely to do the unexpected and to change at the speed of light. Human beings can move about furtively, or wait in a concealed position, in a shadowy corner, especially with the intention of doing something wrong. But the key thing is to plan well and be vigilant regarding these issues. It is also important, to take due note of the words of Zig Zaglar that, *"Any relationship primarily built on physical attractiveness is predestined to be short lived"*. For me, this is a crucial statement.

With these behind us, let us look at some events that the world has had to put up with. In essence, they have either taken away or added to the lives of some families. I have included these case studies here so that readers can learn from the mistakes of others. In addition, these cases demonstrate that human beings are hardly worth trusting one hundred percent. You should be on your guard, without being paranoid, always, for human being can change at any time. Further, human beings can hide their true intentions while they pretend otherwise. Challenged, men and women will seek their own survival even at the cost of their so called partner, spouse, or friends.

***

Here is a story from a considerable number of media outlets.

Case study 1

Divorce man who's asking for his kidney back from his divorcing wife (BBC, Internet)

This was a story about a doctor, RB, in the USA, who was undergoing divorce with his wife. They had married in 1990. From the stories, it is clear that the man was deeply in "love" with wife. The wife, it would appear did not share that same feeling toward him or perhaps she changed (I hope you remember the WebMD's word about unpredictability of women). In any case, the story went that he donated a kidney to his wife's need in 2001.

Now that the wife had, "humiliated, betrayed, disrespected and disregarded" him in this divorce, he wanted the kidney back or a substitute payment of US$1.5m to him! This is the "value" of kidney.

The lesson here is that betrayal is a common feature of intimate relationships and sometimes may lead to tragic end and to a lesser extent, divorce. Readers may recall that I mentioned earlier that one of the sore areas of an intimate relationship is what Dr RB sums up as being, "... humiliated, betrayed, disrespected and disregarded...," by his wife and the divorce process. This is also a characteristic of men to feel this way. It is also a feature of men to be emotive about such issues, as well as to make determined efforts to want revenge for such an act of humiliation. The reader may be interested in the fact that this medical doctor had also been prevented from seeing his children---an often bargaining point in divorce/separation/broken relationships, frequently to the disadvantages of men. Preventing a parent from seeing their children is a common issue in the divorce process and can be very protracted. Except when serious harm was being caused to the child, the child loses the parent's guidance and influence that may have been provided but for the prevention. In this case, RB was in deep "pain". This should remind the reader of the consequences of divorce, which were discussed in earlier chapters.

Case Study 2: From a considerable number of media outlets.

This was a popular news item that occurred in the USA in 2006 and until it was disposed of in 2007. What made this story particularly interesting is that it involved the wife of a preacher and pastor. This means that even being a pastor or preacher is not cast iron immunity against relationship challenges and disasters. I used to have the impression that pastoral families lived lives of tranquillity, given the likelihood that they know what is expected of them --- spiritually. In truth, the evidence against my view is staggering, as there are innumerable accounts where the family of pastors have gone either wild or "wayward". Human beings, after all, remain as human beings, vulnerable and self-serving. This story was particularly violent. The wife of the pastor shot him dead. She killed him. But why, one may ask? The allegation was that she had subjected him to sexual abuse during their short marriage. Mind you, there were three young daughters in the relationship.

The issue here is that the desire and intention of the wife clashed in a spectacular was---over sex and physical abuse---with that of the dead pastor. The story went that they had argued the previous night over, guess what, money!

Here is the lesson: that which so spectacularly splits relationships and causes argument, as I have mentioned before, almost always relates to sex or money. These issues (sex and money) surround the outcome of a clash of desires of the partners or spouses. The second lesson is that a couple should affirm and have well *documented agreement* as to how money (and sex) in the family should be managed throughout the duration of the relationship (see the chapter on marriage contact). A couple should be open and honest enough as to the conduct of sex in the relationship. Though Mrs. MW went to prison for the offence, the man had paid dearly with his life and the children were left fatherless (see earlier chapter on the effect of divorce via death).

Case Study 3

Wife killed husband after affair: adultery (BBC)

This story is about, well again, a clash of desires. This was a couple of Asian origin. This is important because of the impact of religion in that part of the world. WC, who lived with her husband in South England, UK, killed her husband with an axe. The reason: S, her husband, had fathered a child with the niece of WC. Prior to that, WC and S had thought that their marriage was over as they were apparently having problems. WC was still hopeful and desired that the husband was going to get back into the marriage. On discovering the adultery or betrayal, and the failed desire of WC, she acted angrily and killed the husband (See chapter on anger and its likely outcomes).

Lesson: anger can destroy and does destroy. Intentions and desire when defeated, can, as WC said, make people "crazy". Usually, when a relationship runs into problems, despite what *WebMD describes as the unpredictability of a woman*, it means that someone somewhere in the relationship has broken the guiding or basic rule that established the relationship. In this case, which appears to be so clear, laws, norms, and desire were broken.

Case Study 4
Sex pact husband killed wife (BBC)

This story is a most out-of-the-ordinary one. A husband, CH, and wife, T, had been married for 18 years. CH and T had for some reason entered into a pact to the effect that T could have "affairs" (see chapter on Names) with younger men, so long as T could also satisfy the sexual needs of CH, despite the "affair".

A perfect trap was therefore set for T. CH monitored the conduct of T.

One day, T told CH that he "was past his sell-by date!" For those readers who may not connect with this statement, let me explain. The "sell-by date" is a guide that product manufacturers and retailers attach to a product, especially food. It suggests that the food is best sold off the shop shelf within a certain period, or that the quality of the food will reach its optimum after the stated date. "The sell by date" is the period during which food/products must be sold. If not, the food must be removed and discarded. Otherwise, it may become unsalable or not suitable for consumption.

Therefore to apply such a description to a man means that he is utterly useless and now ripe to be discarded. On hearing such words, the man, CH, now armed with a gun, in desperation and anger, shot T dead.

Lessons: Words matter. Spoken or expressed words have immense power. Words can kill. Words can encourage the best of deeds or the worst of acts. Many relationships such as this have come to a shameful and tragic end on account of what was said or done.

Once again, as the reader may have noticed, the issue here is with mismanagement of sex issues and most importantly the interference of a third party in the relationship---which may actually not be aware of the destructive impact this indirect interference was having on the relationship.

Note should also be taken that in this case the man's desire and the woman's wish clashed in a formidable way. All these were potent weapons to end a relationship. I wish to remind the reader that the aim of this book is preventive, somehow. Therefore, I will urge that you ensure you do all you can to remain vigilant and to do your homework well before you enter into a relationship, intimate or not. Human beings are particularly difficult beings --- male or female. Be vigilant always. Human beings change without notice.

Case Study 5.

*Husband killed wife over Facebook entry (*from BBC and a number of media outlets and internet).

MF killed his wife over a piece of *unfavourable* information (words and acts). MF and wife had separated for a couple of days. For the reader who may not know the significance of separation in marriage, let me shed more light. It is possible that the couple may come back together again, although they may not. In some territories, a continuous intentional separation whereby they live separate lives, even if they live under the same roof for 2 years, is likely to end in divorce. Now back to this story: a few days shortly after the separation, the wife altered her relationship status on *Facebook* from "married" to "separated" and that she was looking for other men.

On seeing this, the man felt "humiliated and devastated" (the same sets of words again as in case 1) about what she, the wife, had done. In fury, he killed her by stabbing.

Lesson: pathological anger or destructive anger is the main issue here, following public humiliation and perhaps disgrace. Men, as I have mentioned under the characteristics of men, can not stand public humiliation. They may just tolerate it in private settings.

****

Case Study 6

Press Trust of India/Express India

Wife killed her husband on their honeymoon

This story is both pathetic and shocking. This woman, named V, was on honeymoon ten days after her marriage to her husband, named A. Unknown to the husband, he was about to die. It occurred in a deserted place. He was to meet his unfortunate death by strangulation from V and a couple of male conspirators. The real man whom V was in love with was called "A2". He was the chief helper of V in killing A. Lessons: the intention of A was remarkably different from that of V. She never loved A, as she was in love with A2.

It was also possible that V may have been suffering from mental illness without the knowledge of A. I think a thorough enquiry and honest searches, prior to marriage, could, or just may have prevented this tragic death. One is not saying that human beings can not change their minds; they often do. Given the arranged nature of the marriage, it is possible that V may have entered this marriage without the true intention to do so. Therefore, she saw A as an obstacle to her true intention and duly eliminated him. I will be quick to recommend that thorough mental health assessment and enquiries about the true desire of the couple should form one of the bases of tests before marriage. This is not a joke.

Case Study 7

Wife who Pleaded Guilty in Devastating Plot to Have Husband Murdered (Washington Post)

This is one of those cases of back-stabbing, betrayal, plotting, and conspiracy that is so common in intimate relationships. AB alleged that her husband was physically abusing her (see also the section on domestic violence, DV). She did not tell people what had led up to the "abuse". The story later revealed that she had planned to collect the family insurance upon the death of the husband.

It appeared she had conspired to kill the husband by hiring her daughter's boyfriend to carry out the murder. Indeed, it was the daughter's boyfriend who ultimately carried out the act on behalf of the wife and daughter, who were in a joint enterprise to kill.

As part of the treacherous scheme, on the day in question, the daughter alerted the father, at night that an intruder was in the house. It was in fact part of the plot. Conscious of his family's security, the man got up only to meet the attacker by the house door, and was duly beaten without mercy.

Ironically, it was the wife who called the police, but the victim LB held on to the attacker until the police came.

Lesson: whenever a couple no longer shares the same vision (see why marriages fail or succeed), there will be a crack in the relationship. This is what happened here. The wife and husband were pursuing different agendas. She in fact, considered either poisoning the man or using other deadly means to achieve her objective of having her husband killed. The man wanted a family. It would appear that the woman wanted money; power and freedom (see the chapter on gender differences).
Again, money does split the best of friends and relationships. In fact, you may be in a relationship and not in a friendship. A friend, a real friend, as I have said, does not cause harm.

Also, human beings pretend a lot. They may pretend to love you, while in fact, loathsomeness is actually what is in their mind. You need to be very vigilant. You will need to do your homework well if you are to be successful in human relationships.

Sadly, all the children of this couple were present during the ordeal. The lesson here is that the family is most likely to split up, with the daughter and wife going into prison. The husband, who is the victim, will be nursing his injury, and the other children possibly nursing psychological agony and bewilderment as to what life had thrown at them, without their involvement---apparently (See the Chapter on broken marriages, broken relationships). Note as at the time of concluding this book, the criminal wife was awaiting sentencing as she was found guilty at trial. Likely sentence ranges from 5-60years in prison.

***

Case Study 8

(London Metro/Asian Image)

Wife who killed husband with a knife hidden in her burkha

Once again, let us return to one of those types of unpredictable human behaviour---trust betrayed.

This was a case similar but slightly different to one which I have discussed above. It involved a newly married who would not be honest about her true intentions in or pre-marriage arrangement. Again, she may have been coerced into the relationship considering her cultural background. Whatever the circumstances of the relationship before marriage, she was hiding her true intentions from the man, who apparently loved her, so to speak.

MK and MM had been married for 33 days when MK killed her husband MM. It was an arranged marriage. Possibly unknown to MM, MK had a strong attachment to another man. Although MM did not know it, on the day he met his death, MK was carrying the deadly weapon, a knife, hidden in her *burkha*. The *burkha*, for the benefit of some readers, is a piece of clothing that Muslims women wear to cover their bodies, some with facial coverage as well, in observance of religious calling. The premeditated intention was to stab MM to death and she did exactly this. Her aim was to continue the friendship with the real person whom she loved. Subsequently, on the tragic date, she lured her husband into her trap which she had carefully set up. Unknown to the victim, he fell for it and his life ended.

Lesson: when one human intention is in conflict with another, the person may and usually does take measures, legitimate or not, to eliminate the obstruction (see chapter on anger). The reason is that human beings tend to avoid being unhappy if their desires are unfulfilled. This is what happened here. Human beings will do everything possible to overcome likely obstacles to happiness. Also, human beings are perfect at hiding their true intentions. A wise person who is going into a relationship should find this out as a matter of priority.

The other lesson here is that being in a relationship does not necessarily mean that your partner loves you. It does not mean that she or he would not harm you. People in relationships, except for the actions of strangers and accidents in life, are the ones who would cost you most harm. They know your strengths and weaknesses. A man's enemy, it is said, is in his own house. After all, has it not been said too that a woman's enemy is in her household?

***

Case Study 9

D and C were in prestigious marriage: A first order royal household and enjoying the trappings that come with royalty. This royal house is a leading light amongst monarchies and it has stood the test of time. Nevertheless, when it comes to matters of sex, back-stabbings, treachery, human failings, intimate relationship do not respect royalty. So the story turned out to be played in the open, to the dismay of the public, who revered this royal house.

While C was courting D, C was at more of an advantage because of C's link to the throne of power. He was also having an "affair" with another person called C1. Ultimately, C and D celebrated a glistening wedding which was one of the most glamorous events the world had ever seen. C continued his affair with C1. By now the matrimony between D and C had become "crowded" because of C1. D could no longer take it. C and D fell out and divorced! Imagine this, though not unheard of, in *this* royal household! Meanwhile, C and D had two young children.

To cut a long story short, D died a tragic accidental death. Guess what - the road was opened for C1 and C to actually fulfil their long held ambition to get married. They did so, but in controversial circumstances.

The lesson: inviting and involving a third party of whatever form, shape, size, or intention into matrimony is one of the surest means to dissolve your union. Also, except when desires and intentions are satisfied, human beings can present a façade, even to the larger public. Similarly, sex, money and third parties are a deadly intermix and a sure way to end a seemingly solid relationship.

Case Study 10
Some good news at last

"It's not that bad", as the saying goes here in Britain, when it comes to relationships. HC and BC are high profile individuals, both as a couple politically and professionally. For the most of the past 30 years or so they are almost always in the eyes of the public. They became, at some point, the most politically powerful couple in the world. That was some years back. His word, BC's word, was "law". He could do and undo literally. However, there is a "but" in BC's lifestyle. He loved sex, the claim went. There were even claims that BC had a string of escapades. Then the mother of all recklessness developed, that gave new meanings and interpretations to some words in human sexual relationships. The long and short of it is that BC used his power to engage a junior person in his office for an intimate relationship. He was caught red handed and publicly embarrassed.

In spite of all this, the public began to wonder if HC was going to "ditch" BC. She never did. She stood firmly by him. The press and people speculated what might be the reason for the bond between the two. The grapevine went into full gear to enquire why on earth HC did not leave BC. The rumour mill was not short of ideas. Some even said that it was for the political ambition of HC. This may be true, for HC became the chief representative of her country overseas, after failing to capture the highest office in the land that BC previously held. True to projection, BC stood by HC just as HC had stood by BC through thick and thin. In short, they have both stuck together till this day.

The lesson here is that human beings are vulnerable individuals. "Let him/her who has done no wrong, ever, cast the first stone" on BC. If BC and HC had dissolved their union, it could have been more devastating for their careers, dignity, and the offspring they had. They did not allow the influence of third parties, money, and public opinion to permanently damage the relationship. Regardless of the reasons for them sticking together, at least they found a reason to remain as one.

****

Case 11: *Businessman killed by his own employees*
A number of media outlets (BBC, Internet) reported this story.

The maxim that a man's (or woman's) enemy is in his or her house is true for both personal and business relationships. That is to say, the people who are most likely to harm you or conspire to harm you are those who are both close to you and with whom you have a relationship. Here is a very sorry case.
2003: AC was a multi-millionaire businessman in a thriving freight business. He had hired a person known as KR as one of the drivers. Unknown to AC, KR was a criminal with a shady past. Also unknown to AC, KR had an ambition to unseat AC and take over his business. KR carried out this very treacherous act in conspiracy with others. Not only did these conspirators kill AC, they killed his two sons, his wife, and his mother. Worse still, they dumped AC's corpse in the sea to conceal the evidence. In the end the conspirators were caught and sentenced to imprisonment accordingly.

What lessons can we learn from this story?
The first one is that the enemy is always very close by, and almost always in a relationship with the victim. The enemy, pretending to be an honest trustworthy associate, knows the weakness of the victim. Secondly, the traitor in business dealings is no different from one in personal relationships. They sometimes conspire with a third party to achieve their aims. The third but equally important point is that in business

relationships, as in personal associations, you need vigilance and fore-knowledge of the person with whom you are relating. Remember, human beings can conceal their true nature and are adept at hiding their behavioural identity. But, vigilance and diligent searches will reveal what is hidden and their true character.

Case 12. *Murder in the name of love: Children and their guardians/parents* (UK Government).

It is an established fact that a child, in most cases, is in danger of harm or death at the hands of those they know. Of course, in other occasions, the danger is the work of complete strangers.
VC was a child placed under the care of MTK and CM. In short, VC was so abused that MTK and CM were convicted of her murder in 2003 in a case that became a public outrage in the UK, with a huge public inquiry that followed her death. Children, the reader may recall, are not only vulnerable to abuse; they have no self-defences and no choice as to their birth or placement with a particular carer. On this occasion, at least, three major public services (police, NHS, social services) that she had relationships with also failed her. It is all about protecting a quality and valuable relationship.

Here is a comment by the chairman of the inquiry set up to investigate the alleged failures. "The legislative framework is fundamentally sound. The gap is in its implementation. Having considered all the evidence, it is not to the often hapless front-line staff that I direct most criticism for the failure to protect VC True, their performance often fell well short of an acceptable standard of work. But the greatest failure rests with the senior managers and members of the organisations concerned, whose responsibility it was to ensure that the services they provided to children such as V(C) were properly financed, staffed and able to deliver good quality services to children and families. They must be accountable."

Lesson: relationships can and do fail. When they do and when trust fails, the results can be serious. In the case of children, the results can be dire. Children are always in need of protection as they can not defend themselves in a one-sided relationship stacked against them. Any abuse of a relationship may end in tragedy as this case and many others have shown. This is even truer when the relationship is not as valued as it should be.

From these case studies, it's clear that relationships transcend age. That is children do and for the right reason depends on adult to survive and remain healthy. Also, relationship is no respecter of political positions as we saw in the cases. Similarly, being in the royal palace does not immune individuals and couples from the effects that relationships may bring. Geographically, be it in Asia, Africa, Europe or America, human beings remain the same and behave in similar ways saves for differences in culture. How, then can one sum of these observations? Let us see.

CHAPTER TWENTY SIX
Conclusion

"Your success or failure in life is a direct reflection of the relationship that you keep and the ones that you don't".
Joel Akande

As the reader can now clearly undertand from what I have written here, it is clear that human beings are very complex to deal with. The first things to note are that to deal with other human beings requires considerable intuition, (honest) manouvering, vilgilance, and foresight. Many individuals and couples have tried and failed in forming relationships. Many, who have been badly hurt, when they failed, have taken revenge on other people. Some have decided not to try again.Societies and individuals, buisneses, as well as the families have and may continue to pay the price for these failings.

The second thing is that, human beings often hide their true intentions. While, future events may dictate a change of tact in the course of the relationship, the relationship will fail if the change in tactics is going to cause harm to the partner in the relationship. However, despite the harm that may be caused, a relationship may survive if both couples share a common vision and same agenda even though strategy and tactics differ. Not only do they have to share a common purpose, the parties should operate with the framework of the rules that bind the relationship. Besides, as human, we do err and as they say, to err is human but to forgive is divine. In no where else is this saying truer than in relationships. Forgivensss of wrongs is a dominant key in stable and prosperous relationships. A stern waring is called for here. Either with a child, spouse, friends, partner, and cohabitants or with any other person, a relationship should aspire first not to cause harm. That will be enough even if *actively* loving the other is not possible. It is when selfishness, intention to harm, lack of companionship, interference from outsiders, divergence of vision, and distraction from common purpose sets in that in practice, the relationship journey falters.

The most important element in making a success of any relationship is that, trust must never be broken. It is the oil that lubricates the working machinery of any relationship.

As I have mentioned in the book, the reader should consider that, as doctors have said for generations, prevention is better than cure. If a relationship had a fault from the start and you can clearly see this as an uncomfortable difficulty, then why proceeding into committing into the relationship?

There are things that can either build or end a relationship. First among them is your word and actions. Word can encourage towards great success in the face of impossibility or discourage even when success is within reach. It depends on how you want it.

In addition to word, your acts and support for each other in thick and thin are paramount. Afterall, who want to be with another person who betrays him or her? Also, contrary to many peoples's opinion, money and sex are not primary to sustaining a relationship. Depending on their application, either or both combined can be a sword or a shield.

I hope the reader has learned something from this book, which is a summary of over 45 years' experience which I have gathered in different aspects of life. Always remember that a human being may not be what he or she claims or appears to be. Sometimes, a little effort to find out *more (while remaining vigilant always)* about the person may be all that we need. After all, a stitch in time, they say, saves nine, or at least, you should sleep with one of your eyes fully opened!

Let me end with this advice that I have come to know in recent years as a guiding principle. The advice goes like this:

Relationships: Caveat Emptor

"There can only be two alternate reasons for the existence of any relationship: either to provide help and support for, or to exploit the other person/entity. Now human beings are very shrewd at taking advantage of others, especially if ignorant and vulnerable. This exploitation, without doubt, can either be in a pleasurable (usually sexual) mistreatment or financial abuse of the other person(s). In practice, this relationship can be a conduct to induce the other person to work for next to nothing and/or to satisfy the exploiter's hidden dark psychological desires. In all these cases, be warned to exercise caution, always."

Joel Akande

References

Books:

1. Ancient Mesopotamia. Oppenheim, A. Leo. Chicago & London. The University of Chicago Press. 1964

2. *Contraceptive Technology.* Hatcher RA *et al*. 18th rev. edition. New York, NY: Ardent Media, 2004.

3. Everyday life in Babylonia and Assyria. London. Contenau, George. Edward Arnold Publishers Ltd. 1954

4. Dewhurst's Textbook of Obstetrics and Gyneacology for Postgraduates. 5th Ed. Edited by Charles F. Whitfield. Publisher. Blackwell Science.

5. Family Law and Practice. 2007 Nancy Duffield et al. College of Law Publishing. ISBN. 9781905391261

6. Maudsley & Burn's Land Law. Cases and Materials. Eighth Edition . E.H Burn, OUP, Oxford, UK. ISBN 109 876 54 321.

7. Mesopotamia, the civilization that rose out of clay. Fairservis, Walter Ashlin. New York

8. Oxford Texbook of Psychiatry. Michael Gelder et al. ISBN-13: 978-0198528197

9. The History of Human Marriage. Volume: 1. Contributors: Edward Westermarck - author. Publisher: Macmillan. 1921. Page Number: 26.

10. The Holy Bible

11. The Road and the Key to Happiness. Dr Joel A. ISBN-10: 1434368386.   ISBN-13:978-1434368386   Publisher: AuthorHouse (14 Jun 2008).

12.The Supremacy of the Expressed Word. Dr Joel A ISBN-10:1434340481 ISBN-13: 978-1434340481 AuthorHouse (22 Oct 2007)

Journals

1. ABC of mental health: Psychosexual problems
J P Watson, Teifion Davies *BMJ* 1997;315:239-242 (26 July)

2. Anger and fear
HB Danesh Am J Psychiatry 1977; 134:1109-1112

3. Are Women the ``More Emotional'' Sex? Evidence From Emotional Experiences in Social Context
Lisa Feldman Barrett et al
Cognition And Emotion, 1998, *12* (4), 555± 578

4. Are Women Really More Talkative Than Men?
Matthias R. Mehl, Simine Vazire, Nairán Ramírez-Esparza, Richard B. Slatcher, James W. Pennebaker
Science 6 July 2007:Vol. 317. no. 5834, p. 82,
DOI: 10.1126/science.1139940

5. Children of Divorce: Recent Findings Regarding Long-Term Effects and Recent Studies of Joint and Sole Custody
Judith S. Wallerstein PhD, Janet R. Johnston PhD
Pediatrics in Review.1990; 11: 197-203.

6. Coping with loss
Separation and other problems that threaten relationships
Robert S Weiss. BMJ 1998; 316:1011-1013 (28 March)

7. Social and Emotional Outcomes of Child Sexual Abuse: A Clinical Sample in Turkey .

Burcu Ozbaran, Serpil Erermis, Nagehan Bukusoglu, Tezan Bildik, Muge Tamar, Eyyup Sabri Ercan, Cahide Aydin, and Saniye Korkmaz Cetin. Journal of Interpersonal Violence 2008, doi:10.1177/0886260508323663

7.Substance misuse: alcohol, tobacco, inhalants, and other drugs. Yvonne Bonomo, Jenny Proimos
BMJ 2005;330(7494):777 (2 April),
doi:10.1136/bmj.330.7494.777

8.Cycle of child sexual abuse: links between being a victim and becoming a perpetrator M. Glasser et al.
The British Journal of Psychiatry (2001) 179: 482-494

9.Effects of parental divorce and memories of family problems on relationships between adult children and their parents
PS Webster and AR Herzog.
Journals of Gerontology Series B: Psychological Sciences and Social Sciences, Vol 50, Issue 1 S24-S34, Copyright © 1995 by The Gerontological Society of America

10.Environmental impacts of divorce
Eunice Yu and Jianguo Liu
Center for Systems Integration and Sustainability, Department of Fisheries and Wildlife, Michigan State University, East Lansing, MI 48823-5243

11.Gender differences in masking negative emotions: Ability or motivation? Davis, Teresa L.
Developmental Psychology. Vol 31(4), Jul 1995, 660-667.

12.Health-related behaviors and the benefits of marriage for elderly persons .BS Schone and RM Weinick The Gerontologist, Vol 38, Issue 5 618-627

13.Hominid cranium from Homo: Description and taxonomy of Homo Alemseged, Z., Coppens, Y., Geraads, D. (2002). -323-1976-896". *Am J Phys Anthropol* 117 (2): 103–12. doi:10.1002/ajpa.10032. PMID 11815945

15. Impact of child sexual abuse on mental health Prospective study in males and females. Josie Spataro. The British Journal Psychiatry *(2004) 184: 416-421*

16. Legal practice course guides: Business law. Ed. J.Scott Sclorach and Jason Ellis. 2006-2007. Oxford University Press.

17. Mental Health Outcomes Following Recent Parental Divorce The Case of Young Adult Offspring
Teresa M. Cooney , Jane Kurz
Journal of Family Issues, Vol. 17, No. 4, 495-513 (1996) DOI: 10.1177/019251396017004004

18. Self- and Partner-Perceptions of Interpersonal Problems and Relationship Functioning. Colleen Saffrey et al.
Journal of Social and Personal Relationships, Vol. 20, No. 1, 117-139 (2003) DOI: 10.1177/02654075030201006

19. Stoneking, Mark; Soodyall, Himla (1996). "Human evolution and the mitochondrial genome". *Current Opinion in Genetics & Development* 6 (6): 731–6. Doi 10.1016/S0959-437X (96)80028-1.

20. Teenage sexual **intercourse** and pregnancy
H A Curtis, C J Lawrence, J H Tripp
Archives of Disease in Childhood 1988; 63:373-379; doi:10.1136/adc.63.4.373

21. The effects of divorce and separation on mental health in a national UK birth cohort

M. Richards , R. Hardy and M. Wadsworth From the MRC National Survey of Health and Development, University College London Psychological Medicine (1997), 27:1121-1128 Cambridge University Press Cambridge University Press

22. The effect of divorce on fathers: an overview of the literature JW Jacobs. Am J Psychiatry 1982; 139:1235-1241

23. The Long-Term Effects of Child Sexual Abuse by Female Perpetrators .A Qualitative Study of Male and Female Victims Myriam S. Denov.Journal of Interpersonal Violence, Vol. 19, No. 10, 1137-1156 (2004) DOI: 10.1177/0886260504269093

Research and Published Articles

1.1,000 Federal Benefits of Marriage?An Analysis of the 1997 GAO Report Joshua K. Bakeri

2.Convention on the Rights of the Child. Office of the High Commission for Human Rights. United Nations. Adopted and opened for signature, ratification and accession by General Assembly resolution 44/25 of 20 November 1989.

3.GAO/OGC-97-16 Defense of Marriage Act. GAO United States General Accounting Office. Washington, D.C. 20548 Office of the General Counsel B-275860 January 31, 1997.

4.*Gender and Power.* Women Call the Shots at Home; Public Mixed on Gender Roles in Jobs.*By Rich Morin And D'vera Cohn, Pew Research Center, September 25, 2008*

Websites

http://abcnews.go.com/Technology/Story?id=3348076&page=1

http://articles.directorym.co.uk/Business_Relationships-a966613.html

http://aspe.hhs.gov/hsp/07/marriageonhealth/rb.htm

http://www.asianimage.co.uk/uk/3873495.Newlywed__hid_knife_under_burka_/

http://cc.msnscache.com/cache.aspx?q=wife+killed+husband+with+knife+hidden+in+burkha&d=76036573454849&mkt=en-US&setlang=en-US&w=f828dc08,29168eae

http://www.divorcerate.org/divorce-rate-japan.html

http://www.dictionary.com

http://edition.cnn.com/2009/TECH/02/03/myspace.sex.offenders/index.html

http://en.wikipedia.org/wiki/Human_beings

http://en.wikipedia.org/wiki/Rights_and_responsibilities_of_marriages_in_the_United_States#Rights_and_benefits

http://www.expressindia.com/news/fullstory.php?newsid=69607

http://extension.unh.edu/Family/Documents/divorce.pdf

http://family.findlaw.com/marriage/marriage-resources/le19_4_1.html

http://forbes.com

http://law.jrank.org/pages/1178/Family-Relationships-Crime-Siblings-crime.html

http://marriage.about.com/cs/sex/a/sexfrequency.htm

http://marriageandfamily-allie.blogspot.com/2007/02/marriage-and-cohabitation.html

http://news.bbc.co.uk/1/hi/business/6083814.stm

http://news.bbc.co.uk/1/hi/uk/4308313.stm

http://news.bbc.co.uk/1/hi/world/americas/7818751.stm

http://news.bbc.co.uk/1/hi/world/americas/7906616.stm

http://pewsocialtrends.org/pubs/717/gender-power

http://uk.news.yahoo.com/18/20090206/tuk-husband-ends-marriage-on-facebook-co-a7ad41d.html

http://uk.news.yahoo.com/4/20090129/tuk-couple-poisoned-at-restaurant-dba1618.html

http://uk.news.yahoo.com/4/20090209/tuk-record-numbers-report-sexual-abuse-dba1618.html

http://www.asu.edu/clas/iho/lucy.html

http://www.cba.org/bc/public_media/family/162.aspx

http://www.cdc.gov/nchs/fastats/divorce.htm

http://www.cedr.com/conflict/services/relationships.php

http://www.dailymail.co.uk/femail/article-419040/Women-talk-times-men-says-study.html

http://www.dailymail.co.uk/news/article-1079510/Children-broken-homes-times-likely-suffer-mental-troubles-says-Government-study.html

http://www.esrcsocietytoday.ac.uk/ESRCInfoCentre/research/centres/BRASS.aspx?ComponentId=9052&SourcePageId=19472

http://www.forbes.com/2003/10/08/cz_af_1008health.html

http://www.foreverfamilies.net/xml/articles/benefitsofmarriage.aspx?&publication=full

http://www.newyorker.com/archive/1998/02/02/1998_02_02_030_TNY_LIBRY_000014853

http://www.nuwireinvestor.com/wiki/pages/the-financial-advantages-and-disadvantages-of-marriage.aspx

http://www.professorshouse.com/family/relationships/saying-I-do.aspx

http://www.sciaga.pl/tekst/57309-58-advantages_and_disadvantages_of_being_married

http://www.sciencemag.org/cgi/content/full/317/5834/82

http://www.statistics.gov.uk/cci/nugget.asp?id=322

http://www.thepensionservice.gov.uk/state-pension/serps/home.asp

http://www.theweekmagazine.com/

http://www.unhchr.ch/html/menu3/b/k2crc.htm

http://www.victoria-climbie-inquiry.org.uk/News_Update/news_update.htm

http://www.washingtonpost.com/wp-dyn/content/article/2008/11/25/AR2008112501051.html

http://www.washingtonpost.com/wp-dyn/content/article/2009/02/20/AR2009022003964.html

http://www.webmd.com/mental-health/estrogen-and-womens-emotions

https://openaccess.leidenuniv.nl/dspace/bitstream/1887/12585/8/More-or-less-together06-Belgium.pdf

Books by the same author

1. The Road and the Key to Happiness

Award-Winner in the Psychology category of the National Best Books 2008 Awards, sponsored by USA Book News
Imagine if you are looking for something that is clearly within your grasp. Something that is not lost, yet you cannot find it and you are desperately looking for it. It can be frustrating. This is

what it feels like when you are searching for happiness. The good news is that this book sets out to help you find *the* answer to *the* question that is also on the lips and minds of billions of people in the world: *What is happiness and how do I achieve it?* Based on scientific thoughts and new concepts, as well as clinical experiences, the book will help you to find your happiness following a step-by-step logical approach. To find out more, please begin to read this insightful and beautifully written piece of work.

2. *The Secret And Supremacy Of The Expressed Word*

Award-Winner in the Christian book category of the National Best Books 2008 Awards, sponsored by USA Book News.

ISBN: 9781434340481

Written in plain language, *The Secret And Supremacy Of The Expressed Word* is about the incredible power that lies in the words that we, as individuals, speak, write and sign every day. Our words are the most powerful tools that exist. Based on solid scientific research, as well as citing authoritative sources and distilled from various real life experiences, the book also touches on our words even before we express them, in a process that is otherwise called *intention*. Critically, the book examines the characteristics of our words. The author concluded that the words - in our minds, in our mouths, in our hands or bodies – are living things! The writer took great pains to explain, for the benefit of the reader, how our words achieve their spectacular effects, which includes creative, reproductive and transformative abilities. Thus, nothing will ever exist or be created without our words preceding them.

The Secret and Supremacy of the Expressed Word takes the reader through the step-by-step process of 'how to benefit from' the spectacular power of words. Many examples are given for the reader to follow.

The book will appeal to all, including individuals who want to change things in their life, positive thinkers, clinicians, Christians and non-Christians, scientists and all enquiring minds who want to know about our words, and those who want to advance in life, or those who are simply puzzled by events around them - young or old.

Purchases
The book is available through www.amazon.com, www.myexpert.com and in more than 20,000 book outlets across the world. More information and updates can be obtained from www.myeexpert.com.

Up-coming Book in the series
1. Your Health in Your Hands.
Comprehensive Guide to Healthy Living

This is a book that is based on thorough clinical work and Scientific evidence but presented to the reader in very plain easy- to-understand language that the reader can easily identify with.
It takes the reader through the entire life cycle starting from pre-conception to the time of the final living hour.

The author believes, having treated thousands of patients in decades of his clinical career, that as individuals and families, we can indeed lead a healthy lifestyle in the manner described by such authorities as World Health Organization (WHO).

Many practical ideas that are discussed in the book are backed up by established authorities: yet several of the concepts that are in the book are new to the publishing world.
More information and updates can be obtained from www.myeexpert.com Here, the reader can also preview some of the contents in this well written book.

Index of Keywords   Page
Adolescence   64
Affair   27
Agreement   42, 156
Anger   153
Anxiety   163
Belligerence   156
Benefits   84
Bitterness   116, 126
Blindness   80, 171
Broken marriages   113
Child abuse   306
Cohabitation   87, 106
Common law spouse   94
Communication   189
Companionship   35
Compatibility   41
Conflict   115
Cooling-off   211, 218
Counselling   212
Crime   229, 278
Criminal   283, 315
Crisis   198
Culture   204
Cystic fibrosis   25, 173
Death   203
Deceit   75
Depression   86-88
Desire   101-115
Divorce   112-131
Domestic violence   115, 207, 239, 310
Drugs   69, 74, 136
Extended family   273
Financial: advantages, disadvantages   55, 84, 94
Freedom   99, 107
Freewill   44
Friends   62, 65, 71
Friendship   365
Frustration   297, 310
Gangs   136

GAO (General Accounting Office)	104
Genetic Diseases	25, 174
Guardian	216, 273
Happiness, failure	48-49, 313
Health	86
Help meet	31, 101
Hurt	60
Imprisonment	138
Inheritance	98, 254
In-Laws	110, 120
Insecurity	148
Intention	153
Intercourse	201, 220
Intimacy	225
Leadership	208
Legal advantages, disadvantages	102
Litigation	192
Loneliness	92
Loner	109
Love	75
Loyalty	280
Maintenance	301
Medical, impact of	125
Mental health, impact on	125
Money	241, 245
Parenthood	275
Pension	97
Platonic	263
Poems	302
Poverty	134
Premarital: sex, children, contract	133
Pre-nuptial Agreement	253
Property	60, 96
Prostitution	136
Psychological	312
Purpose	36
Questionnaire	181
Quotes	218
Relatives	141
Religious	317

Reproduction	221
Serenity	235
Sex	220
Shyness	67
Sibling	273
Sickle cell	193
Single	13, 85
Snare	220
Social ties	93
Society	146
Stalking	319
Tax	96
Teen	137
Tools	242
Vision, shared	188

"Great ideas often receive violent opposition from mediocre mind" Albert Einstein

www.ingramcontent.com/pod-product-compliance
Lightning Source LLC
Chambersburg PA
CBHW020329240426
43665CB00043B/192